Nāmācārya

The Life of

Śrīla Haridāsa Ṭhākura

Hare Kṛṣṇa
Hare Kṛṣṇa
Kṛṣṇa Kṛṣṇa
Hare Hare
Hare Rāma
Hare Rāma
Rāma Rāma
Hare Hare

Nāmācārya

The Life of
Śrīla Haridāsa Ṭhākura

Rūpa-Vilāsa dāsa

BOOKWRIGHTS PRESS
CHARLOTTESVILLE, VIRGINIA, USA

Published by

Bookwrights Press
Charlottesville, VA, USA
publisher@bookwrightspress.com

Book design by Sākṣi Gopāla Dāsa
Cover design by Māyāpriya Devī Dāsī
Typeset in Balaram font

Cover photos: Front–The smiling face of Haridāsa Ṭhākura greets the pilgrim to the most holy spot of Phuliyā where Haridāsa Ṭhākura eternally engages in *bhajana*. Back–Prior to Lord Caitanya's appearance, Haridāsa Ṭhākura lived near Śāntipura in Phuliyā in a cave-like dwelling established for him by Śrī Advaita Ācārya. In this place he chanted over 300,000 names daily.

ISBN hardbound: 978-1-880404-50-8
ISBN paperback 978-1-880404-51-5

Readers are invited to write to the author: rupavi1008@yahoo.com

Other books by the author:
A Ray of Vishnu
The Seventh Goswami
Babaji Maharaja
Without Fear

This book is dedicated to

His Divine Grace

A. C. Bhaktivedanta Swami Prabhupāda

—my eternal spiritual master—
who delivered the merciful teachings of the
Vaiṣṇava *ācāryas* to the suffering world.
I pray that he may be a little pleased with this
attempt to glorify the *Nāmācārya*,
Śrīla Haridāsa Ṭhākura.

From: *Śrī Caitanya-caritāmṛta Antya-līlā*
4.102 and 4.103,
spoken by Śrīla Sanātana Gosvāmī:

āpane ācare keha, nā kare pracāra
pracāra karena keha, nā karena ācāra

"Some behave very well but do not preach the cult of Kṛṣṇa consciousness, whereas others preach but do not behave properly."

'ācāra', 'pracāra',—nāmera karaha 'dui' kārya
tumi—sarva-guru, tumi jagatera ārya

"You simultaneously perform both duties in relation to the holy name by your personal behavior and by your preaching. Therefore you are the spiritual master of the entire world, for you are the most advanced devotee in the world."

Purport by His Divine Grace
A.C. Bhaktivedanta Swami Prabhupāda:

"Sanātana Gosvāmī clearly defines herein the bona fide spiritual master of the world. The qualifications expressed in this connection are that one must act according to the scriptural injunctions and at the same time preach. One who does so is a bona fide spiritual master. Haridāsa Ṭhākura was the ideal spiritual master because he regularly chanted on his beads a prescribed number of times. Indeed, he was chanting the holy name of the Lord 300,000 times a day. Similarly, the members of the Kṛṣṇa consciousness movement chant a minimum of sixteen rounds a day, which can be done without difficulty, and at the same time they must preach the cult of Caitanya Mahāprabhu according to the gospel of *Bhagavad-gītā As It Is*. One who does so is quite fit to become a spiritual master for the entire world."

From: *Śrī Hari-nāma-cintāmaṇi*
Spoken by: Śrīla Haridāsa Thākura

"The *smṛti* says that anyone who chants the holy name, whether with faith or neglect, attracts the merciful attention of Lord Krsna. The name is the purest form of knowledge, the best of all *vratas* or vows and the highest meditation. It gives the ultimate auspicious results and is the most sublime renunciation. Chanting is a matchless spiritual activity, the holiest of pious activities, and the supreme path of self-realization. It offers the greatest liberation and goal. The holy name is divine and situated in the paramount spiritual realm, it is superexcellent devotional service and the best purifying agent, showering love of Godhead. It is the essence of all scriptures, the cause of everything, the Supreme Absolute Truth, the most worshipable object and acts as the supreme spiritual instructor and guide."

harer nāma harer nāma
harer nāmaiva kevalam
kalau nāsty eva nāsty eva
nāsty eva gatir anyathā

IN THIS AGE OF KALI THERE IS NO alternative, there is no alternative, there is no alternative for spiritual progress than the holy name, the holy name, the holy name of the Lord."

Bṛhan-nāradīya Purāṇa
[cited: *Śrī Caitanya-caritāmṛta Ādi-līlā* 7.76]

Contents

Chapter Four

TRIAL AND TRIBULATION

Chapter Five

SOLITARY WORSHIP OF THE LORD

Chapter Six

THE LORD'S SAṄKĪRTANA

Chapter Seven

JAGANNĀTHA PURĪ

Chapter Eight

GLORIOUS REVELATIONS AND DEPARTURE

tṛṇād api sunīcena
taror api sahiṣṇunā
amāninā mānadena
kīrtanīyaḥ sadā hariḥ

ONE SHOULD CHANT THE HOLY NAME OF the Lord in a humble state of mind, thinking oneself lower than the straw in the street. One should be more tolerant than a tree, devoid of all sense of false prestige and ready to offer all respects to others. In such a state of mind one can chant the holy name of the Lord constantly."

Śrī Śrī Śikṣāṣṭaka, verse 3
by Lord Caitanya
Śrī Caitanya-caritāmṛta Antya-līlā 20.21
[cited: *Śrī Caitanya-caritāmṛta Antya-līlā* 3.207]

Introduction & Acknowledgments

BY THE GRACE OF ŚRĪLA PRABHUPĀDA and the *guru-paramparā*, I wrote some books from 1988–1990: *A Ray of Vishnu*, *The Seventh Goswami*, and *Bābājī Mahārāja*. These three books represented an attempt to glorify some of the great personalities that prominently adorn the altars of the International Society for Kṛṣṇa Consciousness and many Gauḍīya Vaiṣṇava temples all over the world: Śrīla Bhaktisiddhānta Sarasvatī Ṭhākura, Śrīla Gaura Kiśora dāsa Bābājī Mahārāja, Śrīla Bhaktivinoda Ṭhākura, and Śrīla Jagannātha dāsa Bābājī Mahārāja. The above titles constituted the initial offerings of what I hoped would be a series called *Lives of the Vaiṣṇava Ācāryas*.

Now, 19 years later, by the inspiration and mercy of Śrīla Prabhupāda, I am presenting a fourth book in an attempt to glorify one of the greatest of all *ācāryas*, the Nāmācārya, Śrīla Haridāsa Ṭhākura. I have no qualification to do this, just a desire. Years ago, a prominent *sannyāsī* strongly objected to my writing about Śrīla Bhaktisiddhānta Sarasvatī Ṭhākura, since, the *sannyāsī* reasoned, I was a *gṛhastha*, and Śrīla Sarasvati Ṭhākura was a lifelong celibate and renunciant. How could I be so presumptuous as to imagine that I had the qualification to write about such a personality? At the time, I felt somewhat chastened and intimidated by his remarks. However, my rationale then, and now, is that writing about and glorifying great souls who create *śraddhā* (faith) in my heart and the hearts of others, and whom I revere and honor, is not only permissible, but authorized. After receiving the gift of faith, to not glorify such great souls might even be classified as miserly. I do not want to be a miser; thus, this offering, though imperfect, is made in a spirit of reciprocation and appreciation.

Perhaps it is just a case of "fools rush in, where angels fear to tread"; however, I have been meditating on writing about the Nāmācārya for 18 years, so I will take my chances and hope for Śrīla Haridāsa Ṭhākura's and Śrīla Prabhupāda's causeless mercy. This book is dedicated to Śrīla Prabhupāda, and I hope it brings him some pleasure.

There are quite a number of persons who must be thanked for their help: His Divine Grace A.C. Bhaktivedanta Swami Prabhupāda who, despite all my failings, has never left my heart, despite its unfortunate condition; Dayānanda Prabhu, my old friend and senior God-brother, who guided, corrected, and instructed me in innumerable ways: scriptural, cultural, historical, technical, and philosophical; and my wife, Śarad-bihārī Prabhu, who is my friend and support through thick and thin, despite all my shortcomings; without her tolerance, love, and care I could not have written this book. I also want to thank Līlā-śakti Prabhu who provided my wife, my sons, and I with friendship, a home, and a desk in Leicester and encouraged me to write. Janānanda Swami read some of the chapters, offering critical review and encouragement, and a wonderful painting by the Orissan artist Ramesh Mahajana, painted in 2007. Varṣāṇā Swami provided inspiration and the foreword to this book. Jagannātha Miśra Prabhu sent me some vivid and unique paintings of Ṭhākura Haridāsa, as well as some very helpful Bengali translations. Dozens of photographs of sites connected to the Namācārya's *līlās* were supplied by Jñānagamya Prabhu, Nāma-kīrtana Prabhu, and Viśvambhara Prabhu. Sākṣi Gopāla Prabhu did the design and layout and helped me through all the rigors of the original publication. Without him, this book would never have been presented in such a refined and artistic manner. I offer my sincerest thanks to the Vaiṣṇava who donated the entire cost of the original Torchlight printing, but wishes—out of humility—to remain anonymous. I must finally thank all the readers who, over the years, have encouraged me again and again with appreciation for the previous volumes and prodded me to produce more. I thank you all, named and unnamed.

The following books were of tremendous help and were the basis of this biography:

• *Śrī Caitanya-caritāmṛta* by Kṛṣṇadāsa Kavirāja Gosvāmī, translated and purported by His Divine Grace A.C. Bhaktivedanta Swami Prabhupāda, Bhaktivedanta Book Trust, 1974.

• *Śrī Caitanya-bhāgavata* by Vṛndāvana dāsa Ṭhākura, purported by Śrīla Bhaktisiddhānta Sarasvatī Ṭhākura, translated and edited by Bhumipati Prabhu and Puṇḍarīka Vidyānidhi Prabhu, Vrajraj Press, 1998—2005.

• *Sree Krishna Chaitanya* by Professor Nisikanta Sanyal, Madras Law Journal Press, 1933.

• *The Divine Name* by Raghava Caitanya Prabhu, published by Raghava Caitanya Das, A/5 Anandasram, Proctor Road, Bombay-7, printed by P.H. Raman at the Associated Advertisers and Printers, Ltd., 505 Arthur Road, Tardoo, Bombay-7, 1954.

•*Shri Chaitanya's Teachings Part I*, by Śrīla Bhaktisiddhānta Sarasvatī Ṭhākura, Sree Gaudiya Math, 1975.

•*The Holy Name & Ṭhākur Haridās* by Śrīla Bhaktisiddhānta Sarasvatī Ṭhākura, Sree Gaudiya Math, 1998.

•*Śrī Nāmāmṛta The Nectar of the Holy Name*, compiled from the writings of His Divine Grace A.C. Bhaktivedanta Swami Prabhupāda by Śubhānanda Prabhu, Bhaktivedanta Book Trust, 1982.

•*Vaiṣṇavism (Contemporary Scholars Discuss the Gauḍiya Tradition)*, edited by Steven J. Rosen, FOLK Books, 1992.

•*Hare Krishna, Hare Krishna Five Distinguished Scholars on the Hare Krishna Movement in the West*, edited by Steven J. Gelberg, Grove Press, 1983.

•*Vaiṣṇavism in Bengal 1486—1900* by Dr. Ramakanta Chakrabarty, Sanskrit Pustak Bhandar, Calcutta, 1985.

This book was completed on October 14, 2008, Śrī Kṛṣṇa Śāradīyā Rāsayātrā, Disappearance of Śrī Murāri Gupta, and the first day of the month of Kārtika.

Foreword

by His Holiness Varṣāṇā Swami

I.

UPON HEARING THE DIVINE GLORIES and astounding effects of chanting the holy name(s), many people take it up, overlooking or minimizing important instructions about the process of chanting. Some make a show of spiritual advancement, displaying the shadows of various ecstasies, while lacking the basic moral and religious prerequisites needed to achieve the many benedictions which are achieved with offenseless chanting and the even more spectacular gifts which are bestowed at the level of pure chanting. Their examples only create obstacles in the proper development of the faith of others.

All true religions agree that the holy names of God are the most potent of *mantras*. It is the elixir of life, the divine antidote to the disease of material existence (*bhava-roga*). As with any medicine, a qualified healer is required to prescribe the proper dosage and a compatible lifestyle. The holy name is the supreme remedy; its prescribing physician, Śrī Guru, prescribes the dose; and the injunctions of *śāstra* [scripture] establish the lifestyle to be followed.

In Kali-yuga, various religions, with all their different names for the same God, are prone to the quarrel and hypocrisy that marks this age. With this sectarian tendency of asserting that only one group has all the answers, the very means of purifying the false ego (the universal process of chanting the holy names of God) becomes confused with sectarian sentiments and is therefore neglected by otherwise very sincere seekers. Thus, many good and honest people turn away from religion, finding more integrity, sanity, morality, kindness, and love in materialistic society.

Seeing the world in such an unfortunate condition, the Supreme Healer sent Haridāsa Ṭhākura, His perfect and empowered representative, to this earthly realm to set an impeccable example of integrity in holy life. All his words, actions, and thoughts flowed in complete dedication to practicing and preaching the topmost, universal method of self-realization in this age.

Haridāsa Ṭhākura's life and activities personify how one should apply the *yuga-dharma* (universal religious process for a particular age) in the present era. A careful investigation of his life sheds light on all the details of that chanting process. To achieve the best possible result from chanting requires the knowledge, guidance, example, and instruction of a liberated soul. Haridāsa Ṭhākura was a teacher, by example, of perfect chanting—therefore, he was awarded the title Nāmācārya, one who is the teacher, by perfect example, of the chanting of the holy name.

Śrī Caitanya Mahāprabhu fulfilled a multitude of His purposes through His favorite agents. Through the life of Haridāsa Ṭhākura, He taught the world the glories of relationship with the holy name (*sambandha*), the proper way to practice the chanting process (*abhideya*), and the final goal and realization (*prayojana*) reached by the chanting process.

To realize *sambandha-jñāna* in relation to chanting is to understand that the name and the named are nondifferent:

nāma cintāmaṇiḥ kṛṣṇas
caitanya-rasa-vigrahaḥ
pūrṇaḥ śuddho nitya-mukto
'bhinnatvān nāma-nāminoḥ

"The holy name of Kṛṣṇa is transcendentally blissful. It bestows all spiritual benedictions, for it is Kṛṣṇa Himself, the reservoir of all pleasure. Kṛṣṇa's name is complete, and it is the form of all transcendental mellows. It is not a material name under any condition, and it is no less powerful than Kṛṣṇa Himself. Since Kṛṣṇa's name is not contaminated by the material qualities, there is no question of its being involved with *māyā* [the illusory potency]. Kṛṣṇa's name is always liberated and spiritual; it is never conditioned by the laws of material nature. This is because the name of Kṛṣṇa and Kṛṣṇa Himself are identical."[1]

When chanting, the beginner must try to understand that he is in direct association with the Supreme Personality of Godhead, Śrī Kṛṣṇa and remember always that he is a menial servant of the Lord. Until he does so, he chants at the *nāma-aparādha* or offensive stage.

To realize *abhideya-jñāna* in chanting is to be aware of offenses to the holy name and avoid all offenses in chanting including: *nāma-aparādha*, *seva-aparādha*, *Vaiṣṇava-aparādha*, *guru-aparādha*, *dhāma-aparādha*, etc. By accomplishing this, one moves from offensive chanting to offenseless chanting. One must also chant a prescribed number of rounds daily.

To realize *prayojana-jñāna* in chanting means to come to the stage of *uttama-adhikārī*, the stage at which one chants in *bhāva* [ecstasy] and ultimately *prema* [pure love of God]. Haridāsa Ṭhākura was a completely liberated person who chanted in pure *prema-bhakti*, and thus he was *jagad-guru*, a teacher who was fit to instruct the entire universe in the art of pure chanting.

The scriptures and teachers of all true religions warn against false prophets outwardly cloaked as sheep, but inwardly possessing the consciousness of ravenous wolves. To detect the true identity of real *sādhus* (saintly persons), one must evaluate their words and actions for consistency and integrity.

Those who pose as religious teachers, hoping to gain honor and wealth, personify religious hypocrisy – an offense to the holy name. Those who follow such persons, based on the external symbols and titles adopted by them, fail to attain the favor of Kṛṣṇa. Both such teachers and students cause undue disturbance to society.[2]

Thus, it is the duty of Vaiṣṇavas to remain neutral while regarding the external markings of spiritual status, and instead to seek the indications described by *śāstra* [scripture] of an inner love for God. They should associate with and serve those genuine *sādhus* recognized by this test.

The eternal universal religion, *sanātana-dharma*, emphasizes that every living entity has a right to perfection, not by a change in external dress or ritualistic behavior, but by purification of consciousness. A contending opinion has evolved amongst the Indian *brāhmaṇas* of Kali-yuga: they believe persons born in other castes are ineligible for liberation. To their minds, the best that one may do is to cultivate sufficient credentials (good *karma*) to attain a birth as a *brāhmaṇa* in a future lifetime. This sinister conception is a false one, since spiritual development does not hinge on birth, but rather on the quality and activity of the practitioner.

The nature of the material world is that everything, even the practice of a divinely ordained social and religious system (*varṇāśrama*), deteriorates with time, becoming subject to the selfish aspirations and misconceptions of conditioned souls. When there is a sufficient decline in religious observance and a predominant rise in irreligious practice, the Lord either appears Himself or sends an authorized, empowered agent of His to rectify the situation.

Under the foster care of Kali, many demonic persons take birth in *brāhmaṇa* families to wreak havoc and destruction on the social order and to disturb the peace and influence of the simple, pious people. The *brāhmaṇas*, as the highest order of *varṇa* [social class], are traditionally meant to guide the other three castes in matters of spiritual life. If such *brāhmaṇas* become degraded and fall from the spiritual standards, then the rest of society, who are dependent on their guidance, will follow the same course.

The scriptures advise avoiding even the sight of a *brāhmaṇa* who has no devotion to Viṣṇu, as they are the true "untouchables."[3] Whereas a devotee, even if born outside the social order, uplifts and sanctifies all souls throughout the world by his saintly dealings and spiritual influence.

In order to dissipate various misconceptions developed over the ages that have perverted the pure Vedic perspective, the Supreme Lord makes suitable arrangements for His most illustrious, empowered, and unconquerable servants to appear on earth in humble circumstances.

Thus, Lord Brahmā, unto whom the Lord had first imparted Vedic knowledge from within his heart; from whose four mouths the four *Vedas* first vibrated in this universe; who bestowed upon Nārada the Vedic wisdom which he repeated to the sage Vyāsa; that best of the *brāhmaṇas*, the original guru, father and co-creator of this universe, took birth in a family of the Islamic faith.

Through the example of his life, all of the fortified and well-defended misconceptions regarding the eternal religion and occupation of souls were smashed to pieces. His faith and dedication to chanting the holy name dispelled the darkness of Kali, attracted Lord Caitanya to descend, and entitled him to the epithet *nāmācārya* [teacher of the holy name], which was awarded by the Lord Himself.

II.

How was it that Haridāsa Ṭhākura came to take birth in a humble family of Muslims? There is naturally a great history behind this extraordinary situation. In the childhood pastimes of Kṛṣṇa, an enormous serpent, the unconquerable Aghāsura, who was considered the embodiment of intolerance and of cruelty[4], was effortlessly slain by the Lord. The *devatās* (the demigods) were astonished by this wonderful feat of the Lord. They had previously felt terrified when Agha merely glanced upwards.

Brahmā saw the potency of the Supreme Personality in Kṛṣṇa, but he was bewildered by the intimate sweetness of loving exchanges between Śrī Kṛṣṇa and the *gopas* [cowherd boys]. Observing their picnics, Brahmā noticed that the *gopas* would taste the various delicacies packed by their mothers, and if a preparation was especially tasty they would offer it to Kṛṣṇa, who would lovingly eat their remnants!

Brahmā knew very well that his father, Lord Nārāyaṇa [Viṣṇu], would never eat remnants from the hands of mere cowherd boys. Yet who, other than Nārāyaṇa, possessed the potency to kill Aghāsura? Devising a strategy to determine for himself who the child might be, Brahmā stole the calves and cowherd boys. He hoped that seeing Kṛṣṇa's reaction would help him ascertain the child's true identity.

Thereafter, unbeknownst to Brahmā, Kṛṣṇa expanded Himself into exact duplicates of all the boys and calves for one year. Later, when this trick of the Lord was revealed to Brahmā by all of the duplicates of the boys and calves expanding into Viṣṇu forms (to Brahmā's total bewilderment and astonishment), he came to know that Kṛṣṇa is the source of Nārāyaṇa. He was made privy to this confidential knowledge and also discovered that the beauty, sweetness, and charm of Śyāmasundara covers and excels the power, glory, and majesty of Viṣṇu.

Following this epiphany, Lord Brahmā came before Kṛṣṇa to glorify Him as the Supreme Personality of Godhead. Brahmā revealed his heart's desire, "The greatest possible good fortune that could ever befall me would be to take any birth in this forest of Gokula. Then my head could be bathed by the dust falling from the lotus feet of any of its residents. Their entire life and soul is the Supreme Personality of Godhead, Mukunda, the dust of whose lotus feet is searched for in the Vedic *mantras*."[5]

Kṛṣṇa did not respond with so much as a glance, but thought to Himself, "Who is this four-headed being, and where has he come from? What is he doing here? What is he saying? I am busy looking for my calves. I am just a cowherd boy and do not understand all this."[6]

Brahmā thought it best to depart rather than disrupt Kṛṣṇa's *līlā* any further, and Kṛṣṇa approved his leaving by silence only.

Brahmā regretted his offense deeply, but Kṛṣṇa did not console him or respond to his prayers. It was a period of deep suffering for Brahmā, but he accepted it as a challenge to find the deeper goal and purpose of life, that would make his situation worth living through. In his repentance he found his ultimate role in life. Brahmā contemplated Kṛṣṇa's next appearance in this world, in a form richly endowed with the compassion and love of Śrīmatī Rādhārāṇī, Kṛṣṇa's eternal consort. He felt a calling to surrender to that Golden Lord and serve in His most merciful mission. Answering that calling gave meaning to his pain, and he returned to Earth deeply determined, this time in Navadvīpa-dhāma, undertaking austerities with a desire to achieve Lord Gaurāṅga's mercy. Brahmā's activities as the humblest and purest of saints forms the substance of the book you are about to read.

III.

Soon after Haridāsa Ṭhākura had concluded his earthly pastimes and returned to Lord Caitanya's *nitya-līlā* (eternal pastimes), Mahāprabhu also withdrew from the sight of mortals, plunging the Earth into unprecedented darkness. Some great luminaries appeared thereafter to reflect the Golden Avatāra's munificent rays, but as they too ascended (to the Lord's realm), the dense darkness of Kali-yuga set in once again.

Those who might conclude that Lord Caitanya's influence has faded would not be guilty of entirely faulty reasoning. But, those reaching such a conclusion have not fathomed the depth of Lord Caitanya's gardening metaphor. To understand the nature of gardening, it is important to know the stages and seasons in the life of a seed.

Lord Caitanya's pastimes are likened to seeds which impregnated the earth with the initial life force for pastimes to follow. Those pastime seeds had the power to inaugurate a golden age within the iron age, a *prema-yuga* within the Kali-yuga.

The dawning of that glorious fruition is now on the horizon. As thousands of *mleccha*-born Vaiṣṇavas [devotional offspring of the meat-eating humans] from around the world unite on the sacrificial altar of the holy name to echo the *saṅkīrtana* of Lord Caitanya, it is natural to reflect on one of the seeds which Lord Caitanya planted—the life of Haridāsa Ṭhākura.

In time, darkness always gives way to light, for knowledge can only be covered for a while (temporarily) by the cloud of illusion. Before the dawn of creation, when Brahmā was born in darkness, Kṛṣṇa implanted the seed of Vedic wisdom in his heart. That seed sprouted and grew into subsequent pastimes in which the ripened fruit of Vedic knowledge was revealed and distributed, culminating in the life and teachings of Haridāsa Ṭhākura.

The seeds of that fruit were again covered and in time fructified in the fulfillment of Lord Caitanya's own prediction and desire that "The holy name will be spread to every town and village of the Earth."[7] As the seeds from the fruit of the desire tree, known as the holy name, take root and spread, the whole world is uplifted by its unfailing influence. In the cooling shade of that desire tree, untold millions will find shade and shelter from the scorching effects of conflict and suffering.

The effects of Haridāsa Ṭhākura's life can be witnessed today by seeing the masses embrace the one great philosophy of equality. Many persons are taking initiation into the universal and eternal religion of divine service, the congregational chanting of the holy names. Seeing the outcastes of all lands being drawn irresistibly to the lotus feet of Bhakti devī [goddess of devotion], thus achieving eternal life in Vṛndāvana [the supreme spiritual abode], we bow down again to the dust of the feet of Haridāsa Ṭhākura, who revealed to the world, in pastime (example) and precept, the untold glories of the holy name. We also bow down to His Divine Grace A.C. Bhaktivedanta Swami Prabhupāda who, following in the Nāmācārya's footsteps, expanded and continued what he had begun by spreading the chanting of the holy name to every town and village of the world.

Endnotes

1 *Padma Purāṇa*, as cited in *Śrī Caitanya-caritāmṛta Madhya-lila* 17.133.

2 *śruti-smṛti-purāṇādi-pañcaratna-vidhiṁ vinā // aikāntikī harer bhaktir utpātāyaiva kalpate* "Devotional service to the Lord that ignores the authorized Vedic literatures like the *Upaniṣads*, *Purāṇas*, *Nārada-Pañcarātra*, etc., is simply an unnecessary disturbance in society." (*Bhakti-rasāmṛta-sindhu* 1.2.101)

3 *Padma Purāṇa*, spoken by Lord Śiva:

kim atra bahunoktena brāhmaṇa ye hy avaiṣṇavaḥ
teṣāṁ sambhāṣaṇaṁ sparśaṁ pramādenāpi varjjayet
śvapākam iva nekṣeta loke vipram avaiṣṇavam
vaiṣṇavo varṇa bāhyo 'pi punāti bhuvana-trayam

"There is no need to speak further on this. Even by mistake one should not touch or speak to those *brāhmaṇas* who have no devotion for the Supreme Lord. If a person born in a *brāhmaṇa* family is an *avaiṣṇava*, a nondevotee, one should not see his face, exactly as one should not look upon the face of a *caṇḍāla*, or dog-eater. However, a Vaiṣṇava found in *varṇas* other than *brāhmaṇa* can purify the three worlds."

4 *Śrī Kṛṣṇa-saṁhitā* by Śrīla Bhaktivinoda Ṭhākura.

5 *Śrīmad-Bhāgavatam* 10.14.34, Prayers by Lord Brahmā.

6 *Śrīmad-Bhāgavatam* 10.14.42, commentary by Śrīla Viśvanātha Cakravartī Ṭhākura.

7 *Śrī Caitanya-bhāgavata Antya* 4.126, *pṛthivīte āche yata nagarādi grāma sarvatra pracāra haibe mora nāma:* "In every town and village, the chanting of My name will be heard."

hare kṛṣṇa hare kṛṣṇa kṛṣṇa kṛṣṇa hare hare
hare rāma hare rāma rāma rāma hare hare
iti ṣoḍaśakaṁ nāmnāṁ kali-kalmaṣa-nāśanam
nātaḥ parataropāyaḥ sarva-vedeṣu dṛśyate

HARE KṚṢṆA, HARE KṚṢṆA, KṚṢṆA KṚṢṆA Hare Hare/ Hare Rāma, Hare Rāma, Rāma Rāma, Hare Hare—these sixteen names composed of thirty-two syllables are the only means to counteract the evil effects of Kali-yuga. In all the *Vedas* it is seen that to cross the ocean of nescience there is no alternative to the chanting of the holy name.

Kali-santaraṇa Upaniṣad
[cited *Śrī Caitanya-caritāmṛta Ādī-līlā* 7.76]

Preface

IN LATE 15TH CENTURY BENGAL, roughly comprised of what is now known as Bangladesh and West Bengal (along with parts of Bihar, Tripura and Orissa, where Bengali remains the native language), the socio-religious climate was complex, with many competing forces at work. Bengal was under Muslim rule due to the Turko-Afghan invasion. The Vaiṣṇava scholar Steven Rosen states in his book *The Life and Times of Lord Chaitanya*, (citing the historian Dilip Kumar Mukherjee): "...Wave after wave of alien hordes had come from across the Hindukush Mountains, and, after an orgy of pillaging, raping and slaying, made themselves masters of the country."

Initially, there was an attempt to convert by sword, but in the end conversion to Islam or other religious cults was often effected by the policies of the rigid caste system and, in particular, the *smārtas* (caste *brāhmaṇas*) who considered that birth in a *brāhmaṇa* family was sufficient to confer an exalted religious and social status. This fallacious notion created a tendency in the other castes to embrace Islam due to its more liberal social philosophy. The Muslim conquest of Bengal had greatly disturbed Hindu society. Thousands upon thousands of Hindus had been converted to Islam either by force or by a desire for upward social mobility (which was impossible under the rigid caste system enforced by the caste conscious *smārtas*).

The *smārta brāhmaṇas* kept a tight grip on what they thought was orthodox Hinduism, by establishing incredibly complex ritualistic performances, which became increasingly numerous. Without a sophisticated knowledge of Sanskrit and a long study of all the complex rituals, no one could effectively challenge their authority. However, other popular folk-cults sprang up in answer, propagating concocted forms of demigod worship like those of Manasā, Caṇḍī, and Dharma. Tantric (black magic) rituals became popular, and Tāntrika Kaulācāra, with its rituals involving wine and flesh, became prominent and posed a challenge to the Hindu society. The Tantrics even claimed that Kṛṣṇa worship was Tantric in origin, which alarmed the *smārtas* as well as the Vaiṣṇavas, who were at that time a minority in Navadvīpa.

The *smārtas* (much like the Biblical Pharisees) were interested in maintaining their position of authority, due to the lucrative nature of performing the rituals thought to be essential by many members of Hindu society. Since many of the non-Vedic cults did not directly challenge their authority, some *smārta* recognition was afforded them.

Dr. Ramakanta Chakravarti writes: "The *smārta* recognition of some of the un-Vedic cults reflected their popularity. Secondly, these cults did not challenge the social or ritual supremacy of the *brāhmaṇas*, or the brāhmiṇical priests. Thirdly, the brāhmiṇical recognition of some of these cults probably signified a half-hearted attempt on the part of the *brāhmaṇas* to establish some sort of social integration of the Hindu castes and sects."[1]

"The rituals [of the *smārtas*] had become a trade with vested interests. The singular fact was that the Sultanate of Bengal did not interfere with them...The predominance of the Hindu rituals and the continuance of the Mohammedan autocracy were perhaps complementary developments."[2]

Thus, the *smārtas* did not want the status quo to change. Despite challenges from the folk cults and the Tantrics, they maintained their supremacy with the aid of the Moghul administrators. As thousands of Hindus had been converted into Islam, the only response of the *smārtas* was to stress on *śuddhi* or purification. The rituals were made into formal writs which were compulsory for all Hindus. They never recognized the necessity of preaching Hinduism to the fringe of Hindu society (the lower castes). Such *brāhmaṇas* never considered that this program could be effective in buttressing and enriching Hindu society. Dr. Chakravarti writes: "...the intelligent *brāhmaṇas*...either lacked the courage to adopt that programme, or lacked the intelligence to think of it. Their whole purpose was to categorize, describe and multiply useless rituals...It has also been clearly stated by Barbosa that the Hindus of the upper castes were regularly embracing Islam with a view to receiving favour from the ruling Muhammadans..."[3]

In short, due to spiritual blindness and lack of spiritual intelligence, as well as material motivations for wealth, social prestige and distinction, the *smārtas* utterly neglected the actual spiritual welfare of the people, as well as their own welfare.

Śrīla Bhaktisiddhānta Sarasvatī Ṭhākura summarizes this difficult period of history as follows:

> "It is necessary to have some idea of the state of society in Bengal at that period in order to be able to understand the significance of the Thakur's [Haridāsa's] appearance. The caste-system had lost all its propriety and its so-called purity was only another name for oppressive practices due to the grossest abuse of its principles.

The views regarding religion that were then upheld by the public opinion of the so-called religious communities were nothing but the infuriated expression of sectarian rancour. On the one hand, the rotten Hindu society [was] swollen with the lower grades of its own strata and, [on the other], in the name of religion, they endeavoured merely to realise selfish ambitions. Their practice of religion took the forms of hostility to Vaishnavas and attacks on the Sanatana Dharma--the Eternal Religion of all Jivas. The meanness of the selfish contempt for the true faith [and] wanton cruelty [expressed] showed all the virulence of a chronic disease that had penetrated to the very bones and marrow of the Hindu society. On the other hand, the narrow-minded Yavana *sampradaya* [Muslim community] was enacting scenes of malice, hatred, aggression and oppression towards the Hindu community. The Yavana society, failing to appreciate the true greatness of Hinduism, never desisted from its persistent and many-sided activities against the religion of the Hindus. The Aryas and Yavanas of Bengal were acting towards each other on the conviction that the dharma of man was based on the principle of mutual animosity leading to unjustifiable attacks on the mode of worship of each by the other. The contending passions of the two parties brought untold suffering on society in Bengal. Generally people were devoid of all religious association and were demoralised by every form of luxury which they held in high estimation along with the pleasures of the world and material power. External display had become so prominent in all the religious practices of the Hindus that it would be no exaggeration to say that there was not a single person who had any sympathy for the method of artless devotion. Under the impression that the attainment of the kingdom of the next world was a feat as difficult as the crossing of the highest mountain peaks, the difficult methods of yoga, arduous *vratas* 'vowed observances' such as Chandrayana etc., severe *brahmacharya* and *sannyasa* 'asceticism' etc. were pointed out as the paths leading to *bhukti* 'enjoyment' or *mukti* 'annihilation.' As they had doubts regarding the possibility of attainment of the trivial fruits of *dharma*, *artha* and *kama* by offensive taking of the Name and of *mukti*, the goal of the so-called Vedantist practices, by taking the dimly perceived Name, the Hindus had absolutely no respect for the straight path of devotion."[4]

Thus, in 15th century Bengal there was tremendous social and religious ferment, and Lord Caitanya's appearance during this period, as well as Haridāsa Ṭhākura's 35 years earlier, had a tremendous religious as well as social impact amongst all the above clashing religious forces. Many Muslims were infuriated at the idea that a Muslim like Haridāsa Ṭhākura could convert to Hinduism, which was considered to be a crime punishable by death as we shall later see in this book.[5] The *smārtas* were outraged that a person from the meat-eating race could become a prominent preacher and leader amongst *brāhmaṇas*. They felt that the purity of their practices and their leadership in Hindu society were threatened. However, due to the pure principled behavior of Haridāsa Ṭhākura, the Tantrics also felt that their sensuous doctrine was being threatened and their target audience (the lower castes) was being seduced away from them[6] by Śrī Caitanya Mahāprabhu and His followers like Haridāsa Ṭhākura.[7]

Haridāsa Ṭhākura was reviled, abused, and persecuted for many years, although he also received the support of many pious and sincere persons from all levels of society. Śrīla Prabhupāda comments: "There are many examples in history of devotees of the Lord who risked their lives for the spreading of God consciousness. The favorite example is Lord Jesus Christ. He was crucified by the nondevotees, but he sacrificed his life for spreading God consciousness. Of course, it would be superficial to understand that he was killed. Similarly, in India also there are many examples such as Ṭhākura Haridāsa and Prahlāda Mahārāja. Why such risk? Because they wanted to spread Kṛṣṇa consciousness, and it is difficult."[8]

Once Haridāsa Ṭhākura joined forces with Śrī Caitanya Mahāprabhu, there was a tremendous renaissance of the pure principles of Vaiṣṇavism, and thousands of persons from the *brāhmaṇa* community, as well as Muslims, Tantrics and the folk cults all united under the banner of Śrī Caitanya's philosophy, which was, in fact, the original, universal essence of Vedic teaching: *varṇa* (class) was based on qualifications and symptoms, never birth. All human beings (in fact all living entities) are souls, and anyone who sincerely practiced the principles of Vaiṣṇavism should be accepted not only as a Vaiṣṇava but better than a *brāhmaṇa*. This philosophy, despite being solidly grounded in the Vedic scriptures, was considered revolutionary. There was a tremendous reaction to it, and controversies, violence, and struggle broke out and have continued to the present day. Śrīla Bhaktisiddhānta Sarasvatī Ṭhākura spoke out very strongly against what he called "brāhmaṇism" and, at one point, while leading a procession of Vaiṣṇavas in Navadvīpa, was stoned for his beliefs. On several other occasions his life was directly threatened.

Śrīla A.C. Bhaktivedanta Swami Prabhupāda comments:

"So the birthright brahmanism is not applicable at the present moment. The sacred thread inaugurated by my Guru Maharaja according to *pancaratrika* system and *Hari-bhakti-vilasa* by Srila Sanatana Gosvami must continue. It does not matter whether the priestly class accepts it or not. When my Guru Maharaja Bhatisiddhanta Sarasvati Gosvami Prabhupada introduced this system, it was protested even by His inner circle of God-brothers and friends. Of course He had actually no God-brothers, but there were many disciples of Bhaktivinode Thakura who were considered as God-brothers who protested against this action of my Guru Maharaja, but He didn't care for it. Actually one who takes to chanting Hare Krsna mantra offenselessly immediately becomes situated transcendentally, and therefore he has no need of being initiated with sacred thread, but Guru Maharaja introduced this sacred thread because a Vaisnava was being mistaken as belonging to the material caste. To accept a Vaisnava in material caste system [birth] is [a] hellish consideration (*naraki buddhi*).

> Therefore, to save the general populace from being offender to a Vaisnava, he persistently introduced this sacred thread ceremony, and we must follow his footsteps...This system introduced by my Guru Maharaja is a chance for all the members of the society, scientifically based and applied, apart from the exploitative sentiment of birthright 'caste' system, to become actually situated on the transcendental platform."[9]

The pure Vedic conception of social division, on the basis of actual qualifications and symptoms, has historically created conflict due to the attachment for control and mundane social prestige of materialistic religionists. Such attachment generated hatred for genuine *sādhus* and even their murder in some instances. Thus, this hagiography[10] shall attempt to portray the heroic activities of Śrīla Haridāsa Ṭhākura, who consistently risked his life to rescue others from illusion and suffering created by misidentification of the self with matter. Just as Jesus Christ was crucified for straightforwardly telling the truth and exposing the hypocrisy of the Pharisees and other cheating religionists, so also for the same "crime" Haridāsa Ṭhākura was beaten in 22 marketplaces, despite exhibiting all the pure symptoms of an empowered and liberated soul.

His story has everything: love, conflict, drama, temptation, philosophy, ecstasy, reversal of fortune, tragedy, victory, inspiration, and transcendence. His essential teaching proposes that the happiness that we seek and, indeed the lives that we hope to create for ourselves, can all be found in the syllables of the *mahā-mantra*: Hare Kṛṣṇa Hare Kṛṣṇa Kṛṣṇa Kṛṣṇa Hare Hare Hare Rāma Hare Rāma Rāma Rāma Hare Hare. This eternal truth has as much relevance today as it did more than 500 years ago. The message is as eternal as the messenger, Haridāsa Ṭhākura, who continues to instruct us even today.

Nāmācārya Śrīla Haridāsa Ṭhākura

In 1871, Śrīla Bhaktivinoda Ṭhākura wrote the following while absorbed in meditation on the *samādhi* of Haridāsa Ṭhākura:

On Haridas Samadhi
(A Saragrahi Vaishnava)

O! Born of Moslem parents, Haridas!
And trained in youth in Moslem creed,
Thy noble heart to Vaishnava truth did pass!—
Thy holy acts thy candour plead!

Is there a soul that cannot learn from thee
That man must give up sect for God?
That thoughts of race and sect can ne'er agree
With what they call Religion broad?

Thy love of God and brother soul alone
Bereft thyself of early friends,—
Thy softer feelings oft to kindness prone
Led on thyself for higher ends!!

I weep to read the Kazees[11] and their men
Oft persecuted thee, alas!
But thou didst nobly pray for th' wicked then!
For thou wert Vaishnava Haridas!!

And God is boundless grace to thee, O man!
United thee to one who came
To save the fallen souls from Evil's plan
Of taking human souls to shame.

And he it was who led you all that came
For life eternal, —holy, —pure!
And gave you rest in Heaven's enduring name
And sacred blessing ever sure!

Thy body rests upon the sacred sands
Of Swargadwar near the sea,
Oh! Hundreds come to thee from distant lands
T' enjoy a holy, thrilling glee!

The waters roar and storming winds assail
Thy ears in vain, Ah! Vaishnava soul!
The charms of Brindaban thy heart regale,
Unknown the wheel of time doth roll!!

He reasons ill who tells that Vaishnavas die
When thou art living still in sound.
The Vaishnavas die to live and living try
To spread a holy life around!

Now let the candid man that seeks to live
Follow thy way on shores of time,
Then posterity sure to him will give
Like one song in simple rhyme!

Endnotes

1 Dr. Ramakanta Chakravarti, *Vaiṣṇavism in Bengal*, Sanskrit Pustak Bhandar, 1985, p. 31.

2 Dr. Ramakanta Chakravarti, *Vaiṣṇavism in Bengal*, Sanskrit Pustak Bhandar, 1985, p. 32.

3 Dr. Ramakanta Chakravarti, *Vaiṣṇavism in Bengal*, Sanskrit Pustak Bhandar, 1985, pp. 35, 36.

4 Srila Bhaktisiddhanta Sarasvati Thakura, *The Holy Name and Thakur Haridas*, Sri Gaudiya Math, 1998, pp. 1, 2.

5 According to Shariya, Moslem Law, apostasy is punishable by death, and some contemporary Muslims who follow Shariya impose this penalty on an apostate.

6 The governments at that time enforced a feudal system. Heads of recognized religious groups were given tax exemption and even awarded lands, along with their own "serfs." Thus, the serfs who worked the lands would pay taxes to the religious heads, to the Mahants, Thakurs, Swamis, or whatever they might be called according to locale. When a new group like the Caitanya movement threatened the faith of their followers, the Hindu religious leaders were concerned with potential loss of income. Later, a similar tension existed between Śrīla Bhaktisiddhānta Sarasvatī Ṭhākura and the Gauḍīya Vaiṣṇava Gosvāmī families, who were in some cases prominent landowners.

7 Richard Eaton, *The Bengal of Śrī Caitanya Mahāprabhu, Vaisnavism: Contemporary Scholars Discuss the Gaudiya Tradition*, edited by Steven J. Rosen, FOLK Books, 1992, pp. 174, 175, "...the true adversaries of the Caitanya movement at that time were the *brāhmaṇas* of the *śākta* cults—the devotees of Caṇḍi and Manasā. In their view, the whole *kīrtana* tradition not only caused public disturbances, but lacked scriptural authority. Secondly, they accused Caitanya of identifying himself with God. Thirdly, that he had usurped from *brāhmaṇas* their own monopoly over the use of *mantras*. And, finally that his group was attracting followers from among the lower classes. Now I find this last remark very significant because it hints at the social basis of the Caṇḍi and Manasa sects at the time. In other words, *śākta brāhmaṇas* or *smārta brāhmaṇas*, seem to have viewed the low classes as their natural constituency, and they saw Caitanya as threatening to cut in on their potential clientele. So I think this, really, was at the basis of their complaints to the Kazi."

8 *Bhagavad-gita* 11.55, purport *BG As It Is* (audio).

9 ACBS letter, 70-11-28.

10 [Greek *hagios* holy] Hagiography is defined as "the biography of a saint," but it carries the additional connotation of "a biography that overpraises its subject." Generally hagiographies, as rendered by worshippers and followers of such saints, tend to extol the glories of saintly personalities and to overlook biographical details that would expose character flaws or anomalies. Such works tend to be viewed with cynicism and are treated as historical fiction or myth. Scholars favoring empiricism in historical narrative tend towards extreme skepticism when they are confronted with either miracles or a life of flawless spiritual purity.

Therefore, what is to be made of this account of Haridāsa Ṭhākura, whose life is so well-documented in the medieval works of *Śrī Caitanya-caritāmṛta* and *Śrī Caitanya-bhāgavata*, both of which are based on eyewitness accounts of the activities of this Vaiṣṇava saint? Are the eyewitnesses all deluded beings who exaggerated to create a good story? Implicit assumptions are made: if persons are said to display miracles, extraordinary goodness, sublime saintliness, or total selflessness, then such acts and qualities must, *a priori*, be exaggerations or lies. Such thinking displays an egocentric and unwarranted prejudice—*ātmavan manyate jagat*—we think others must think or behave as we do. This is muddled thinking. One may not have met such a saint, but that does not prove that such a person does not exist. This book presents that person the skeptics have not met: the Nāmācārya, Haridāsa Ṭhākura.

[11] A kazi (kazee) is a local judge who adjudicates based on Shariya (Moslem Law) which was established shortly after the time of Mohammad. As such, a kazi took the role of the local executive, legislative, and judicial government rolled into one.

Abbreviations Key

BG	-	*Bhagavad-gītā As It Is*
CB	-	*Śrī Caitanya-bhāgavata*
CC	-	*Śrī Caitanya-caritāmṛta*
MG	-	*Kṛṣṇa Consciousness The Matchless Gift*
NOD	-	*Nectar of Devotion*
NOI	-	*Nectar of Instruction*
RTW	-	*Renunciation Through Wisdom*
SSR	-	*The Science of Self Realization*
TLK	-	*Teachings of Lord Kapila, the Son of Devahūti*

HARIDĀSA ṬHĀKURA IS KNOWN AS *Nāmācārya* because it is he who preached the glories of chanting *hari-nāma*, the holy name of God. By using the words *tomāra avatāra* ("your incarnation"), Śrī Caitanya Mahāprabhu confirms that Haridāsa Ṭhākura is the incarnation of Lord Brahmā. Śrīla Bhaktisiddhānta Sarasvatī Ṭhākura says that advanced devotees help the Supreme Personality of Godhead in His mission and that such devotees or personal associates incarnate by the will of the Supreme Lord. The Supreme Lord incarnates by His own will, and, by His will, competent devotees also incarnate to help Him in His mission. Haridāsa Ṭhākura is thus the incarnation of Lord Brahmā, and other devotees are likewise incarnations to help in the prosecution of the Lord's mission.

Śrī Caitanya-caritāmṛta Antya-līlā 11.25 purport.

HARIDĀSA WAS BORN IN A LOW-CLASS family just as Prahlada was born in a demoniac family and Hanumān was born in a monkey family. The demigods desire the touch of Haridāsa and even Mother Gaṅgā desires that Haridāsa immerse in her waters. What to speak of his touch, just by seeing Haridāsa one is released from the bondage of fruitive activities. Indeed, even if one sees a person who has taken shelter of Haridāsa, he is freed from material bondage."

Caitanya-bhāgavata Ādi-khaṇḍa 16.241–244

Ṛcīka Muni's son, who was named Brahmā, became a *yavana* due to his father's curse. The great-souled Brahmā, who was cursed by his father, Ṛcīka, and Brahmā, the universal creator, met together as Haridāsa. Prahlāda came and united with them as well. These three mingled together as Śrī Haridāsa Mahājana."

Prema-vilāsa, chapter 24

Chapter One

Advent & Identity

Advent

THE ADVENT OF HARIDĀSA ṬHĀKURA is shrouded in mystery. Although there is very little definitive information about his early life, something can be gleaned from the main biographical sources: *Śrī Caitana-bhāgavata* by Vṛndāvana dāsa Ṭhākura and *Śrī Caitanya-caritāmṛta* by Kṛṣṇadāsa Kavirāja Gosvāmī, as well as other authoritative books. He was born in the Village of Budhan in the District of Jessore in East Bengal (now in Bangaladesh) to a Muslim family. The names of his mother and father, his early education, how he passed his boyhood, etc., all remain unknown. He appeared some 30 to 35 years prior to Śrī Caitanya Mahāprabhu.

Professor Nisikanta Sanyal[1] states: "Thakur Haridas made his appearance in this world in about the year 1451 A.D. (1372 Sakabda), thirty-five years before the Advent of Sree Chaitanya, in the village of Budhan in the district of Jessore. He came of a Muhammedan family and in some manner, of which we do not possess any trustworthy record, obtained very early in life the mercy of a Vaishnava who initiated him into the religion of all souls." The professor finishes his summary of the Ṭhākura's early life by stating: "He, thereupon, left his parents' house and his kin, and came to Benapole where he made a small hut and lived therein."[2]

Rāghava Caitanya Prabhu[3] tells us little more: "There are no authentic records of his antecedents, his parents, boyhood, education, etc. He was born in a Muslim family. We know him under the name of 'Haridas,' which literally means 'a servant of Sri Hari.' Though born of a Muslim family, he possessed an inexplicable aptitude for taking the Name of Sri Hari. Hence, violating the rules of Muslim society, he incessantly repeated Sri Hari's Name. He felt it was the sole support of his life. Having lost all attachment to worldly life even when very young, Thakur Haridas left his native village."[4]

Śrīla Bhaktisiddhānta Sarasvatī Ṭhākura writes:

> "In these dark days of Bengal thirty or thirty-five years in advance of the appearance of Bhagavan Sri Chaitanyadeva, in order to help the transcendental activities of Him Who is Love Himself, the four-faced Virinchi (Brahma) appeared in a non-Hindu Yavana family in the Village of Budhan...We do not learn anything about the boyhood of Thakur Haridas from authoritative works. No reliance can be placed on recent books on the subject that offer fictitious accounts bearing the names of ancient authors. In the opinion of some, the appearance of Brahma in a non-Hindu Ya-

> vana family was in expiation of the offence of stealing the calves. There are some again who hold that Sri Prahlada Maharaj became visible under the name of Haridas. When he grew up in years, Thakur Haridas, giving up the social customs and principles of the Yavana [Muslim] family was found constantly taking the Name of Sri Hari. The writers who have recorded the lila of those days are silent as regards the agent by whose instigation Thakur Haridas was initiated in the rite of the Name of the Godhead, transgressing the rules of Yavana society and also as regards the person whose mercy he obtained[5]. We, therefore, feel a certain degree of apprehension in adducing proofs in support of those facts after the lapse of such a long period. Haridas ascertained that to pray to God without any selfish object giving up all mundane expectations and impulses is the only duty of life. After having arrived at this decision, though still very young, Thakur Haridas left Budhan and taking up his residence in a solitary cell close to Budhan began loudly taking the Name of Krishna."[6]

In the above statement by Śrīla Sarasvatī Ṭhākura, he appears to express ambivalence about whether Haridāsa Ṭhākura is Brahmā or Prahlāda Mahārāja. This is due to his fidelity to the previous *ācāryas* who have given different opinions about Haridāsa Ṭhākura's identity, and who have also accepted both the possibility and reality of one spiritual being having multiple identities or personalities. Śrīla Kavi-karṇapūra Gosvāmī, the exalted son of Śrīla Śivānanda Sena; Śrīla Svarūpa Dāmodara Gosvāmī, the personal secretary of Śrī Caitanya Mahāprabhu; and Śrīla Murāri Gupta Prabhu, the incarnation of Hanumān, have all accepted this latter principle in their writings. What's more, Śrīla Murāri Gupta Prabhu and Śrīla Svarūpa Dāmodara Gosvāmī both kept extensive notes on all the activities of Śrī Caitanya Mahāprabhu and His associates which are considered to form the authoritative basis of subsequent biographies by Vṛndāvana dāsa Ṭhākura (*Śrī Caitanya-bhāgavata*) and Kṛṣṇadāsa Kavirāja Gosvāmī (*Śrī Caitanya-caritāmṛta*).[7]

Thus, what would constitute a severe derangement of the mind on the material plane (a person possessing multiple personalities) is normative, ecstatic, and non-conflicting on the spiritual plane. In the "Whose Who" of Caitanya-līlā (*Śrī Gaura-gaṇoddeśa-dīpikā*) by Śrīla Kavi-karṇapūra, some of Mahāprabhu's associates are said to be composed of one, two, or even three or more personalities or identities of liberated souls serving in the eternal kingdom of Goloka Vṛndāvana!

Vṛndāvana dāsa Ṭhākura states:

"Haridāsa Ṭhākura appeared in the Village of Budhana, and as a result that province is filled with *kīrtana* even today." Śrīla Bhaktisiddhānta Sarasvatī Ṭhākura comments: "Haridāsa Ṭhākura is an eternally perfect associate of the Lord. He appeared in a Mohammedan family, in the village of Budhana, within the district of Jessore. Due to his mercy, many persons in the district of Jessore obtained piety and became faithful to the chanting of Kṛṣṇa's holy names."[8]

Identity

In the *Navadvīpa-dhāma-mahātmya*, Śrīla Bhaktivinoda Ṭhākura has written the following: "In the Dvāpara-yuga Nandanandana Śrī Kṛṣṇa was herding the cows through Vraja-dhāma in the company of his cowherd boyfriends when Brahmā decided to test the Lord out of a desire to see His majestic form and opulences. He stole both Kṛṣṇa's cows and calves, as well as his friends and hid them for a year in the caves of Sumeru Mountain. But a year later, when Brahmā returned to Vraja, he was astonished to see that Kṛṣṇa was still there with both His friends and cows. Brahmā immediately understood his error and began to regret his rash action. He fell down at Kṛṣṇa's feet and begged him for forgiveness. Kṛṣṇa responded by mercifully revealing His divine opulence. He who appears in the Dvāpara-yuga as Nandanandana Śrī Kṛṣṇa descends again in the Kali-yuga as Gaurāṅga, taking on the mood and luster of Rādhārāṇī in order to display the most magnanimous pastimes. Brahmā was afraid that he might commit the same offense during Gaurāṅga's incarnation so he went to Antardvīpa, the central island of Navadvīpa, and began to meditate. The Lord understood his mind and so came to him in the form of Gaurāṅga and said, 'During my incarnation as Gaura, you will be born in a family of *mlecchas* and will preach the glories of the Holy Name and bring auspiciousness to all living beings.'"

There are some additional statements about Haridāsa Ṭhākura that may be found in *Advaita-prakāśa* and other literatures, which are not included in this book. This is due to Śrīla Bhaktisiddhānta Sarasvatī Ṭhākura's opinion that *Advaita-prakāśa* is not dependable as a source of information. He states in his introduction of *Śrī Caitanya-caritāmṛta*: "There are several other new books or books that were written a little later (such as Jayānanda's *Caitanya-maṅgala*, Govinda Dāsa's *kadacā*, *Vaṁśī-śikṣā*, *Advaita-prakāśa* and *Nityānanda-vaṁśa-vistāra*). Although it is said that these books are old, we have no interest in them. They are distinct in the way that they are incorrect in their philosophical truths and conclusions. Their narrow-minded, evil intentions are obvious and highly noticeable due to the absence of any effort [of] proper teachings in them. The *Caitanya-caritāmṛta* is said to be the original book, and these *āpa-granthas* (bogus books) are not recognized."

The above statement by Śrīla Sarasvati Ṭhākura may seem a trifle harsh to the reader. However, the *sahajiyās*, groups of spiritual sentimentalists (pseudo-devotees), who sprang up after the disappearance of Śrī Caitanya Mahāprabhu and His principal followers, created great obstacles in the preaching of Śrīla Bhaktivinoda Ṭhākura and Śrīla Bhaktisiddhānta Sarasvatī Ṭhākura. Such so-called devotees composed many literatures about Lord Caitanya and His followers which had, as their primary source, their fertile imaginations. Later, a group of Calcutta publishers called the "Batatalas"[9] published more than 50 of the *sahajiyās'* spurious works during the years 1815 to 1899. These books came to be viewed by many people as the definitive works concerning Lord Caitanya and His associates. The service performed by Śrīla Bhaktivinoda Ṭhākura and Śrīla Bhaktisiddhānta Sarasvatī Ṭhākura was to publish and propagate the actual authorized works written by the contemporaries of Mahāprabhu and their disciples. Anything not in conformance with such eyewitness accounts or accounts from authorized biographers was rejected. Some of the *sahajiyā* works made claims for their own antiquity (even to the extent of publishing their creative fictions in the names of Śrīla Rūpa and Sanātana Gosvāmīs), but the erroneous conclusions and speculative assumptions of such books revealed their undependable nature. At their worst, such *sahajiyā* authors were *gañjā* smokers, black arts tantrics, and practitioners of illicit sex in imitation of *rasa-līlā*; at best, such sentimentalists deviated from the pure teachings of the Six Gosvāmīs of Vṛndāvana and concocted various spiritual practices and writings. Discarding such tainted accounts, Śrīla Bhaktisiddhānta Sarasvatī Ṭhākura strictly adhered to the conclusions of the Six Gosvāmīs and their followers.

Regarding Haridāsa Ṭhākura's previous identity, *Gaura-gaṇoddeśa-dīpikā* states:

> "Ṛcīka Muni's son Brahmā Mahātapaḥ and Prahlāda Mahārāja combined to appear as Haridāsa Ṭhākura in Lord Caitanya's pastimes. In the book *Caitanya-carita*, Murāri Gupta explains that one morning Mahātapaḥ gave an unwashed *tulasi* leaf to his father, who became so angry at him for this that he cursed him. Because of this Mahātapaḥ took birth in a *yavana* family as the great devotee Haridāsa Ṭhākura." (*GGD* texts 93—95)

The Gauḍīya Vaiṣṇava community generally accepts the conclusions of *Śrī Gaura-gaṇoddeśa-dīpikā* due to its being composed by Śrīla Kavi-karṇapūra Gosvāmī, the son of Śrīla Śivānanda Sena, the exalted follower of Śrī Caitanya Mahāprabhu. Śivānanda Sena was the provider and protector of the devotees from Bengal when they traveled to see Lord Caitanya in Jagannātha Purī. He is an eternal associate of the Lord as affirmed by Kṛṣṇadāsa Kavirāja Gosvāmī[10], and in Kṛṣṇa-*līlā* he is a combined form of two *gopīs*, namely Vīrā-devī and Dūtī-devī. Śivānanda Sena's wife is the *vraja-gopī* named Bindumatī[11]. One of the three exalted sons of Śivānanda Sena was Śrīla Kavi-karṇapūra Gosvāmī. All of Śivānanda Sena's sons are eternal associates of the Lord as explained by Kṛṣṇadāsa Kavirāja Gosvāmī.[12] Śrīla Kavi-karṇapūra Gosvāmī is also known as Purī dāsa and Paramānanda Sena. He is the author of many exalted works, including *Ānanda-vṛndāvana-campū*, *Ālaṅkāra-kaustubha*, and the great epic *Caitanya-candrodaya-nātaka,* and was personally empowered by Śrī Caitanya Mahāprabhu to write authoritative books. Murāri Gupta, the incarnation of Hanumān,[13] appeared as a physician in Lord Caitanya's pastimes and is also the author of *Caitanya-carita*, a wonderful description of Śrī Caitanya Mahāprabhu and kept elaborate notes which formed the basis of many subsequent biographical works. Anything written by him is accepted as authoritative by the Gauḍīya Vaiṣṇavas.

In the *Prema-vilasa*, chapter 24, composed by the disciple of Śrīmatī Jāhnavā-devī, Nityānanda dāsa, he concurs with the descriptions by Kavi-karṇapūra Gosvāmī and Bhaktivinoda Ṭhākura and also states that Prahlāda Mahārāja appeared with two(!)Brahmās:

"Ṛcīka Muni's son, who was named Brahmā, became a *yavana* due to his father's curse. The great-souled Brahmā, who was cursed by his father, Ṛcīka, and Brahmā, the universal creator, met together as Haridāsa. Prahlāda came and united with them as well. These three mingled together as Śrī Haridāsa Mahājana."

Śrīla Prabhupāda states: "On the *mahā-prakāsa* day, Lord Caitanya Mahāprabhu embraced Haridāsa Ṭhākura and informed him that he was nondifferent than an incarnation of Prahlāda Mahārāja."[14]

Vṛndāvana dāsa Ṭhākura does not attempt to resolve the previous identity of Haridāsa Ṭhākura. He simply states: "Someone said, 'Haridāsa is like four-headed Brahmā.' Another person said, 'He is the manifestation of Prahlāda.' Haridāsa is certainly an exalted devotee. He enjoys his pastimes amongst the associates of Lord Caitanya."[15]

According to certain writers, Haridāsa Ṭhākura was born in a *brāhmaṇa* family. They say his father's name was Sumatī and his mother's name was Gaurī; that his parents died when he was young; and that he then went to live with a Muslim couple named Khan in the village of Halimpur about five miles from his birthplace on the other bank of the Salai River. Such people say that was why he was brought up in an Islamic environment. However, Śrīla Bhaktisiddhānta Sarasvatī Ṭhākura does not give any credence to such theories, stating: "Some people compose imitation literatures in which they claim that Haridāsa Ṭhākura was born in a seminal *brāhmaṇa* family, and thereby they attribute to him insignificant mundane social considerations, born from their own ignorance. Such imaginary truth is always contrary to historical facts."[13]

Śrīla Bhaktisiddhānta Sarasvatī Ṭhākura expresses his irritation in the above quote concerning persons attempting to ascribe mundane social importance to Haridāsa Ṭhākura. Such attempts are actuated by a desire to deny his birth in a Muslim family and to give him what they consider a more noble position as a seminal *brāhmaṇa*. Haridāsa Ṭhākura was already exalted beyond the imaginations of such authors of whimsical and fallacious accounts. So many imaginary literatures had been published by the Batatalas, as referenced earlier in this chapter, and such literatures had nothing to do with truth or historical fact. Śrīla Sarasvatī Ṭhākura wanted to be sure that no one took such ill-motivated accounts seriously.

Although there are various views about Haridāsa Ṭhākura's previous identity and antecedents, it is generally understood that his life parallels the activities of Prahlāda Mahārāja who took birth in a *daitya* family but was completely absorbed in chanting the Holy Name from early childhood. Prahlāda was persecuted and ultimately delivered by the Lord, as was Haridāsa. Yet Haridāsa Ṭhākura's life also parallels the activities of Brahmā, who had an unparalleled capacity to perform meditational austerities. Haridāsa Ṭhākura was famous amongst all the Vaiṣṇavas, because he chanted 300,000 names of the Lord daily without fail. Haridāsa Ṭhākura is an eternally perfect associate of the Lord; that much is certain, and he is among the greatest of Śrī Caitanya Mahāprabhu's exalted associates.

In an incident to be described later in this narration, a snake charmer, empowered by Śrī Anantadeva, spoke of the glories of Haridāsa:

> "On the order of the Lord, Haridāsa was born in a low-class family to show that birth in a high caste or good family is useless. If a devotee of the Lord is born in a low-class family, he is still worthy of worship. This is the verdict of the scriptures. And if someone is born in a high-class family but does not worship the lotus feet of Śrī Kṛṣṇa, then his high birth is useless and he falls to hell. Haridāsa thus took birth in a low-class family to prove the words of the scriptures. Haridāsa was born in a low-class family just as Prahlāda was born in a demoniac family and Hanumān was born in a monkey family. The demigods desire the touch of Haridāsa and even mother Gaṅgā desires that Haridāsa immerse in her waters. What to speak of his touch, just by seeing Haridāsa one is released from the bondage of fruitive activities. Indeed, even if one sees a person who has taken shelter of Haridāsa, he is freed from material bondage. If I glorify Haridāsa for a hundred years with a hundred mouths I would still not reach the end of his glories. You are all fortunate, for because of you I received an opportunity to glorify Haridāsa. I assure you that one who simply chants the name of Haridāsa without offense will certainly attain the abode of Kṛṣṇa."[17]

Endnotes

[1] Professor Nisikanta Sanyal was a disciple of Śrīla Bhaktisiddhānta Sarasvatī Ṭhākura. Although he appears to have deviated from the pure teachings of Śrīla Sarasvatī Ṭhākura after his guru's departure, his book *Sree Krishna Chaitanya* was a very scholarly treatise which pleased Śrīla Sarasvatī Ṭhākura very much, so much so that he wrote a lengthy intro-

duction for it, a philosophical masterpiece, exposing the impossibility of understanding transcendental personalities by a narration of historical incidents. He praises the professor's explanations by saying: "The author has wisely delineated these crucial points in the Instructive Life of the Lord." Śrīla Prabhupāda wrote: "I am glad to learn that Donald has purchased Prof. Sanyal's book Krishna Caitanya. Late Prof. N. K. Sanyal was my Godbrother and his book Krishna Caitanya is approved and authoritative. Keep it very carefully and we may publish in Back to Godhead some articles from the book. It will help us a great deal because my Spiritual Master has given His approval to this book. Please keep it carefully and when I return I shall see to it."
(Letter to Brahmananda 67-03-14, San Francisco)

[2] Sanyal, Nisikanta, *Sree Krishna Caitanya*, The Madras Law Journal Press, 1933, p. 239.

[3] Rāghava Caitanya Prabhu was a disciple of Śrīla Bhaktisiddhānta Sarasvatī Ṭhākura. He has written a very nice book about chanting the holy name of Kṛṣṇa, called *The Divine Name,* with great feeling and philosophical acumen, and that book includes a narration, from authorized sources, of the life of Haridāsa Ṭhākura.

[4] Rāghava Caitanya dāsa, *The Divine Name*, Associated Advertisers and Printers, Ltd., Bombay, 1954.

[5] Dr. Sambidananda Das, one of Śrīla Sarasvati Ṭhākura's disciples, was one of the preachers sent to London in 1934. He received his doctorate from London University, and the thesis for the doctorate was entitled *The History and Literature of the Gaudiya Vaishnavas and Their Relation to Other Medieval Vaishnava Schools.* This thesis was later published as a book by the Sree Gaudiya Math in Madras in 1991. In the portion of the book concerning Haridāsa Ṭhākura, he writes: "According to *Prema-vilasa* (XXIV), he was initiated by Advaita [Ācārya], and [according] to Abhirama Sakhanirya, he was the disciple of Abhirama Thakura of Khanakul Krishnagar. Krishnadas Kaviraj puts him among the disciples of Sri Chaitanya Himself." (pg. 298) Therefore, on the point of initiation, there is no universal agreement about who the *dīkṣā-guru* of Haridāsa Ṭhākura was. Certainly, Advaita Ācārya was a *śīkṣā-guru*, what to speak of Lord Caitanya. Abhirama Ṭhākura was an exalted and extraordinary follower of Śrī Nityananda Prabhu, who was much loved and revered by all of the followers of Lord Caitanya and Lord Nityānanda. Thus, the initiator remains a mystery.

[6] Śrīla Bhaktisiddhānta Sarasvatī Ṭhākura, *The Holy Name and Thakur Haridasa*, Sree Gaudiya Math, 1998, pp. 2, 3.

[7] Śrīla Kavi-karṇapūra, *Śrī Gaura-gaṇoddeśa-dīpikā*, translation by Kuśakratha dāsa, The Kṛṣṇa Library, Vol. 11, 1987.
Śrīla A.C. Bhativedanta Swami Prabhupāda, *Srimad Bhagwatam*, Canto I, Introduction, League of Devotees, 1962: "The Lord's early life was recorded by one of His chief devotees and contemporaries, namely Śrīla Murāri Gupta, a medical practitioner of that time, and the later part of the life of Śrī Caitanya Mahāprabhu was recorded by His private secretary Śrī Dāmodara Gosvāmī, or Śrīla Svarūpa Dāmodara, who was practically [the] constant companion of the Lord at Purī. These two devotees recorded practically all the incidents of the Lord's activities, and later on all the books regarding the Lord, as above mentioned, were composed on the basis of *kaḍacās* (notebooks) by Śrīla Dāmodara Gosvāmī and Murāri Gupta."

[8] *Śrī Caitanya-bhāgavata (CB) Adi* 16.18, text and purport, commentary by Śrīla Bhaktisiddhānta Sarasvatī Ṭhākura, translation by Bhumipati dāsa, editing by Puṇḍarīka Vidyānidhi dāsa, Vrajraj Press, 1998, p. 484.

[9] Dr. Ramakanta Chakravarti, *Vaisnavism in Bengal (1486—1900)*, Sanskrit Pustak Bhandar, 1985, pp. 392,393.

[10] *Śrī Caitanya-caritāmṛta (CC) Adi* 10.52, 54.

[11] *Śrī Gaura-gaṇoddeśa-dīpikā (GGD)*, text 176.

[12] *CC Adi* 10.62, text and purport.

[13] *GGD*, text 91.

[14] *CC Adi* 17.71, purport.

[15] *CB Madhya* 10.104—107.

[16] *CB Adi* 16.142, purport.

[17] *CB Adi* 16.237—247.

etan nirvidyamānānām
icchatām akuto-bhayam
yoginām̐ nṛpa nirṇītam̐
harer nāmānukīrtanam

O KING, CONSTANT CHANTING OF THE HOLY name of the Lord after the ways of the great authorities is the doubtless and fearless way of success for all, including those who are free from all material desires, those who are desirous of all material enjoyment, and also those who are self-satisfied by dint of transcendental knowledge."

Śrīmad-Bhāgavatam 2.1.11
[Śukadeva Gosvāmī to Mahārāja Parīkṣit]

HARIDĀSA ṬHĀKURA USED TO CHANT the holy name on his beads 300,000 times daily. Throughout the entire day and night, he would chant the sixteen names of the Hare Kṛṣṇa *mahā-mantra*. One should not, however, imitate Haridāsa Ṭhākura, for no one else can chant the Hare Kṛṣṇa *mahā-mantra* 300,000 times a day. Such chanting is for the *mukta-puruṣa*, or liberated soul. We can follow his example, however, by chanting sixteen rounds of the Hare Kṛṣṇa *mahā-mantra* on beads every day and offering respect to the *tulasī* plant. This is not at all difficult for anyone, and the process of chanting the Hare Kṛṣṇa *mahā-mantra* with a vow before the *tulasī* plant has such great spiritual potency that simply by doing this one can become spiritually strong. Therefore, we request the members of the Hare Kṛṣṇa movement to follow Haridāsa Ṭhākura's example rigidly. Chanting sixteen rounds does not take much time, nor is offering respects to the *tulasī* plant difficult. The process has immense spiritual potency. One should not miss this opportunity."

Chapter Two

Deliverance of the Prostitute

Solitary Chanting

AFTER LEAVING HIS HOME, Haridāsa Ṭhākura stayed for some time in the forest of Benāpola, which was situated in the area of the village of Benāpola, in the district of Yaśohara, which is now in Bangladesh. He constructed a cottage in a solitary spot in the forest, planted a *tulasī* plant and began to constantly chant the Hare Kṛṣṇa *mahā-mantra*: Hare Kṛṣṇa Hare Kṛṣṇa Kṛṣṇa Kṛṣṇa Hare Hare Hare Rāma Hare Rāma Rāma Rāma Hare Hare, a formula composed of the 16 names of the Lord and formed of 32 syllables. Such chanting of God's holy name is called *tārak brahma nāma*, or "the name that helps one cross beyond the ocean of illusion." The Ṭhākura chanted throughout the entire day and night.

Śrīla A.C. Bhaktivedanta Swami Prabhupāda comments:

"Haridāsa Ṭhākura used to chant the holy name on his beads 300,000 times daily. Throughout the entire day and night, he would chant the sixteen names of the Hare Kṛṣṇa *mahā-mantra.* One should not, however, imitate Haridāsa Ṭhākura, for no one else can chant the Hare Kṛṣṇa *mahā-mantra* 300,000 times a day. Such chanting is for the *mukta-puruṣa*, or liberated soul. We can follow his example, however, by chanting sixteen rounds of the Hare Kṛṣṇa *mahā-mantra* on beads every day and offering respect to the *tulasī* plant. This is not at all difficult for anyone, and the process of chanting the Hare Kṛṣṇa *mahā-mantra* with a vow before the *tulasī* plant has such great spiritual potency that simply by doing this one can become spiritually strong. Therefore, we request the members of the Hare Kṛṣṇa movement to follow Haridāsa Ṭhākura's example rigidly. Chanting sixteen rounds does not take much time, nor is offering respects to the *tulasī* plant difficult. The process has immense spiritual potency. One should not miss this opportunity."[1]

To maintain himself, Haridāsa Ṭhākura would go to a *brāhmaṇa's* home and beg for some food. His saintly presence, activities, and practices began to attract a following amongst the local inhabitants, and news of his glories also began to be broadcast to other regions.

Rāghava Caitanya Prabhu comments:

"All the virtuous inhabitants of the village regarded Thakur Haridas as a great saint. They were greatly impressed by the various marks of devotion which they had never witnessed [on others] and his extraordinary love for the Holy Name. He gained within a short time great popularity...amongst the local people. His reputation spread even to distant places. People from distant places collected there to have a sight of the saint. They rendered him various services and tried to follow his soul-stirring instructions."[2]

Chapter Two : Deliverance of the Prostitute

The Envious Rāmacandra Khān

However, the local administrator of those parts and a holder of large tracts of land named Rāmacandra Khān became agitated at the Ṭhākura's growing influence. He was envious of Vaiṣṇavas, and Kṛṣṇadāsa Kavirāja Gosvāmī calls him the chief of the atheists. He could not tolerate that such respect was being given to the Ṭhākura, so he designed a plan with the help of his ill-intentioned friends.

Śrīla Bhaktisiddhānta Sarasvatī Ṭhākura comments:

> "The sight of Haridas endeavouring with a singleness of purpose to take the Name aroused the feeling of hostility in the malicious section of Hindu society. The pure-hearted people were delighted with the spectacle of Haridas' unprecedented love for the Name; but the evil impulses of certain persons imbued with [the] mischievous instincts of brutes were not subdued. One of the leaders of this body of haters of devotees formed the resolution of devising a method of defiling Haridas. This man, by [the] name [of] Ramachandra Khan, was very well-known in those parts. He had also an immense following, and great material prosperity made him proud. Under the advice of several mean-minded friends he prepared to engage himself in an evil deed. He [Haridas], an alien, had come to reside in the village of Ramachandra. Without offering to support the evil deeds of Ramachandra, he was always occupied with the Name of Hari. [Although] born in a Yavana family, he uttered vocatives of the Sanskrit language in calling God. The Name uttered by him, because he prayed with a loud voice, penetrated into the auricular cavities of persons like Ramachandra Khan, etc., and such hearing, [in] the opinion of Ramachandra Khan, being clearly against the shastras, Ramachandra volunteered to create trouble for Haridas."[3]

In the above commentary by Śrīla Bhaktisiddhānta Sarasvatī Ṭhākura, he notes the malicious behavior of those persons in the "higher castes" that was commonly exhibited toward those of lower castes and births. Rather than being enlivened by the wonderful spiritual success story of Śrīla Haridāsa Ṭhākura, Rāmacandra Khān and others of his ilk reacted in an envious way, like animals defending their territory. In this case it was not so much territory as prestige and social standing that was being defended. This was contrasted with the reaction of the more pious members of Hindu society of that locale who were clearly delighted to see the spiritual advancement of the Ṭhākura and considered themselves fortunate to have his association. Haridāsa Ṭhākura (in the minds of the demonic section) would be made to suffer for the misfortune of being an outsider (an alien) in every sense: he was a Muslim, he was not from that part of the country, and he was engaging in a "controversial" practice—chanting the holy names of God!

Kṛṣṇadāsa Kavirāja Gosvāmī states: "By no means could he find any fault in the character of Haridāsa Ṭhākura. Therefore, he called for local prostitutes and began a plan to discredit His Holiness."[4]

Rāghava Caitanya Prabhu comments:

> "Unfortunately Ramchandra Khan took Haridas Thakur to be a mere beginner in the devotional field—a weak-minded emotionalist who could be made an easy victim to the temptations of the world. Puffed up with the vanities of wealth, youth and rank, he did not understand the marvelous glories of the devotees of Sri Hari. Having full faith in his newly invented plan, Ramchandra Khan secured the help of the best prostitutes of the locality, and asked them to spoil the character of Thakur Haridas. He promised them huge rewards. All these prostitutes, except one, did not accept the offer and retired; but one of them, a young and [the] most beautiful amongst the whole lot, ventured to accept the offer and assured him [of] success by bringing ruin on the character of Thakur Haridas in three days' time."[5]

Śrīla Bhaktisiddhānta Sarasvatī Ṭhākura writes:

"Ramachandra thought that Haridas was [a] weak-minded young man like himself...engaged in uttering the Name of Hari merely under the impulse of the moment, [who] had become a *sadhu* being denied the possession of objects of sensuous gratification, and, therefore, would be drawn away from the path of holiness by the actual contact of any object of sensuous desire; and thinking thus and gaining over a certain harlot by holding out the prospect of pecuniary reward, he sent her to the solitary cell of Thakur Haridas."[6]

Rāmacandra Khān had made severe miscalculations not only about the character of Śrīla Haridāsa Ṭhākura, but about his own importance. Although it is true that there are many pretenders in the dress of saintly persons, who utilize saffron cloth as a pretext to fill their bellies and live a comfortable life of sensual indulgence, Śrīla Haridāsa Ṭhākura bore absolutely no relation to such cheaters. Rāmacandra Khān, due to the bewilderment of wealth, ignorant followers, and local prestige also imagined himself to be a person of great intelligence and a keen judge of human character. He arrogantly fantasized that he was spiritually evolved and that Haridāsa Ṭhākura's activities were not authorized by the scriptures. He reached this conclusion by consulting his own cynical mind and a number of his sycophantic followers. His previous experience had repeatedly proved to him that if you can discover a man's weakness, it is easy enough to entrap and expose him as an ordinary sensuous person, driven by the senses and mind to indulge in sense pleasure. Being such a proud materialist and driven by demonic tendencies, Rāmacandra Khān could not tolerate anyone in his locale who didn't show him suitable signs of awed recognition and fawning respect. Therefore, he desired to destroy the credibility of the "ignorant" followers of the Ṭhākura by exposing him as an ordinary person. Śrīla

Haridāsa Ṭhākura, being spiritually absorbed, had not given any thought to creating relationships with local rulers and politicians. His sole intent was the constant ecstatic glorification of Kṛṣṇa. Nonetheless, Haridāsa was well aware of the full scope of Khān's intentions at the very moment his unfortunate plan was put into motion. It is clear that Rāmacandra Khān could conceive of nothing as tempting as an attractive young woman. Generally people imagine that others think and feel the way they do: *ātmavan manyate jagat*—everyone thinks of others according to their own tendencies or predilections. Thus, the foolish politician imagined that his plans were infallible, because the ultimate temptation in the form of a beautiful woman was being placed before a "sentimental" person masquerading as a *sādhu*.

Rāmacandra Khān told the prostitute, "My constable will go with you so that as soon as he sees you with Haridāsa Ṭhākura, immediately he will arrest him and bring both of you to me." But the young girl replied, "First let me have union with him once; then the second time I shall take your constable with me to arrest him."[7]

Temptation

That evening the prostitute dressed herself very attractively and approached Haridāsa Ṭhākura at sunset. After offering obeisances to the *tulasī* plant, she approached the doorway of the hut and offered obeisances to Haridāsa Ṭhākura and then remained standing in the doorway.

Rāghava Caitanya Prabhu writes: "She then slowly sat down at his doorstep. She exhibited her body to Haridas Thakur in various gestures and postures like one mad with sensuous passions."[8]

She spoke to him very sweetly as follows: "My dear Ṭhākura, O great preacher, great devotee, you are so beautifully built, and your youth is just beginning. Who is the woman who could control her mind after seeing you. I am eager to be united with you. My mind is greedy for this. If I don't obtain you, I shall not be able to keep my body and soul together."[9]

Haridāsa Ṭhākura replied, "I shall accept you without fail, but you will have to wait until I have finished chanting my regular rounds on my beads. Until that time, please sit and listen to the chanting of the holy name. As soon as I am finished, I shall fulfill your desire."[10]

Haridāsa Ṭhākura did not deceive her; in fact, it will be revealed that he chose his words carefully. The prostitute sat with Haridāsa while he chanted until dawn and then she returned to Rāmacandra Khān with the news of the Ṭhākura's promise. The next night she returned, and the Ṭhākura gave her many assurances. "Last night you were disappointed. Please excuse my offense. I shall certainly accept you. Please sit down and hear the chanting of the Hare Kṛṣṇa *mahā-mantra* until my regular chanting is finished. Then your desire will surely be fulfilled."[11]

After offering her obeisances to the *tulasī* plant and Haridāsa Ṭhākura, she sat down at the door. Hearing Haridāsa Ṭhākura chanting the Hare Kṛṣṇa *mantra*, she also chanted, "O my Lord Hari, O my Lord Hari."

Śrīla A.C. Bhaktivedanta Swami Prabhupāda comments:

> "Herein one can clearly see how a Vaiṣṇava delivers a fallen soul by a transcendental trick. The prostitute came to pollute

Haridāsa Ṭhākura, but he took it as his duty to deliver the prostitute. As clearly demonstrated here, the process of deliverance is very simple. With faith and reverence the prostitute associated with Haridāsa Ṭhākura, who personally treated her material disease by chanting the Hare Kṛṣṇa *mahā-mantra*. Although the prostitute had an ulterior motive, somehow or other she got the association of a Vaiṣṇava and satisfied him by occasionally chanting in imitation, 'O my Lord Hari, O my Lord Hari.' The conclusion is that associating with a Vaiṣṇava, chanting the holy name of the Lord and offering obeisances to the *tulasī* plant or a Vaiṣṇava all lead one to become a transcendental devotee who is completely cleansed of all material contamination."[12]

Nevertheless, by the end of the night, the prostitute was feeling restless. Seeing this, the Ṭhākura spoke to her as follows: "I have vowed to chant ten million names in a month. I have taken this vow, but now it is nearing its end. I thought that today I would be able to finish my performance of *yajña* [sacrifice], my chanting of the Hare Kṛṣṇa *mantra*. I tried my best to chant the holy name all night, but I still did not finish. Tomorrow I will certainly finish, and my vow will be fulfilled. Then it will be possible for me to enjoy with you in full freedom."[13]

The prostitute again returned to Rāmacandra Khān and tendered her report. On the following day she came earlier than usual, at the beginning of the evening. After offering her obeisances to the *tulasī* plant and Haridāsa Ṭhākura, she sat down on the threshold, hearing his chanting and chanting herself.

Haridāsa Ṭhākura assured her, "Today it will be possible for me to finish my chanting. Then I shall satisfy all your desires."[14]

* * *

Conversion

The night ended, but by Haridāsa Ṭhākura's association the mind of the prostitute had changed. Śrīla Bhaktisiddhānta Sarasvatī Ṭhākura comments: "...watching the manifestation of the supernatural force of the character of Haridāsa, the heart of the sinful woman was changed."[15]

The transformation of the prostitute was profound. It is described in the *Caitanya-śikṣāmṛta* by Śrīla Bhaktivinoda Ṭhākura that the association of a *madhyama-adhikārī* is sufficient to create *śraddhā,* or faith. However, by association with an *uttama-adhikārī*, symptoms of *bhāva* (ecstasy) may be experienced. Although the prostitute is described in the texts and commentary above in very severe terms: "sinful," "fallen," etc., in the modern age, young men and women indulge in random acts of sex, gambling, intoxication, etc. as a matter of course, without the promise of reward and with very little thought of the possible consequences. Therefore, their minds and hearts are very covered and dull even when compared to the young prostitute's. Śrīla Prabhupāda rescued many such men and women who were indulging in behavior much worse than the young woman sent by Khān, and yet Śrīla Prabhupāda was able, by the "supernatural force" of his character, to give them a taste of spiritual ecstasy and set them on the path of liberation and pure devotional service. By experiencing the higher taste of Kṛṣṇa consciousness, layers of ignorance are shattered and real life begins. The young girl, who had been born into a culture of respect for saintly persons, was deeply affected by the powerful atmosphere of divine love which emanated from Śrīla Haridāsa Ṭhākura.

Now purified, she fell at the feet of Haridāsa Ṭhākura and confessed that Rāmacandra Khān had sent her to tempt him for sex. The young girl, terrified at the temerity of what she had done, began to plead with Haridāsa that she wanted his shelter. She felt that she had committed many sins, topped off by this attempt to cause a saint to break his vows. She begged for deliverance.

Śrīla Haridāsa Ṭhākura replied, "I know everything about the conspiracy of Rāmacandra Khān. He is nothing but an ignorant fool. Therefore his activities do not make me feel unhappy. On the very day Rāmacandra Khān was planning his intrigue against me, I would have left this place immediately, but because you have come to me, I stayed here for three days to deliver you."

The prostitute said, "Kindly act as my spiritual master. Instruct me in my duty by which to get relief from material existence."

The Ṭhākura replied, "Immediately go home and distribute to the *brāhmaṇas* whatever property you have. Then come back to this room and stay here forever in Kṛṣṇa consciousness. Chant the Hare Kṛṣṇa *mantra* continuously and render service to the *tulasī* plant by watering her and offering prayers to her. In this way you will very soon get the opportunity to be sheltered at the lotus feet of Kṛṣṇa."[16]

Haridāsa Ṭhākura knew by the inner direction of the Lord in the heart exactly what Rāmacandra Khān had planned, but he had stayed just for the chance of rescuing the young girl, who was, at her heart's core, innocent. The proof of her sincerity will shortly be revealed.

Śrīla Bhaktisiddhānta Sarasvatī Ṭhākura comments:

> "The heart of the merciful Haridasa was touched. He forgot all about the bad profession of the harlot—the unworthy object of the lust of many—and deciding that she was eligible for taking the *maha-mantra* of the Name of Hari in the manner that is free from offence, rescued her from the deep well of sensuality. Such mercy is not met with anywhere except [in] the heart of a Vaishnava. All praise to Haridasa! May your mercy be appreciated by all the people of the world..."[17]

In his commentary on this incident, Professor Sanyal raises the issue of whether the conversion of the prostitute was simply an exercise in blind sentimentality on her part.

This concept of religious sentimentalism has its parallel in other religious traditions where, in the intense atmosphere of the "revival" of faith, one dedicates himself with great fervor to be "born again" or to transform his or her life. After a few days, the idea is given up, and the former life of sense indulgence is renewed. In Sanskrit, the expression *śmāśana-vairāgya* (crematorium renunciation) is used to illustrate a similar principle. One goes to the burning ghat (crematorium) and reflects on the temporality of human existence. He/she decides to be dedicated to spirituality more seriously. After a few weeks, the initial enthusiasm dissipates and the inspiration is lost.[18] The professor rejects this idea that her renunciation was sentimental, explaining:

> "The harlot was not 'converted' by speculative arguments addressed to the mind but simply by listening to the Name of Hari from the lips of Thakur Haridas and chanting the Same herself in his company. She had apparently the advantage of possessing at the very outset a natural regard for Thakur Haridas and for his advice and also for the holy Tulasi. This was the only antecedent condition of her redemption. Was it, therefore, blind and traditional faith that actually saved her in this crisis?

"The answer must be in the negative. Those, who are most officiously given to the cult of *blind faith*, are not necessarily attracted towards the actual devotee. The affinity for the true soul is itself a spiritual, that is to say perfectly self-conscious, impulse. It must be most carefully distinguished from the blind, material impulse which is so common and which, as a matter of fact, is the worst form of obstacle in the way of the realisation of spiritual life. The instinctive affinity of the harlot for Haridas is an activity of the soul and as such is, therefore, perfectly moral, perfectly self-cognisant and categorically different from sensuous sentimentality that ordinarily passes in this world as 'blind' faith. Faith is the instinctive attitude of the soul towards the Truth and can, therefore, never be blind. It is the blind who in their blindness confound true faith with the counterfeit ware with which alone they happen to be, unfortunately for themselves, only too familiar.

"Real faith can alone lead one to the presence of a pure soul. The material mind cannot reach the proximity of a sadhu. The harlot possessed the spiritual faculty by which it was possible for her to really approach Thakur Haridas."[19]

Regarding Haridāsa's instructions to the former prostitute to distribute all of her possessions to qualified *brāhmaṇas* and take up his example of chanting and worshipping *tulasi*, Śrīla Prabhupāda comments: "Everything actually belongs to Kṛṣṇa, but so-called civilized men unfortunately think that everything belongs to them. This is the mistake of materialistic civilization. The prostitute (*veśyā*) has earned money by questionable means, and therefore Haridāsa Ṭhākura advised her to distribute to the *brāhmaṇas* whatever she possessed."[20]

The order given by Haridāsa for the young woman to take up a life of such severe renunciation and self-abnegation might strike many readers as impractical or impossible to follow. However, he had bestowed such powerful mercy upon her that she was able to fully surrender to his instructions. Kṛṣṇa promises in the *Bhagavad-gītā* that whoever fully surrenders to Him will be protected from the results of all sinful reactions and attain the platform of fearlessness, due to being completely protected at every moment by Kṛṣṇa. The former prostitute had complete faith in this principle and Kṛṣṇa's pure representative Haridāsa Ṭhākura.

Śrīla Prabhupāda comments:

> "Modern civilization, however, is interested neither in Kṛṣṇa nor in getting relief from sinful acts. Therefore, men are suffering. Surrender is the ultimate instruction of *Bhagavad-gītā*, but for one who cannot surrender to the lotus feet of Kṛṣṇa, it is better to chant the Hare Kṛṣṇa *mantra* constantly, under the instruction of Haridāsa Ṭhākura. In our Kṛṣṇa consciousness movement we are teaching our followers to chant the Hare Kṛṣṇa *mantra* continuously on beads. Even those who are not accustomed to this practice are advised to chant at least sixteen rounds on their *tulasī* beads so that they might be trained. Otherwise, Śrī Caitanya Mahāprabhu recommended: 'One should chant the holy name of the Lord in a humble state of mind, thinking oneself lower than the straw in the street. One should be more tolerant than a tree, devoid of all sense of false prestige, and ready to offer all respect to others. In such a state of mind one can chant the holy name of the Lord constantly. *Sadā* means 'always.' Haridāsa Ṭhākura says, *nirantara nāma lao*: 'Chant the Hare Kṛṣṇa *mantra* without stopping.' Although Kṛṣṇa wants everyone to surrender to His lotus feet, because of people's sinful activities they cannot do this... [they] cannot suddenly surrender to the lotus feet of Kṛṣṇa. Nevertheless, if they begin chanting the Hare Kṛṣṇa *mantra* and rendering service unto the *tulasi* plant, they will very soon be able to surrender. One's real duty is to surrender to the lotus feet of Kṛṣṇa but if one is unable to do so, he should adopt this process, as introduced by Śrī Caitanya Mahāprabhu and His most confidential servant, Śrīla Haridāsa Ṭhākura. This is the way to achieve success in Kṛṣṇa consciousness."[21]

After instructing his disciple in this way, Haridāsa Ṭhākura stood up and left, continuously chanting the holy name. Thereafter, the prostitute distributed whatever possessions she had to the *brāhmaṇas*. Śrīla Prabhupāda explains at length the benefits of this type of charity which might strike some persons as extreme or irrational.

> "All the girl's possessions had been earned by professional prostitution and were therefore products of her sinful life. When such possessions are given to *brāhmaṇas* and Vaiṣṇavas who can engage them in the service of the Lord because of their advancement in spiritual life, this indirectly helps the person who gives the charity, for he is thus relieved of sinful reactions...A Vaiṣṇava guru accepts money or other contributions, but he does not employ such contributions for sense gratification. A pure Vaiṣṇava thinks himself unfit to help free even one person from the reactions of sinful life, but he engages one's hard-earned money in the service of the Lord and thus frees one from sinful reactions. A Vaiṣṇava guru is never dependent on the contributions of his disciples. Following the instructions of Haridāsa Ṭhākura, a pure Vaiṣṇava does not personally take even a single paisa from anyone, but he induces his followers to spend for the service of the Lord whatever possessions they have."[22]

Haridāsa Ṭhākura's disciple strictly executed the orders of her spiritual master. She shaved her head, and wearing only a single cloth, stayed at her master's former hermitage, chanting the *mahā-mantra* throughout the day and night 300,000 times. She worshipped the *tulasi* plant and only ate what she received as alms; if nothing was supplied, she fasted. In this way she conquered her senses and symptoms of love of God manifested in her person. She became a celebrated devotee, became extremely elevated, and many stalwart devotees came to see her.

Śrīla Prabhupāda comments:

> "...when a prostitute or any other fallen soul becomes a Vaiṣṇava, stalwart devotees are interested in seeing them. Anyone can become a Vaiṣṇava if he or she follows the Vaiṣṇava principles. A devotee who follows these principles is no longer on the material platform. Therefore, it is one's strict adherence to the principles that should be considered, not the country of one's birth. Many devotees join our Kṛṣṇa consciousness movement from Europe and America, but one should not therefore consider them European Vaiṣṇavas or American Vaiṣṇavas. A Vaiṣṇava is a Vaiṣṇava and should therefore be given all the respect due a Vaiṣṇava."[23]

Like the prostitute, many modern Vaiṣṇavas were prostitutes to materialistic society, dedicated followers of the hedonistic principles of "...eat, drink, and be merry for tomorrow we die." Such atheistic notions have eaten into the very vitals of contemporary society. Having understood the spiritual responsibility of the human form of life, the Vaiṣṇavas of the modern era also adopt a serious level of renunciation like the former prostitute. Although they may not come up to her standard, they are very reluctant to stoop to the lower levels of mindless hedonism practiced in their former lives. This is only possible by the mercy of a pure Vaiṣṇava like Śrīla Prabhupāda.

Some persons foolishly think that Kṛṣṇa's formula (*Bhagavad-gītā* 4.13) which puts the emphasis on quality and activity (*guṇa* and *karma*) is insufficient and that birth (*janma*) is a more important consideration. This pathetic idea has been current for many centuries. All of the stalwart *ācāryas*, including Haridāsa Ṭhākura, the Six Gosvāmīs and their followers, Śrīla Bhaktivinoda Ṭhākura, Śrīla Bhaktisiddhānta Sarasvatī Ṭhākura, Śrīla A.C. Bhaktivedanta Swami Prabhupāda and all great Vaiṣṇavas in the lineage of Śrī Caitanya Mahāprabhu have taught this principle from

Bhagavad-gītā: that qualification is based on one's practical activities and qualities. The great Vaiṣṇava stalwarts never care a fig for the paltry mundane arguments offered by persons motivated by a material desire for false prestige and bewildered by bodily consciousness. When the people saw the great Vaiṣṇavī's sublime character, they were astonished and appreciated all the more Haridāsa Ṭhākura's influence, offering him obeisances and glorification.

In contemporary western society, the emphasis on birth is often supplanted by an emphasis on wealth, power, beauty, intelligence, fame, etc. Those who have such opulences, generated by their previous pious acts (*karma*), imagine that they have been placed in a special category or have even been empowered by God. They consider that possessing such opulences indicates their God-given or fate-driven superiority as humans, and that others should recognize them as such and defer to them in every way. However, simply possessing opulence does not signify or guarantee its appropriate use. When such qualities are utilized to exploit other humans, animals, plants, or the earth itself for sensuous pleasure, thus reinforcing the illusory sense of being the cynosure of all eyes and worthy of adulation, profit, and distinction, such childish, ignorant egotism merely highlights the full implication in illusion of such fools: *māyayāpahṛta-jñānā*—their knowledge is stolen by the illusory energy. Their fate is dark, unless they are fortunate enough to receive the merciful intervention of a pure soul.

The Fate of Rāmacandra Khān

Rāmacandra Khān was infuriated by the failure of his scheme. Although he had previously been a non-devotee and an atheist, now he became completely demoniac. Śrīla

Prabhupāda compares him to Rāvaṇa who, although born of a *brāhmaṇa* father, Viśvaśravā, became an *āsura* (demon) by offenses to Lord Rāma and His greatest devotee, the Vaiṣṇava Hanumān. Thus, by Rāmacandra Khān's offenses committed to Haridāsa Ṭhākura and others, he was doomed. He cultivated a burning hatred toward Vaiṣṇavas throughout his life and eventually gathered the bitter fruits of his cultivation.

When Lord Nityānanda later toured Bengal to preach love of God on the order of Lord Caitanya, He came to the house of Rāmacandra Khān and sat down on the altar of the Durgā-maṇḍapa. The courtyard soon filled up with crowds of people. Rāmacandra Khān, considering it beneath him to make a personal appearance to receive his exalted guest, sent a servant. The servant informed the Lord: "My dear sir, Rāmacandra Khān has sent me to accommodate You in some common man's house. You might go to the house of a milkman, for the cow shed is spacious, whereas the space here in the Durgā-maṇḍapa is insufficient because You have many followers with You."[24]

In so many words the servant, acting as the representative of Rāmacandra Khān, was telling Lord Nityānanda to go away. When Lord Nityānanda heard this, He became angry and left that place. Laughing loudly He spoke as follows: "Rāmacandra Khān has spoken rightly. This place is unfit for Me. It is fit for cow-killing meat-eaters."[25] He then left the home of Rāmacandra Khān and "his" village as well. Rāmacandra Khān was so obnoxious in his attitude that he had the dirt in the place where Nityānanda Prabhu sat dug up. He tried to "purify" the area by sprinkling it with water mixed with cow dung. Nevertheless, his mind remained unsatisfied.

Within a short time the unfortunate Rāmacandra who had been trying to avoid paying his income tax to the Mogul government was punished severely. The government's minister of finance came to his residence. He stayed in the Durgā-maṇḍapa and killed a cow and cooked the meat there. He arrested Rāmacandra Khān and his wife and sons, and then continuously plundered the house and village for three days. In the same spot that had been refused to Lord Nityānanda, the minister cooked the flesh of a cow for three consecutive days. Then the next day he left, accompanied by his followers. The Mohammedan minister took away Rāmacandra Khān's position, wealth, and followers. For many days the village remained deserted.

Śrīla Bhaktisiddhānta Sarasvatī Ṭhākura describes the incident in more graphic terms:

> "Consequently, when Lord Nityananda with His entourage of Vaishnavas arrived a few days afterwards in the *mandapa* of Ramachandra, the evil-disposed Ramachandra, treating Him with contempt, said that his spacious *mandapa* would not accommodate Him and His *gosthi* (personal adherents) but that he was prepared to house Him in his *gostha* (cowshed). On hearing this, the Lord went away to another village. By means of this load of iniquity, which now reached its full weight, Ramachandra speedily brought down upon himself the most terrible destruction. In consequence of delay, prompted by avarice in the payment of revenue to the Mohammedan ruler of the country, the Yavana monarch forcibly entered his *mandapa*, polluted it for good by slaughter of animals and other similar acts; plundered all the wealth of Ramachandra; and finally spat into his mouth and even compelled him to swallow objectionable blood and flesh of animals, etc. Ramachandra was made aware by this event that his temporary greatness had been the merest of trifles. Such greatness, the existence of which is liable to be destroyed in a moment, can never be the permanent means of obtaining the highest good."[26]

Rāghava Caitanya Prabhu remarks:

> "Ramchandra Khan lost his caste, his wealth, his relations and everything he possessed as his own. Offences, when committed against devotees of the Lord, are not forgiven even by Bhagavan Himself. They are the worst impediments in the path of God-realisation. Offences committed against the bhaktas bring along with them manifold sufferings, not only to the person concerned, but even to many others. Over and above this, it brings complete destruction of the place, i.e., the village or township itself."[27]

In many ways modern materialists are worse off than Rāmachandra Khān. Like Rāvana, Rāmacandra Khān was personally rebuked by the Lord. He immediately received the results of his impiety, and he could appreciate the gravity of his fall from his former opulent position. Modern materialists appear to enjoy the protection of the demonic forces of Kali, so they generally are not seen to be suffering the results of abominable acts like cow killing and exploitation of the earth and other living beings. Without intercession by compassionate Vaiṣṇavas, however, their fate will be very bleak. Vaiṣṇavas do not eagerly anticipate the suffering of materialists or materialistic society, which is under the protection of the forces of Kali. Rather the Vaiṣṇavas take shelter of powerful devotees like Haridāsa Ṭhākura and seek to follow his example by introducing materialists to the medicinal and nectarine effects of chanting Hare Kṛṣṇa.

This incident describing the transformation of a prostitute into a great Vaiṣṇava and the destruction of Rāmacandra Khān contains a number of instructive lessons. Perhaps the first and foremost is the power of chanting the *mahā-mantra* when done so in the association of a *mahā-bhāgavata* and with sincerity and faith. The young woman had certainly committed many sins and was motivated by greed to approach the Ṭhākura. In spite of her passion for wealth and possessions, she possessed an excellent quality: she had a natural instinct to respect *sādhus* and the sacred *tulasi*.

Rāghava Caitanya Prabhu comments:

> "She was not a scholar in any sense. She was neither convinced nor converted by polemics or a show of miracle or supernatural powers. Her reformation was brought about by the simple method of listening to the Holy Name and Its repetition, and her natural receptive disposition completed the work. A spiritual aspirant must possess a natural instinct to pay due respect to sadhus and other godly objects. They must never underestimate them on any ground...The words emanating from the lips of pure devotees are not material sounds. They are, on the contrary, transcendental sounds capable of producing the most marvellous experiences in the heart of submissive listeners. An aspirant who longs to follow the path of God-realisation must submissively hear the Holy Name uttered by genuine sadhus. After serving the devotee, the Holy Name is to be accepted from him as his special favour, and [The Name] is to be chanted constantly in the holy company full observing all his instructions."[28]

Thus, the second significant understanding which can be derived from these incidents is that without sufficient piety, which can only be generated by the piety of association with saintly persons, it is not possible to take up the path of *bhakti*.

This principle is discussed at length by Kṛṣṇadāsa Kavirāja Gosvāmī in the *Caitanya-caritāmṛta*:

> "There are unlimited conditioned souls who are bereft of Lord Kṛṣṇa's service. Not knowing how to cross the ocean of nescience, they are scattered by waves, time and tide. However, some are fortunate to contact devotees, and by this contact they are delivered from the ocean of nescience, just as a log, floating down a river, accidentally washes upon the bank."[29]
>
> "By good fortune, one becomes eligible to cross the ocean of

nescience, and when one's term of material existence decreases, one may get an opportunity to associate with pure devotees. By such association, one's attraction to Kṛṣṇa is awakened."[30]

In the purport to the above verse, Śrīla Prabhupāda, citing the explanation of Śrīla Bhaktivinoda Ṭhākura, states:

> "Is this *bhāgya* (fortune) the result of an accident or something else? In the scriptures, devotional service and pious activity are considered fortunate. Pious activities can be divided into three categories—pious activities that awaken one's dormant Krsna consciousness are called *bhakty-unmukhī sukṛti*. Pious activities that bestow material opulence are called *bhogonmukhī*, and pious activities that enable the living entity to merge into the existence of the Supreme are called *mokṣonmukhī*. These last two awards of pious activities are not actually fortunate. **Pious activities are fortunate when they help one become Kṛṣṇa conscious. The good fortune of *bhakty-unmukhī* is attainable only when one comes into contact with a devotee. By associating with a devotee willingly or unwillingly, one advances in devotional service, and thus one's dormant Kṛṣṇa consciousness is awakened.**"

Kṛṣṇa also states in *Śrīmad-Bhāgavatam* 11.20.8 to Uddhava, just prior to His departure from the material world:

> "Somehow or other, if one is attracted to talks about Me and has faith in the instructions I have set forth in *Bhagavad-gītā*, and if one is actually detached from material things and material existence, his dormant love for Me will be awakened by devotional service."[31]

ENDNOTES

[1] *CC Antya* 3.100, purport.
[2] Rāghava Caitanya dāsa, *The Divine Name*, p. 16.
[3] Śrīla Bhaktisiddhānta Sarasvatī Ṭhākura, The *Holy Name and Thākur Haridās*, Sree Gaudiya Math, p. 4.
[4] *CC Antya* 3.104.
[5] Rāghava Caitanya dāsa, *The Divine Name*, p. 17.

[6] Śrīla Bhaktisiddhānta Sarasvatī Ṭhākura, *The Holy Name and Thākur Haridās*, Sree Gaudiya Math, pp. 4, 5.
[7] *CC Antya* 3.107, 108.
[8] Rāghava Caitanya dāsa, *The Divine Name*, p. 18.
[9] *CC Antya* 3.112, 113.
[10] *CC Antya* 3.114, 115.
[11] *CC Antya* 3.120, 121.
[12] *CC Antya* 3.122.
[13] *CC Antya* 13.124—126.
[14] *CC Antya* 13.129.
[15] Śrīla Bhaktisiddhānta Sarasvatī Ṭhākura, *The Holy Name and Thākur Haridās*, p. 6.
[16] *CC Antya* 3.131—137.
[17] Śrīla Bhaktisiddhānta Sarasvatī Ṭhākura, *The Holy Name and Thākur Haridās*, p. 6.
[18] *CC Madhya* 16.238 purport. "The word *markaṭa-vairāgya*, indicating false renunciation, is very important in this verse. Śrīla Bhaktisiddhānta Sarasvatī Ṭhākura, in commenting on this word, points out that monkeys make an external show of renunciation by not accepting clothing and by living naked in the forest. In this way they consider themselves renunciants, but actually they are very busy enjoying sense gratification with dozens of female monkeys. Such renunciation is called *markaṭa-vairāgya*—the renunciation of a monkey. One cannot be really renounced until one actually becomes disgusted with material activity and sees it as a stumbling block to spiritual advancement. Renunciation should not be *phalgu*, temporary, but should exist throughout one's life. Temporary renunciation, or monkey renunciation, is like the renunciation one feels at a cremation ground. When a man takes a dead body to the crematorium, he sometimes thinks, "This is the final end of the body. Why am I working so hard day and night?" Such sentiments naturally arise in the mind of any man who goes to a crematorial *ghāṭa*. However, as soon as he returns from the cremation grounds, he again engages in material activity for sense enjoyment. This is called *śmaśāna-vairāgya*, or *markaṭa-vairāgya*."
[19] Nisikanta Sanyal, *Sree Krishna Chaitanya*, pp. 570, 571.
[20] *CC Antya* 3.136 purport.
[21] *CC Antya* 3.137 purport.
[22] *CC Antya* 3.139 purport.
[23] *CC Antya* 3.142 purport.
[24] *CC Antya* 3.152, 153.

Chapter Two : Deliverance of the Prostitute

[25] *CC Antya* 3.155.
[26] Śrīla Bhaktisiddhānta Sarasvatī Ṭhākura, *The Holy Name and Thākur Haridās*, pp. 7, 8.
[27] Rāghava Caitanya dāsa, *The Divine Name*, p. 25.
[28] Rāghava Caitanya dāsa, *The Divine Name*, pp 26, 27.
[29] *CC Madhya* 22.43.
[30] *CC Madhya* 22.45.
[31] Some religions, like Calvinism in the West, and *smārta-brāhmanism* in the East, believe that one comes to God via a spiritual destiny. Some people analyze the early development of ISKCON by citing the use of psychedelic drugs, the rise of the counterculture, and youthful disinterest in the religion of their birth. The above statements of the *ācāryas*, however, oppose psychological or social predisposition toward spirituality. One's desire to associate with devotees and accumulate piety (perform pious acts) that awaken *bhakti* are the two critical factors mentioned here. Other psychological or sociological perspectives belie a perception darkened by the filter of materialism.

evaṁ-vrataḥ sva-priya-nāma-kīrtyā
jātānurāgo druta-citta uccaiḥ
hasaty atho roditi rauti gāyaty
unmāda-van nṛtyati loka-bāhyaḥ

WHEN A PERSON IS ACTUALLY ADVANCED and takes pleasure in chanting the holy name of the Lord, who is very dear to him, he is agitated and loudly chants the holy name. He also laughs, cries, becomes agitated and chants just like a madman, not caring for outsiders."

Śrīmad-Bhāgavatam 11.2.40
Kavi to Mahārāja Nimi
[cited: *Śrī Caitanya-caritāmṛta Madhya-līlā* 9.262]

nāma cintāmaṇiḥ kṛṣṇaś
caitanya-rasa-vigrahaḥ
pūrṇaḥ śuddho nitya-mukto
'bhinnatvān nāma-nāminoḥ

THE HOLY NAME OF KṚṢNA IS TRANSCENdentally blissful. It bestows all spiritual benedictions, for it is Kṛṣna Himself, the reservoir of all pleasure. Kṛṣṇa's name is complete, and it is the form of all transcendental mellows. It is not a material name under any condition, and it is no less powerful than Kṛṣṇa Himself. Since Kṛṣṇa's name is not contaminated by the material qualities, there is no question of its being involved with *māyā*. Kṛṣṇa's name is always liberated and spiritual; it is never conditioned by the laws of material nature. This is because the name of Kṛṣṇa and Kṛṣṇa Himself are identical."

Padma Purāṇa

GOPĀLA CAKRAVARTĪ BECAME FURIOUS and shouted, "If one is not liberated by *nāmābhāsa*, then you may be certain that I shall cut off your nose."

The Ṭhākura accepted the arrogant *brāhmaṇa's* challenge, calmly replying: "If by *nāmābhāsa* liberation is not available, certainly I shall cut off my [own] nose."

Śrī Caitanya-caritāmṛta Antya 3.198, 199

Chapter Three

Nāmābhāsa, Advaita Ācārya, & Māyā

Nāmābhāsa & Gopāla Cakravartī

FROM THE FOREST OF BENĀPOLA, HARIDĀSA Ṭhākura walked to Cāndapura where he stayed with Balarāma and Yadunandana Ācāryas. Cāndapura is situated near the confluence of the Ganges and Yamunā rivers at Saptagrāma in the district of Hugli, West Bengal. Balarāma Ācārya and Yadunandana Ācārya were the family priests of the two brothers, Hiranya and Govardhana Majumadār, who were, respectively, the father and uncle of Raghunātha, who was later to become the great renounced follower of Lord Caitanya, Raghunātha dāsa Gosvāmī. Raghunātha dāsa was a child at the time of his first meeting with Haridāsa Ṭhākura.

The two brothers, Hiranya and Govardhana, had the title of Majumadār, due to their being accountants or treasurers of the royal revenues of the Nawab, the king of Bengal. Śrīla Bhaktisiddhānta Sarasvatī Ṭhākura refers to Hiranya and Govardhana as "multimillionaires" and the glory of the *kāyastha* community [experts in managing business and governmental affairs]. They were the greatest friends and patrons of the *brāhmaṇas* residing in Navadvīpa. Haridāsa Ṭhākura lived with Balarāma Ācārya who considered himself the Ṭhākura's servant and disciple, and Kṛṣṇadāsa Kavirāja Gosvāmī notes that: "...he kept Haridāsa Ṭhākura in the village with great care and attention."[1]

According to Rāghava Caitanya Prabhu, Balarāma Ācārya had a special cottage constructed where Haridāsa Ṭhākura performed his chanting. The Ṭhākura accepted *prasāda* daily at the house of Balarāma Ācārya. At this time Raghunātha dāsa, who was a young boy engaged in studies, came to him every day. Kṛṣṇadāsa Kavirāja Gosvāmī writes: "Naturally Haridāsa Ṭhākura was merciful towards him, and because of the merciful benediction of this Vaiṣṇava, he later attained the shelter of Śrī Caitanya Mahāprabhu's lotus feet."[2]

The Majumadār brothers lived in a palatial building[3], a portion of which was a public assembly hall. Balarāma Ācārya, through a series of humble entreaties, convinced the Ṭhākura to come to a meeting of scholars and *brāhmaṇas*, as well as many local celebrities. The Ṭhākura arrived to a warm welcome and was showered with respect, due to the appreciation of those learned gentlemen for Haridāsa Ṭhākura's great austerities in the chanting of three *lakhs* of holy names daily (more than 190 rounds). The ensuing discussions centered on the glories of the holy name. Kṛṣṇadāsa Kavirāja Gosvāmī describes the assessment of the assembled scholars in regard to the holy name and the ensuing response from Śrīla Haridāsa Ṭhākura:

"Some of them said, 'By chanting the holy name of the Lord, one is freed from the reactions of all sinful life.' Others said, 'Simply by chanting the holy name of the Lord, a living being is liberated from material bondage.'

"Haridāsa Ṭhākura protested, 'These two benedictions are not the true result of the chanting the holy name. By actually chanting the holy name without offenses, one awakens his ecstatic love for the lotus feet of Kṛṣṇa.'[4]

"When a person is actually advanced and takes pleasure in chanting the holy name of the Lord, who is very dear to him, he is agitated and loudly chants the holy name. He also laughs, cries, becomes agitated and chants just like a madman, not caring for outsiders."[5]

The above verse from *Śrīmad-Bhāgavatam* was spoken by Śrī Narada Muni to Vasudeva to teach him *Bhāgavata-dharma.* Śrīla Prabhupāda explains in the purport to *Śrī Caitanya-caritāmṛta Ādi-līlā* 7.93: "Vasudeva had already achieved the result of *Bhāgavata-dharma* because Lord Kṛṣṇa appeared in his house as his son, yet in order to teach others, he desired to hear from Śrī Nārada Muni to be enlightened in the process of *Bhāgavata-dharma.* This is the humbleness of a great devotee."

Lord Caitanya cites this verse in his discussions with Prakāśānanda Sarasvatī, and remarks that His *guru* had repeatedly instructed Him that this verse was the essence of all the *Bhāgavatam*'s instructions.[6] This point (that love of God is the ultimate goal of Kṛṣṇa consciousness) is elaborated on by Śrīla Viśvanātha Cakravartī Ṭhākura in his *Śrīmad-Bhāgavatam* commentary called *Caitanya-manjusa:*

ārādhyo bhagavān vrajeśa-tanayas tad-dhāma vṛndāvanaṁ
ramya kācid upāsana vraja-vadhū-vargeṇā va kalpitā
śrīmad bhāgavataṁ pramāṇam amalaṁ premā pumartho mahān
śrī-caitanya mahāprabhor matam idaṁ tatrādarāḥ na paraḥ

"The Supreme Personality of Godhead, the son of Nanda Mahārāja, is to be worshiped along with His transcendental abode, Vṛndāvana. The most pleasing form of worship for the Lord is that which was performed by the *gopīs* of Vṛndāvana. *Śrīmad-Bhāgavatam* is the spotless authority on everything, and **pure love of God is the ultimate goal of life for all men**. These statements, for which we have the highest regard, are the opinion of Śrī Caitanya Mahāprabhu."

Śrīla Prabhupāda repeatedly cites the phrase *premā pumartho mahān* from the verse above throughout his commentaries. This is an important point to understand. One who does not understand this point does not understand the essence of Śrī Caitanya Mahāprabhu's teachings.

Haridāsa Ṭhākura continued his explanation:

"Liberation and extinction of the reactions of sinful life are two concomitant byproducts of chanting the holy name of the Lord. An example is found in the gleams of morning sunlight.

"As the rising sun immediately dissipates the world's darkness, which is deep like an ocean, so the holy name of the Lord, if chanted once without offenses, can dissipate all the reactions of a living being's sinful life. All glories to that holy name of the Lord, which is auspicious for the entire world." [Rupa Gosvami's *Padyavali*, text 16][7]

After reciting the above, the Ṭhākura requested the learned scholars to explain the meaning of the verse. The scholars humbly deferred to the Ṭhākura for the explanation, considering his understanding superior to their own.

"Haridāsa Ṭhākura said, 'As the sun begins to rise, even before visible, it dissipates the darkness of night. With the first glimpse of sunlight, fear of thieves, ghosts and demons immediately disappears, and when the sun is actually visible, everything is manifest, and everyone begins performing his religious activities and regulative duties. Similarly, the first hint that offenseless chanting of the Lord's holy name [*nāmābhāsa*] has awakened dissipates the reactions of sinful life immediately. And when one chants the holy name offenselessly, one awakens to service in ecstatic love at the lotus feet of Kṛṣṇa. Liberation is the insignificant result derived from a glimpse of awakening of offenseless chanting of the holy name.'

"While dying, Ajāmila chanted the holy name of the Lord, intending to call his son Nārāyaṇa. Nevertheless, he attained the spiritual world. What then to speak of those who chant the holy name with faith and reverence?" (*Śrīmad-Bhāgavatam* 6.2.49)

"Liberation, which is unacceptable for a pure devotee, is always offered by Kṛṣṇa without difficulty."

"My devotees do not accept *sālokya, sārṣṭi, sārūpya, sāmīpya*, or oneness with me—even if I offer these liberations—in preference to serving Me." (*Śrīmad-Bhāgavatam* 3.29.13)[8]

After hearing his explanations, an initial hush fell over the assembly, but then the handsome and learned *brāhmaṇa* Gopāla Cakravartī strongly objected to the Ṭhākura's glorification of the holy names. Gopāla Cakravartī was employed by the Majumadār brothers as a bearer of money and letters to the *Nawab* or king. His official position was chief tax collector, and he was required to present 12 *lakhs* of rupees annually to the *Nawab* in Gauḍa for the royal treasury. He was a very handsome man, learned, young, and arrogant, and he became very angry and critical upon hearing the statements of the Ṭhākura:

"O assembly of learned scholars, just hear the conclusion of the emotional devotee. After many millions upon millions of births, when one is complete in absolute knowledge, one still may not attain liberation, yet this man says that one may attain it simply by the awakening of a glimpse of the holy name."[9]

Śrīla Prabhupāda translates the Bengali term *bhāvukera* in the above statement as "of an emotional person." Rāghava Caitanya Prabhu translates the term as "this sentimentalist,"[10] and Professor Sanyal gives it an even stronger (and more insulting meaning): "one whose trade is to amuse people by dance and song."[11] These varied translations try to capture the disparaging and insulting nature of the remarks of the doomed offender, Gopāla Cakravartī.[12]

Haridāsa Ṭhākura replied to the foolish statement of the tax collector: "Why are you doubtful? The revealed scriptures say that one can attain liberation simply by a glimpse of offenseless chanting of the holy name. For a devotee who enjoys the transcendental bliss of devotional service, liberation is most insignificant. Therefore, pure devotees never desire to attain liberation.

"'My dear Lord, O master of the universe, since I have directly seen You, my transcendental bliss has taken the shape of a great ocean. Being situated in that ocean, I now realize all other so-called happiness, including even *brahmānanda*, to be like the water contained in the hoofprint of a calf.'" (*Hari-bhakti-sudhodaya* 14.36)[13]

Gopāla Cakravartī became furious and shouted, "If one is not liberated by *nāmābhāsa*, then you may be certain that I shall cut off your nose."

The Ṭhākura accepted the arrogant *brāhmaṇa's* challenge, calmly replying: "If by *nāmābhāsa* liberation is not available, certainly I shall cut off my [own] nose."[14]

A great tumult erupted in the assembly hall. The Majumadār brothers chastised the foolish tax collector, and Balarāma Ācārya sharply rebuked him saying, "You are a foolish logician. What do you know about the devotional service of the Lord? You have insulted Haridāsa Ṭhākura. Thus, there will be a dangerous position for you. You should not expect anything auspicious."[15]

Rāghava Caitanya Prabhu provides a more colorful translation of Balarāma Ācārya's remarks: "Fool of an ass! You boast much of your learning; what do you know about *bhakti*? This is not the place for your verbal jugglery. You have dug your own grave by insulting the great Haridas Thakur. Inevitable perdition is soon to befall you. None can help."[16]

In the purport to the text of Gopāla's unfortunate remarks, Śrīla Prabhupāda refers to *ghaṭa-paṭiyā* philosophy which literally means "interested in the pot and the earth." This philosophy is ascribed to Māyāvādīs who think that everything is one, i.e. pots and earth are non-different. Such an idea is indicative of impaired intelligence or defective discrimination, and Śrīla Prabhupāda comments: "Since Gopāla Cakravartī was a *ghaṭa-paṭiyā* logician, a gross materialist, what could he understand about the transcendental service of the Lord?"[17]

The Majumadārs dismissed the unfortunate Gopāla from their service, demanding that he never darken their door again. All the members of the assembly, including the Majumadārs, fell at the feet of Haridāsa Ṭhākura and begged his forgiveness. The Ṭhākura did not take the incident very seriously, but the Lord did. Within three days the arrogant *brāhmaṇa* was afflicted by leprosy and as a result: "...his highly raised nose melted away and fell off. The *brāhmaṇa's* toes and fingers were beautiful like golden-colored campaka buds, but because of leprosy they all withered and gradually melted away."[18]

Some devotees feel themselves so much in the minority that they await the judgment day when the Lord will punish wrongdoers. Such devotees sometimes feel persecuted by their former friends, family members, or society for their beliefs (at least mentally). They even find themselves eager to witness the destruction of materialistic individuals and societies. However, such immature thoughts are not appropriate for serious devotees. When hearing about the fate of Gopāla Cakravartī, good-hearted devotees do not rejoice in his "just desserts." Rather, they think, "There, but for the grace of God go I."

The question may be raised why, if Haridāsa Ṭhākura did not take the insults of Gopāla Cakravartī seriously, the proud *brāhmaṇa* had to suffer such a severe reaction. From the incident of Durvāsā Muni and Mahārāja Ambarīṣa we can understand that unless an offender approaches the offended Vaiṣṇava and begs his forgiveness, the Lord cannot excuse the offender. This principle was also affirmed in the incident involving Śrīvāsa Ṭhākura and Gopāla Cāpāla. Gopāla Cāpāla continued to suffer for a long time until he approached Śrīvāsa Ṭhākura on the urging of Śrī Caitanya Mahāprabhu and begged to be forgiven for his offenses. Śrīvāsa Ṭhākura unreservedly forgave Gopāla Cāpāla, and thus he was forgiven due to his sincere repentance and readiness to render service to Srivasa Ṭhākura by taking fully to Kṛṣṇa consciousness. Therefore, we can understand that it is not enough that the Vaiṣṇava is not personally aggrieved by an offender; the Lord's anger will not be dissipated unless the offender personally approaches that Vaiṣṇava and humbly submits himself and begs for forgiveness and is prepared to rectify his behavior by serving and satisfying the offended devotee. When the pure-hearted Vaiṣṇava grants his forgiveness whole-heartedly, the Lord is then satisfied, and not otherwise.

The additional element to be considered in this discussion is the element of atonement or rectification. Despite the forgiveness of an advanced devotee being granted, there may still remain an obstacle. There are two items *kṣamā* (forgiveness) and *anugraha* (favor). An offended devotee may grant *kṣamā* quite easily, but that is only part of the rectification. To clarify this point by an example: suppose a devotee is accused of thievery. This status of being a thief is then broadcast widely in the Vaiṣṇava community. Later, it turns out that the accused devotee is completely innocent of the charge. The culprit who falsely named the accused a thief should then approach the offended Vaiṣṇava and apologize.

The offended Vaiṣṇava may readily agree to forgive the offender. However, such an apology is insufficient. The accused devotee's reputation has been spoiled. The accuser, in order to gain the favor of the offended Vaiṣṇava, needs to try to rectify the situation.[19] Therefore, the offender should publish or broadcast the innocence of the accused devotee at least as widely and vigorously as he originally broadcast the so-called guilt of that devotee and enquire also how he may further serve and satisfy the wronged Vaiṣṇava. When the offended devotee becomes fully satisfied, he grants his full-hearted forgiveness (favor) and actually prays to Kṛṣṇa for the deliverance of the offender. Such a bestowal of mercy is called *anugraha*, and is essential for the complete removal of *aparādha*. Meditating on and trying to be the servant of the servant of the Vaiṣṇavas is an additional and important remedy in curing an offensive mentality, because a servant will show respect to all and humbly serve the Vaiṣṇavas. He will not think he is very important; he simply thinks how he can be a better servant of the devotees. This mentality will remove the tendency to commit offenses as well as help to mitigate those offenses inadvertently or unconsciously committed.

Śāntipura: Association with Advaita Ācārya

Haridāsa was aggrieved to hear of Gopāla's condition and was quite prepared to forgive him, but offenses to Vaiṣṇavas not rectified by the offender are intolerable to Kṛṣṇa. Desiring the association of Advaita Ācārya, the Ṭhākura proceeded to Śāntipura where he greeted the Ācārya by falling at his feet. Advaita Ācārya roared when he saw Haridāsa and embraced him and offered him all respect in return.

Advaita Ācārya had a cave-like dwelling constructed for Haridāsa Ṭhākura on the bank of the river Ganges, where they used to regularly meet and discuss the topics of *Bhagavad-gītā* and *Śrīmad-Bhāgavatam*. The Ṭhākura accepted food every day at the home of the Ācārya, and they constantly relished spiritual topics.

Haridāsa became concerned that Advaita Ācārya was showing him so much affection and attention. Advaita Ācārya belonged to the aristocratic *brāhmaṇa* community of Śāntipura, and Haridāsa Ṭhākura was anxious about the social ramifications his association with Advaita Ācārya might produce. Although both of these transcendental Vaiṣṇavas were well aware that social convention is an unimportant consideration when it comes to transcendental hierarchy, still Haridāsa Ṭhākura was always careful to observe social etiquette to preserve the peace and tranquility of society. He was fearful that Advaita Ācārya would be subjected to criticism on his account. Many of the *brāhmaṇas* were very critical that a person born as a Muslim was being treated as a transcendental Vaiṣṇava. Advaita Ācārya, however, was unconcerned and strongly affirmed that by offering respect to Haridāsa Ṭhākura he was behaving strictly according to scriptural principles, and concluded by stating:

"Feeding you is equal to feeding ten million *brāhmaṇas*. Therefore, accept this *śrāddha-pātra*."[20]

Śrāddha is *prasāda* offered to the forefathers at a certain date of the year or month. The *śrāddha-pātra* (the plate offered to the forefathers) is supposed to be offered to the most qualified *brāhmaṇa* in society. Advaita Ācārya showed by this act that a transcendental Vaiṣṇava, regardless of his birth, is greater than a *brāhmaṇa*. This was a significant incident, and one that caused consternation in certain quarters of Śāntipura.[21] However, there are many supporting scriptural statements which affirm that birth is not the determining factor in ascertaining spiritual importance, and Śrīla Prabhupāda comments: "Advaita Ācārya had confidence in the śāstric [scriptural] evidence and did not care about social customs.[22] Advaita Ācārya was highly respected in Śāntipura, both as a *brāhmaṇa* and a highly learned professor of the scriptures. Nevertheless, he was subjected to a good deal of censure and criticism for his honoring of Haridāsa Ṭhākura and for his association with the Vaiṣṇavas of Navadvīpa. He never cared for any of it. He was happy to act strictly on the basis of scriptural principles. The Kṛṣṇa consciousness movement, therefore, is a cultural movement that does not care about local social conventions. Following in the footsteps of Śrī Caitanya Mahāprabhu and Advaita Ācārya, we can accept a devotee from any part of the world and recognize him as a *brāhmaṇa* as soon as he is qualified due to following the principles of Vaiṣṇava behavior."[23]

During this period Advaita Ācārya was absorbed in thinking how the conditioned souls could be delivered. He became very determined that Kṛṣṇa would descend, and with a firm vow began to worship the *śālagrāma-śilā* with Ganges water and *tulasī* leaves, praying for the Lord's descent. At the same time Haridāsa Ṭhākura chanted in his cave on the bank of the Ganges, also praying for Kṛṣṇa's descent. Kṛṣṇadāsa Kavirāja Gosvāmī comments: "Because of the devotional service of these two persons, Lord Śrī Caitanya Mahāprabhu descended as an incarnation. Thus He preached the holy name of the Lord and ecstatic love of Kṛṣṇa to deliver the entire world."[24]

Deliverance of Māyā

During this period of solitary chanting in the cave by the Ganges an extraordinary event transpired, described as "astonishing" and "beyond material reasoning" by Kṛṣṇadāsa Kavirāja Gosvāmī. One moonlit evening as Haridāsa Ṭhākura sat chanting loudly in his cave in the presence of *tulasī,* an extraordinarily beautiful and effulgent woman appeared in the courtyard, her scent perfuming the air. She offered obeisances to *tulasī* and circumambulated her. She then requested that Haridāsa Ṭhākura have union with her and began to "...manifest various postures, which even the greatest philosopher would lose his patience upon seeing."[25]

However, Haridāsa Ṭhākura is described by Kṛṣṇadāsa Kavirāja Gosvāmī as "...immovable, for he was deeply determined."[26] He informed the amazingly beautiful being that he had to first complete his vows of chanting. Utilizing the same tactic as he had earlier with the prostitute sent by Rāmacandra Khān, he engaged her in hearing the chanting for three days. Daily she approached him "...exhibiting various feminine postures that would bewilder the mind of even Lord Brahmā."[27] There is a certain irony in this comparison, since Haridasa Thakura is said to be an incarnation of Lord Brahma. However, in this appearance as a pure Vaiṣṇava, absorbed in the holy names, he was unaffected, having achieved the pinnacle of spiritual development—*prema-bhakti.* The feminine poses exhibited by the extraordinarily beautiful woman "...were just like crying in the forest."[28]

After the third day of waiting, she chided Haridāsa Ṭhākura for giving her false assurances: "...I see that throughout the entire day and night your chanting of the holy name is never finished."

Haridāsa Ṭhākura replied: "My dear friend, what can I do? I have made a vow. How, then, can I give it up?"

The woman then admitted:

"I am the illusory energy of the Supreme Personality of Godhead. I came here to test you. I have previously captivated the mind of even Brahmā, not to speak of others. Your mind alone have I failed to attract. My dear sir, you are the foremost devotee. Simply seeing you and hearing you chant the holy name of Kṛṣṇa has purified my consciousness. Now I want to chant the holy name of the Lord. Please be kind to me by instructing me about the ecstasy of chanting the Hare Kṛṣṇa *mahā-mantra.*

"There is now a flood of the eternal nectar of love of Godhead due to the incarnation of Lord Caitanya. All living entities are floating in that flood. The entire world is now thankful to the Lord. Anyone that does not float in this inundation is most condemned. Such a person cannot be delivered for millions of *kalpas.*

"Formerly, I received the holy name of Lord Rāma from Lord Śiva, but now, due to your association, I am greatly eager to chant the holy name of Lord Kṛṣṇa. The holy name of Lord Rāma certainly gives one liberation, but the holy name of Kṛṣṇa transports one to the other side of the ocean of nescience and at last gives one ecstatic love of Kṛṣṇa. Please give me the holy name of Kṛṣṇa and thus make me fortunate, so that I also may float in the flood of love of Godhead inaugurated by Śrī Caitanya Mahāprabhu."[29]

Māyā, the illusory energy of the Lord, then worshipped the feet of Haridāsa Ṭhākura, and he gave her initiation by requesting her to chant the Hare Kṛṣṇa *mahā-mantra*. After receiving this benediction, Māyā left with great pleasure.

Kṛṣṇadāsa Kavirāja Gosvāmī then addresses his readers who may not take this narration seriously due to insufficient faith. He gives a series of reasons why people should have faith. In many places in the narrations of Vṛndāvana dāsa Ṭhākura and Kṛṣṇadāsa Kavirāja Gosvāmī, it has been described how the eternal associates of Kṛṣṇa like Brahmā, Śiva, the Kumāras, as well as Nārada, Prahlāda, the goddess of fortune and others descended to this world appearing as human beings to taste the nectar of chanting the holy name. What's more, all of these narrations are based on the words of a person of spotless character and pure devotion, namely Svarūpa Dāmodara Gosvāmī, an eyewitness to so many of Śrī Caitanya Mahāprabhu's wonderful pastimes, as well as the testimony of Raghunātha dāsa Gosvāmī who heard directly from Svarūpa Dāmodara Gosvāmī.

"What to speak of others, even Kṛṣṇa, the son of Nanda Mahārāja, personally descends to taste the nectar of love of Godhead in the form of chanting of Hare Kṛṣṇa. What is the wonder if the maidservant of Kṛṣṇa, His external energy, begs for love of Godhead? Without the mercy of a devotee and without the chanting of the holy name of the Lord, love of Godhead cannot be possible. In the activities of Lord Sri Caitanya, the three worlds dance and chant, having coming in touch with love of Godhead. This is the characteristic of His pastimes. The holy name of Kṛṣṇa is so attractive that anyone who chants it—including all living entities, moving and nonmoving, and even Lord Kṛṣṇa Himself—becomes imbued with love of Kṛṣṇa. This is the effect of chanting the Hare Kṛṣṇa *mahā-mantra*."[30]

Kṛṣṇadāsa Kavirāja Gosvāmī concludes:

> "I have heard from the mouth of Raghunātha dāsa Gosvāmī all that Svarūpa Dāmodara Gosvāmī recorded in his notes about the pastimes of Śrī Caitanya Mahāprabhu. I have briefly described those pastimes. Whatever I have written is by the mercy of Śrī Caitanya Mahāprabhu, since I am an insignificant living being. I have described but a fragment of the glories of Haridāsa Ṭhākura. Hearing this satisfies the aural reception of every devotee."[31]

Endnotes

[1] *CC Antya* 3.167.
[2] *CC Antya* 3.170.
[3] It is interesting to note the difference between the attitude of Rāmacandra Khān and that of the Majumadārs. In modern societies around the world there are also those who are opposed, favorable, or indifferent to the Vaiṣṇavas.
[4] *CC Antya* 3.177—179.
[5] *SB* 11.2.40.
[6] This is an extremely important philosophical point: that love of God is the real goal of Kṛṣṇa consciousness. It is on this point that Sri Caitanya Mahāprabhu differed with other Vaiṣṇavas. For example, in South India, Mahāprabhu's discussions with the Tattvavādīs exposed this issue. Mahāprabhu's discussions with Rāmananda Rāya also covered the same important point. A true representative of Mahāprabhu stresses this point. Like Haridāsa Ṭhākura, a Caitanya follower does not necessarily demand that someone give up their wealth or pursue the path of renunciation. He did not do so with the Majumadārs. Rather, the pure devotee insists that the goal of chanting, the goal of Kṛṣṇa consciousness, is love of Kṛṣṇa. Knowledge and renunciation are secondary to Kṛṣṇa devotion.
[7] *CC Antya* 3.180, 181.
[8] *CC Antya* 3.183—189.
[9] *CC Antya* 3.193.
[10] Rāghava Caitanya dāsa, *The Divine Name*, p. 38.
[11] Nisikanta Sanyal, *Sree Krishna Chaitanya*, p. 579.
[12] The translation of *bhāvukera* by Professor Sanyal is reminiscent of Śrīla Prabhupāda's disparaging remarks about those who travel to various places in order to entertain others by beautifully narrating the stories of *Śrīmad-Bhāgavatam*. These reciters receive donations in return for their

"piety." However, the goal of such recitation is not to simply entertain people, but to awaken them to the true *Bhāgavatam* culture of devotional service as Śrīla Haridāsa Ṭhākura is doing here.

[13] *CC Antya* 3.195—197.

[14] *CC Antya* 3.198, 199.

[15] *CC Antya* 3.201.

[16] Rāghava Caitanya dāsa, *The Divine Name*, p.40.

[17] *CC Antya* 3.201 purport.

[18] *CC Antya* 3.209, 210.

[19] As mentioned in the story of Bhṛgu Muni, there are three categories of offenses: mental, verbal, and physical. The atonements are different for each, and the implication is that one should atone for an offense "in kind"; or according to the level of severity. Modern devotees often ritualize offenses by saying things like, "Pardon any offense I might commit in what I am about to say." Many devotees assume that their novice position (or the novice position of others!) gives them the right to offend individuals, leaders, groups, and organizations. Being frivolous, they unwittingly or callously offend others and assume that the more advanced persons are required to forgive such offenses. However, Śrīla Prabhupāda demonstrated both the actions of forgiveness and of intolerance of irreconcilable insolence. The point is that committing offenses, like chanting and worshipping, are not rituals. All services should be done with care and thought. "Guarding against offense" does not imply constant guilt or fear, but this expression implies that *bhakti* is a personal exchange, not a ritual act. In *bhakti* one does not become pure or atone from offense by a ritual like bathing in sacred rivers. One is freed from offense by seeing Kṛṣṇa and His devotees as persons and seeing Kṛṣṇa's personal relationships with His devotees as of topmost importance to Him.

[20] *CC Antya* 3.222.

[21] Dr. Sambidananda Das in his book *The History and Literature of the Gaudiya Vaishnavas and Their Relation to Other Medieval Vaishnava Schools* (Sree Gaudiya Math, Madras, 1991) observes the revolutionary nature of Advaita Ācārya's activities: "To start a practice which was sure to be regarded as a social innovation and the attempt to place a true devotee, to whatever caste he may have belonged at birth, above the so-called brahmanas, in a place like Santipur, a stronghold of brahmana influence, required a certain amount of sacrifice of social esteem. The clear mandate of his [Advaita's] deep scriptural knowledge supported him against enormous odds. In Bengal, particularly during

this period, nobody could dream of ignoring the restrictions of the rigid society, however unsastric they might be, lest the society excommunicate the offender and prevent him from arranging the marriages of his children, especially the daughters, at the proper age, the non-performance of which duty was and is still considered, particularly in the village life, to be the gravest slur on the good name of the family. Moreover, the daily life of any Hindu was made impossible if he incurred the displeasure of his caste. The leaders of caste punish dissenters by preventing the barber, washerman, nurse, shopkeeper and so on from giving them any social services. The punishment which the society inflicted on such offenders was more severe than the penal servitude of the criminal court. No social threats, on wrath of the fanatic ruler of the country, prevented Advaita from doing his duty. He was invincible on the strength of his conviction that God is sure to be pleased with one who seeks to serve Him."

[22] In America and other materialistic societies, some people consider the devotees' behavior and traditional dress to be eccentric. However, devotees like Advaita Ācārya have shown the example of indifference to such criticism. On one hand, religious freedom is encouraged in western countries. On the other hand, Amish, Mennonites, Hasidic Jews, orthodox Muslims, and Hare Kṛṣṇas are sometimes quietly ostracized or even censured due to their traditional dress. Mature devotees know when it is appropriate to remain under cover, so that they are not unproductively persecuted. However, they are also not afraid to assert themselves by wearing traditional clothing like many Sikhs and Muslims do in order to demonstrate pride in their heritage and spiritual values.

[23] *CC Antya* 3.221 purport.

[24] *CC Antya* 3.226.

[25] *CC Antya* 3.238.

[26] *CC Antya* 3.239.

[27] *CC Antya* 3.245.

[28] *CC Antya*.3.246.

[29] *CC Antya* 3.248—258.

[30] *CC Antya* 3.265—268.

[31] *CC Antya* 3.269—271.

jayati jayati nāmānanda-rūpaṁ murārer
viramita-nija-dharma-dhyāna-pūjādi-yatnam
kathamapi sakṛd-āttaṁ muktidaṁ prāṇīnāṁ yat
paramam amṛtam ekaṁ jīvanaṁ bhūṣaṇaṁ me

ALL GLORIES, ALL GLORIES TO THE ALL blissful holy name of Śrī Kṛṣṇa, which causes the devotee to give up all conventional religious duties, meditation and worship. When somehow or other uttered even once by a living entity, the holy name awards him liberation. The holy name of Kṛṣṇa is the highest nectar. It is my very life and my only treasure."

Bṛhad-bhāgavatāmṛta (1.9), by Sanātana Gosvāmī
[cited: *Śrī Caitanya-caritāmṛta Antya-līlā* 4.71]

THE KING AGAIN REQUESTED HARIDĀSA: "O brother, just recite the confession from the Koran, and you'll have nothing to worry about. Otherwise the kazi and his men will punish you, and you'll be forced to recite the Koran anyway. In this way you'll be humiliated."

Haridāsa Ṭhākura replied with absolute faith and conviction: "One cannot do anything other than what the Supreme Lord desires. Know for certain that the Lord awards the results of one's offenses. Even if my body is cut into pieces and I give up my life, I will never give up chanting the Lord's holy name."

Śrī Caitanya-bhāgavata Adi 16.90, 91, 94

Chapter Four

Trial & Tribulation

Ecstatic Manifestations

THE *ŚRĪ CAITANYA-BHĀGAVATA* describes the extraordinary solitary *bhajana* of the Nāmācārya. Haridāsa Ṭhākura was living close to a remote village called Phuliyā near Śāntipura, the home of Advaita Ācārya. The following account of the ecstatic symptoms manifested by Haridāsa Ṭhākura in the course of his daily practice of chanting the holy names is given by Vṛndāvana dāsa Ṭhākura:

> "Haridāsa would continually wander on the banks of the Ganges while loudly chanting the names of Kṛṣṇa. Hāridasa was most renounced in the matter of material enjoyment, and his mouth was always beautified with the chanting of Lord Kṛṣṇa's names. He did not give up chanting the names of Govinda for

> even a moment, and as a result he was constantly manifesting various ecstatic symptoms. Sometimes he danced alone, and sometimes he roared like a mad lion. Sometimes he cried loudly, and sometimes he laughed loudly. Sometimes he roared loudly, and sometimes he fell to the ground unconscious. Sometimes he would utter some unnatural sounds, for which he would later give some profound meaning. He manifested all the different ecstatic symptoms like crying, hairs standing on end, laughing, losing consciousness, and perspiring. As soon as Haridāsa began to dance, these symptoms would all manifest in his body. Haridāsa's entire body became wet, as tears of love flowed from his eyes. Even staunch atheists would offer him respect. Even Brahmā and Śiva were satisfied to see the wonderful manifestation of Haridāsa's hair standing on end. All the *brāhmaṇas* of Phuliyā were overwhelmed upon seeing Haridāsa. While Haridāsa resided in Phuliyā, everyone there developed great faith in him. Haridāsa would regularly take bath in the Ganges and then loudly chant the names of Lord Hari while wandering about."[1]

It is useful to contrast the culture and society that Haridāsa Ṭhākura moved in with our contemporary versions. In modern societies most people are either in their homes, in their places of work, in their automobiles, or in the bustling malls and supermarkets. Religious life is often confined to a ritual weekly observance in a well-established institution of worship. A few, who are viewed as eccentrics, preach on the streets, but most people ignore them. In some cities, a few entertainers perform on the streets or in subways. However, most entertainment comes elegantly and expensively packaged via the various modern media and is exhibited in tightly controlled stadiums and arenas.

In Haridāsa Ṭhākura's time the environment was quite different. The majority of people lived in villages or small towns. People had their windows and doors open. Birds, lizards, and other small animals were free to go in and out of the homes, and sounds of street singers and chanters entered as well. There were traveling storytellers, faquirs, swamis, drama troupes, and others who provide entertainment for the people. Most entertainers, like drama troupes and storytellers incorporated both religious and mundane themes in their presentations. Sometimes mendicants would sing the erotic, spiritual songs of Caṇḍīdāsa or Jayadeva. Some would cry out the names of Govinda, and some would sing Islamic themes or chant the Islamic names of God.

This was the cultural background in which Haridāsa made his home in Phuliyā. Gradually people came to understand that he was indeed a *sādhu*, a saintly person. In contrast to some of those who traveled, sang, and chanted, he did not care at all for his own livelihood. On even closer observation, the people of Phuliyā realized that Haridāsa was situated in the topmost category of those who sincerely chanted the Lord's names and sang about the Lord's pastimes. One can only imagine how, in such a religious society, a common household might hear the names of the Lord as Haridāsa Ṭhākura passed by. People would consider themselves blessed upon hearing his pure, unmotivated, and uninterrupted vibration. They would sometimes marvel at his absorption in and enjoyment of the name, and they would capture some of that enjoyment and in some cases be spiritually transfixed and transformed by the experience. Vṛndāvana dāsa Ṭhākura emphasizes that Haridāsa communicated the enjoyment, the pleasure of the Name of the Lord, and his audience received the experience, not as mundane, but as spiritual ecstasy.

Vṛndāvana dāsa Ṭhākura mentions that the *brāhmaṇas* were overwhelmed at seeing Haridāsa. This is a significant statement, because the *brahmanas* were in a position to criticise him, as his Muslim birth placed him outside the precincts of Hindu society. However, they, too, appreciated his genuine spirituality.

Śrīla Bhaktisiddhānta Sarasvatī Ṭhākura comments, citing the *Bhakti-rasāmṛta-sindhu* by Śrīla Rūpa Gosvāmī, that nine symptoms of ecstatic emotion manifest in the behavior of a pure Vaiṣṇava: forgiveness, concern that time should not be wasted, detachment, absence of false prestige, hope, eagerness, a taste for chanting the holy name of the Lord, attachment to descriptions of the transcendental qualities of the Lord, and affection for those places where the Lord resides. "These are called *anubhāvas*, subordinate signs of ecstatic emotions."[2]

The physical symptoms of ecstatic emotion are described in the 11th Canto of the *Śrīmad-Bhāgavatam*:

> "By chanting the holy name of the Supreme Lord, one comes to the stage of love of Godhead. Then the devotee is fixed in his vow as an eternal servant of the Lord, and he gradually becomes very much attached to a particular name and form of the Supreme Personality of Godhead. As his heart melts with ecstatic love, he laughs very loudly or cries or shouts. Sometimes he sings and dances like a madman, for he is indifferent to public opinion." (*SB* 11.2.40)

In his purport to the verse of the *Ādi-khaṇḍa* of *Śrī Caitanya-bhāgavata* (16.29), Śrīla Bhaktisiddhānta Sarasvatī Ṭhākura further describes the eight transformations of ecstatic love enumerated in the writings of Śrīla Rūpa Gosvāmī: *stambha* (being stunned), *sveda* (perspiring), *romāñca* (hairs standing on end), *svara-bheda* (choking), *vepathu* or *kampa* (trembling), *vaivarnya* (fading of color), *aśru* (weeping), and *pralaya* or *mūrchā* (devastation).[3]

All of the symptoms of an ecstatic devotee of the Lord situated in pure love of God were manifested in the behavior of Haridāsa Ṭhākura. Although shy and retiring by nature, when he was in the grip of spiritual emotion, he would exhibit the loving sentiments of a pure Vaiṣṇava in relation to his Lord. His was not a false show of imaginative ecstasy, but the natural overflow of ecstatic feeling erupting in his heart.

Arrested—Preaching to the Prisoners

Although the people of Phuliyā had high regard and veneration for Haridāsa Ṭhākura, the local *kazi* or cleric[4] was incensed and went to the king of Bengal and complained about Haridāsa Ṭhākura's misbehavior. The "crime" he ascribed to Haridāsa was that although Haridāsa Ṭhākura was born a Muslim, he was following the religion of the Hindus. The king, feeling hostility for such an aberration and at the urging of the *kazi*, immediately had Haridāsa arrested and imprisoned. The residents of Phuliyā felt morose upon receiving this news and lamented their loss very bitterly, as they fully expected that Haridāsa Ṭhākura would be persecuted or even killed for his activities.

Haridāsa was placed in prison like an ordinary criminal, but amongst the prisoners were many pious persons who were joyful at the prospect of getting the association of a *mahā-bhāgavata* like Haridāsa. They persuaded the guards to let them have the audience of the great soul, thinking that their miseries would be dissipated by his presence. When Haridāsa arrived in their company, he glanced at them with compassion and mercy. Haridāsa Ṭhākura's presence was spiritually powerful, charismatic and he was extremely handsome: "...Haridāsa's hands reached to his knees, his eyes were like lotus petals, and his enchanting moonlike face was beyond compare."[5]

As the prisoners offered him their obeisances, ecstatic symptoms manifested in their bodies. When the Ṭhākura observed their devotional sentiments, he smiled in a curious way and gave them an apparently ambiguous blessing:

"Stay there. Stay as you are now."[6] Or as Professor Sanyal translates it: "May you continue to remain in your present condition."[7]

Śrīla Bhaktisiddhānta Sarasvatī Ṭhākura explains the smiling of Haridāsa Ṭhākura in his commentary: "...the smile was a confidential blessing in disguise. Seeing their moroseness, Ṭhākura Mahāśaya said to them, 'I have blessed you with an auspicious smile. Don't consider it otherwise and feel sad.'"[8]

Upon hearing this mysterious benediction, the prisoners became depressed, not understanding the Ṭhākura's intention. Haridāsa Ṭhākura, seeing their distress, offered them reassurances:

> "You have not understood the meaning of the blessings I gave, and therefore you are lamenting. I never award inauspicious benedictions. Carefully try to understand as I explain: As your minds are presently fixed on Kṛṣṇa, let them stay that way forever. Now you can all together constantly chant the names of Kṛṣṇa and think of Kṛṣṇa. Here you have no envy or trouble from others, so you can humbly chant and think of Kṛṣṇa. Otherwise, if you again return to material enjoyment, by bad association you'll forget everything about Kṛṣṇa. One cannot achieve love for Kṛṣṇa as long as he is engaged in sense gratification. You should know for certain that Kṛṣṇa is far away from such persons. The mind that is absorbed in material enjoyment is a great disturbance. Attachment for wife and children are the binding ropes of illusion that lead to death. If by providence a fortunate person achieves the association of a devotee, he gives up his attachment for material enjoyment and

worships Kṛṣṇa. In conclusion, the nature of material enjoyment is that one makes the same mistake again and again. Therefore, I did not mean 'Stay in prison,' but rather stay free from thoughts of material enjoyment and always chant the name of Hari. Do not even slightly lament that I gave you this blessing in an ambiguous way. I glance mercifully on all living entities. May you all have firm devotion for Lord Kṛṣṇa. Don't worry. I guarantee that within two or three days you will be freed. Whether you are a householder or a renunciant—whatever you are—don't forget these instructions at any cost."[9]

Śrīla Bhaktisiddhānta Sarasvatī Ṭhākura purports and summarizes the above statements of Haridāsa Ṭhākura in the following unique words:

"Your present state of mind is auspicious for you, because you have received the opportunity to cultivate Kṛṣṇa consciousness by giving up endeavors for material enjoyment. Therefore always remain engaged in chanting Kṛṣṇa's names and in remembering Kṛṣṇa. If you get freedom from prison life and again indulge in sense gratification, then as a result of associating with wicked persons who are averse to the Lord you will forget the Supreme Lord. As long as the endeavor for material enjoyment is prominent in the living entity, there is no possibility for him to worship Kṛṣṇa. The conditioned souls who are devoid of devotional service to Kṛṣṇa are always merged in topics related to their wives and children, which are the center of their enjoyment. If by the mercy of the lord a person in this dangerous situation meets a saintly person, his taste for material enjoyment will be turned into taste for the service of the Supreme Lord. When one gives up the cultivation of Kṛṣṇa consciousness, then his natural material propensities will submerse him in a mire of offenses. I do not mean that you should remain suffering within this prison, but in your present condition you have the opportunity to constantly chant the holy names of the Lord. Therefore, do not be distressed. The Vaiṣṇavas always bless all living entities with the words: 'May your devotion to the Supreme Lord be fixed.' I consider this the greatest mercy towards the living entities. Your prison life will soon be finished. Never give up your determination for serving the Supreme Lord in any condition."[10]

Trial and Torture

After explaining his merciful benediction to the prisoners, guaranteeing their release and offering them his best wishes, Haridāsa was presented to the king. The king had assumed that Haridāsa Ṭhākura was a charlatan or an ordinary trouble maker, but when the king noted his impressive figure and personality, as well as the charm and effulgence of the heroic Vaiṣṇava, he respectfully offered him a seat. The king then began to simultaneously chide and question Haridāsa Ṭhākura in a familiar way, as one brother to another, since, in his ignorance, that was as much respect as he could muster.

> "My dear brother, why do you have such a mentality? By good fortune you've been born a Muslim, so why do you follow the religious practices of the Hindus? We don't even eat rice that's been touched by Hindus, so why are you degrading yourself? You've been born in a high family. You're transgressing your caste and religion to follow the religion of others. How will you attain salvation? Whatever sinful activities you've unknowingly performed can be cleared by uttering *kalām*."[11]

Śrīla Bhaktisiddhānta Sarasvatī Ṭhākura comments on "uttering *kalām*": "*Kalām*[12] (an Arabic word) means 'word' or 'statement.' *Kalām* [or *Kalām-e-Allah*] refers to a passage from the Koran indicating the acceptance of Mohammed's Islam religion."[13]

Haridāsa Ṭhākura was so amused by the foolish, sectarian sentiments of the king that he began to laugh and commented: "How wonderfully the illusory energy of the Lord acts."[14]

Feeling compassion for the king, upon hearing his pathetic display of ignorance, Haridāsa Ṭhākura began to speak in a universal, nonsectarian way about the Absolute Truth:

> "Listen, dear sir. The Supreme Lord of all is one without a second. The Hindus and Muslims differentiate the Lord only by name, but in spiritual vision the Lord is one. This is confirmed in the *Purāṇas* and the *Koran*. The pure, eternal, nondual, inexhaustible Lord sits in the heart of everyone. That Lord induces everyone to work in a particular way, and everyone in the entire world acts accordingly. The names and qualities of that Lord are chanted by everyone according to their respective scriptural injunctions. The Supreme Lord accepts the devotion of everyone, but if anyone is envious of His children, then He retaliates. Therefore, I am only acting under the inspiration of the Supreme Lord. By his own desire, a Hindu *brāhmaṇa* may also become a Muslim. What can the Hindus do? That is his *karma*. If one is already dead, then what is the use of killing him. Dear sir, now you can judge. If I'm at fault, then you may punish me."[15]

Śrīla Bhaktisiddhānta Sarasvatī Ṭhākura summarizes and comments significantly on certain points made by Haridāsa Ṭhākura in the above passages of *Śrī Caitanya-bhāgavata*:

> "The Supreme Personality of Godhead is one, eternal, nondual, and the Lord of all living entities. That one Lord is the controller of the Hindus, Muslims, young and old, and male and female who are ignorant of the science of the Supreme Lord foolishly oppose each other by concocting two different Gods with separate names, but when they give up such discrimination and difference of opinion and indifferently consider their respective religious scriptures, the *Purāṇas* and the *Koran*, then they will never find such differences in the Absolute Truth."[16]

Śrīla Bhaktivinoda Ṭhākura wisely comments on the topic of sectarian fanaticism:

"As far as we can understand, no enemy of Vaishnavism will find any beauty in the Bhagavat. The true critic is a generous judge, void of prejudices and party-spirit. One who is at heart the follower of Mohammed will certainly find the doctrines of the New Testament to be a forgery by the fallen angel [the devil]. A Trinitarian Christian, on the other hand, will denounce the precepts of Mohammed as those of an ambitious reformer...Party-spirit—that great enemy of truth—will always baffle the attempt of the enquirer, who tries to gather truth from religious works of his own nation, and will make him believe that absolute truth is nowhere except in his old religious book."[17]

Haridāsa Ṭhākura's nonsectarian message, so logically and thoughtfully presented, impressed the king and his retinue very much, and they felt very satisfied by the logic and import of the Ṭhākura's statements. Śrīla Prabhupāda exhibited the same spirit while preaching in Iran in 1976 in a conversation with a Muslim university student named Ali:

Śrīla Prabhupāda: Yes. Name means authorized name, not fictitious. If you chant a fictitious name, that will not be effective. But if you chant the real name of God, then you'll be purified. So if you are chanting the authorized name of God, there is no question of chanting Hare Kṛṣṇa. If you have got the real name of God, chant it. As Caitanya Mahāprabhu says: *nāmnām akāri bahudhā nija-sarva-śaktis tatrārpitā niyamitaḥ smaraṇe na kālaḥ*. God is unlimited; therefore, He must have unlimited names also. There is no question of sectarianism in this movement. We are recommending that you chant the holy name of the Lord. Do it. Is there any objection? Suppose you say that you are Muhammedan. If I say you chant the holy name of God, have you got any objection?

Ali: Oh! No. No. Chanting—I do chant myself!

Śrīla Prabhupāda: Yes, that's all. We are preaching this. We don't say that you become one of us. You chant the holy name of the Lord, that's all.[18]

Like Ali, those assembled in the king's court were satisfied with the statements of Haridāsa Ṭhākura, with one exception: the *kazi* who had originally instigated the complaint. He was a fanatic with an adamantine heart, with no particle of human kindness in it. He insisted on the punishment of Haridāsa Ṭhākura:

"This miscreant will simply create other miscreants, and he'll bring a bad name to the Muslim community. Therefore, punish him in an exemplary way, or at least make him recite the confession from the *Koran*."[19]

Śrīla Bhaktisiddhānta Sarasvatī Ṭhākura comments that the *kazi* incited the king with the following import:

> "The example of following Hindu principles that Haridāsa is setting will certainly bring infamy to the Muslim community, and in the future many Muslims will bring further defamation and disrepute to the Muslim religion by following him. Therefore, you should severely punish him as a warning to others so that this may not happen. Otherwise, Haridāsa should personally repent and beg forgiveness for his actions; then only can he be excused from punishment."[20]

Since the *kazi* was considered both a religious and legal authority, his words carried weight with the king, and his recommendations could not be easily ignored. The fanaticism of the *kazi* is typical of the thoroughly sectarian and narrow view that God's interests can only be defined by the interpretation of religious texts by persons who assert their authority without necessarily having the requisite qualifications. In this case the so-called authority of the *kazi* was not only ecclesiastical, because, in the medieval Islamic tradition, a cleric like the *kazi* had both religious and secular authority. In fact, there was no difference between ecclesiastical and secular law—they were one. Although the *kazi* lacked compassion for all living beings and was without a tinge of love for God, he was still to be obeyed. Such supposed interests of the Lord must be defended (according to such fanatics) by all means, including violence, for the pleasure of the Lord. Professor Sanyal comments:

> "...fanaticism is the result of culpable ignorance due to a radically disloyal and unserving disposition. Recourse to violence, either physical, mental or spiritual, is directly opposed to the Purpose of Krishna, because violence is powerless against the soul who, being of the essence of Krishna, possesses His perfect freedom of will. The freedom of will of the soul is indestructible. He can be reclaimed only by an appeal to his judgment and free will. Those, who advocate violence, are far away from Krishna and perfectly ignorant of their own selves. Faith in Krishna is the natural attitude of the pure soul. Fanaticism is the hypocritical and malicious caricature of spiritual faith by the soul in the state of utter delusion. Fanaticism, being essentially an attitude of opposition to Krishna, is also necessarily intolerant of all loyal servants of the Supreme Lord. It is not by accident that the fanatics crucified Jesus. The fanatics can never tolerate the good will of Krishna towards all His creatures. They pretend to show their love (?) for Krishna by hating His loved ones. The fanatics are bound to hate everybody because they really hate the Supreme Lord Himself. They, therefore, also hate those who are averse to Krishna, not from a sense of loyalty to Krishna, but because they themselves are unmindful of the service of Krishna and want everybody to serve them. Fanaticism always kindles counter-fanaticism in those of its victims who happen to be equally averse to Krishna. But it is powerless to move the servant of Godhead to thoughts of malice against his deluded oppressors."[21]

The king felt that he was in no position to ignore the powerful cleric even though he felt that Haridāsa Ṭhākura's words rang true. With some urgency, he entreated Haridāsa Ṭhākura:

"O brother, just recite the confession from the *Koran*, and you'll have nothing to worry about. Otherwise the *kazi* and his men will punish you, and you'll be forced to recite the *Koran* anyway. In this way you'll be humiliated."[22]

Haridāsa Ṭhākura replied with absolute faith and conviction: "One cannot do anything other than what the Supreme Lord desires. Know for certain that the Lord awards the results of one's offenses. **Even if my body is cut into pieces and I give up my life, I will never give up chanting the Lord's holy name.**"[23]

Professor Sanyal translates the dramatic refusal of Haridāsa Ṭhākura as: "If my body be hacked to pieces, if life itself deserts me, even then I will not give up the Name of Hari." And Rāghava Caitanya Prabhu translates it: "Even if my body is cut to pieces, and my soul leaves the body, I will not give up [the] chanting of Sri Hari-Nama."

Rāghava Caitanya Prabhu comments on this bold and fearless declaration of Haridāsa Ṭhākura: "What a brilliant example of firm determination, and a noble ideal of extraordinary will power! For every aspirant marching towards God realization, this example of Haridāsa Ṭhākura, is like a guiding star." He also comments: "The words of Haridāsa Ṭhākura were like piercing shafts released from a powerful bow. Everyone there was taken by great surprise."[24]

Śrīla Bhaktisiddhānta Sarasvatī Ṭhākura also comments powerfully about the extraordinary statement which expresses the deep conviction and courage of Haridāsa Ṭhākura:

> "This material body, which is received from the mother and father, is not permanent. The life that is averse to the service of Kṛṣṇa and which is presently absorbed in material happiness is also perishable and changeable. But the holy names of the Supreme

> Lord and the Supreme Lord Himself are not two separate objects. Spiritual names are not like the names of material objects that are invented by human beings within the time factor. The spiritual name and the possessor of the name are one. Therefore, I can never give up chanting the holy names and repose my faith in my gross and subtle bodies. The constitutional position of a living entity is that he is the eternal servant of Kṛṣṇa. In other words, every living entity is a Vaiṣṇava. The Vaiṣṇavas have no other activities than chanting the holy names of Śrī Hari. The only duty of both the practitioner and the perfected being is to chant the holy names of the Lord. I cannot give this up to follow manmade social behavior[25]. Even if the result is that society and its administrators torture me as much as they want, I am prepared to tolerate it all with a smiling face. I will never give up the eternal service of Hari to run after temporary material happiness. I have no other activity than congregationally chanting the spiritual names of Kṛṣṇa that I have received through disciplic succession. Both the body and the mind are distinct from 'I,' the owner of the body, because 'I' am eternal, while the body and mind are temporary."[26]

The king was frustrated by Haridasa Thakura's powerful resolve. His hope of saving him from the *kazi's* wrath was now thwarted, and he resignedly turned to the fiery *kazi* and asked, "Now what will you do with him?"[27]

The reply was forthcoming: "He should be beaten in the twenty-two marketplaces [of Ambuya-muluka]. Take his life in this way. That is my opinion. If he survives being beaten in twenty-two marketplaces, then we'll understand that he's actually knowledgeable and his words are true."[28]

Some brutish guards were summoned and instructed by the fanatical and cruel *kazi*:

"Beat him in such a way that he will die. If a Muslim who follows the Hindu religion is killed, then he'll be delivered from that sin."[29]

The king, instigated by the vicious cleric, gave the order, and Haridāsa Ṭhākura was roughly seized. He was taken from market to market and beaten without any mercy. While being beaten, he constantly chanted the holy name in ecstasy. His ecstasy was so intense that he felt no pain. However, seeing the severe beating and torture of a saintly person, the pious people became very distressed. Some of them predicted the destruction of the kingdom.

Śrīla Bhaktisiddhānta Sarasvatī Ṭhākura states:

> "By oppressing the Vaiṣṇavas in this way, great inauspiciousness will soon fall on this kingdom. Simply as a result of torturing the Vaiṣṇavas, the world faces various miseries like famine, drought, plague, and war."[30]

Some of the people cursed the king and the *kazi*, and others were prepared to fight them. Still others offered the Muslim guards bribes in the hope that they could convince the guards to soften their blows and spare Haridāsa Ṭhākura's life or to stop the beating altogether. Nothing any of them said could stop the terrible onslaught. The sinful guards showed no mercy, and they continued beating Haridāsa Ṭhākura with tremendous force from market to market.[31] Still, by Lord Caitanya's merciful arrangement: "Haridāsa felt no pain whatsoever in spite of such heavy beating. The scriptures explain that Prahlāda felt no pain when he was mercilessly beaten by the demons."[32]

Śrīla Bhaktisiddhānta Sarasvatī Ṭhākura comments on this incident with an obvious reference to his own efforts to propagate the *saṅkīrtana* movement:

> "Just as Hiraṇyakaśipu tortured his *mahā-bhāgavata* son, Prahlāda, in various ways (see *Śrīmad-Bhāgavatam* 7.5.33—53 and 7.8.1—13), the sinful Muslims also began to torture

Haridāsa Ṭhākura in various ways. But like Bhakta-rāja Prahlāda, he did not feel a tinge of misery. The quality of tolerance like this is natural for the *mahā-bhāgavatas*. They are so busy in constantly serving the Supreme Lord that incident[s] of the external world like torture cannot give them any anxiety. That is why Śrī Gaurasundara has stated in his *Śrī Śikṣāṣṭaka* that only one who is more tolerant than a tree is able to glorify the topics of Kṛṣṇa, not others. If a practitioner is intolerant, then he will not be able to glorify Hari because we have seen in innumerable cases in this world that persons who are averse to the Supreme Lord have unfairly and unnecessarily attacked the all-auspicious honest preacher engaged in chanting the names of Hari and have tried to close his mouth, which is engaged in glorifying Hari. The sinful society that is intoxicated by pride related with family, caste, wealth, and material education always tried to completely stop glorification of Hari, which is the only Absolute Truth. Even on the dishonest pretext of duplicitously joining the *saṅkīrtana* party in name, they silently oppose chanting the holy names, which are *satya-vastu*, the Absolute Truth."[33]

Upon reading the account of Haridāsa Ṭhākura's torture, some readers might think that such incidents bear no relation to their own attempts to become Kṛṣṇa conscious. "It may be possible for liberated persons like Haridāsa Ṭhākura, the *nāmācārya*, the incarnation of Lord Brahmā, the eternal associate of Lord Caitanya, to undergo such a severe test, but what has any of this got to do with me? I am an ordinary devotee, trying to chant 16 rounds and teach whatever I know to others. How can I be expected to be so tolerant?" Yet, in the 20th and 21st centuries we have many examples of heroic devotees who were prepared to risk everything, including their lives, to fulfill the desires of Śrīla Prabhupāda and the disciplic succession.

Gargamuni Prabhu risked his life in Bangaladesh in 1971 during a war for liberation. Tribhuvanātha Prabhu risked his life in Lebanon in the 1980's, distributing Arabic

Bhagavad-gītās during a civil war. Ananta-śānti Prabhu, Srila Prabhupada's first Russian disciple, risked his life to spread Kṛṣṇa consciousness in Soviet Russia, and was imprisoned and tortured repeatedly. Many other Russian devotees were also imprisoned, tortured, beaten, and even killed in their efforts to spread Kṛṣṇa consciousness. Hlādinī Prabhu was killed by a Liberian terrorist while she was trying to protect the Monrovian Vaiṣṇavas. In Sarajevo, Bosnia, the *saṅkīrtana* devotees there repeatedly risked their lives during the three-year war that took over 100,000 lives. The party was attacked by knife-wielding Muslim soldiers in April of 1996, and several of the devotees were seriously wounded. There are so many other examples of devotees being fire bombed, shot at, knifed, punched, pushed, shoved, spat upon, etc. Books have been and will continue to be written on the risks taken and amazing tolerance exhibited by the 20th and 21st century Vaiṣṇavas.

Devotees should never think that the courage exhibited by Haridāsa Ṭhākura is simply *līlā* and has no bearing on the present *saṅkīrtana* efforts of sincere Vaiṣṇavas. Haridāsa Ṭhākura does have an exalted status as an eternal associate of the Lord, but he was also a *jīva* soul who was firmly determined to serve the Lord unconditionally. His absolutely determined exhibition of free will in Kṛṣṇa's service is magnificent, but it is certainly not irrelevant to any devotee who sincerely tries to serve Kṛṣṇa. In Śrī *Caitanya-caritāmṛta Antya* 3.239, Haridasa Thakura is described as follows:

nirvikāra haridāsa gambhīra-āśaya
balite lāgilā tāṅre hañā sadaya

Haridāsa is described as *nirvikāra*—unmoved or immovable and *gambhīra āśaya*—very deeply determined.

These adjectives illustrate how *gambhīra āśaya* was Haridāsa Ṭhākura's particular qualification—*gambhīra*—very deep and *āśaya*—determination. Haridāsa Ṭhākura was the emblem of humility, tolerance, and tremendous determination. His life is meant to instruct all Vaiṣṇavas, and since his activities cannot be imitated, aspiring Vaiṣṇavas are meant to follow in his footsteps. To spread Kṛṣṇa consciousness requires tolerance, determination, and courage. Without courage, tolerance, and determination, one cannot preach.

Vṛndāvana dāsa Ṭhākura offers a benediction to the reader: "What to speak of Haridāsa himself, even one who remembers his activities is immediately relieved of all material miseries."[34]

As he was being beaten, Haridāsa Ṭhākura was feeling compassion for the sinful guards who were beating him, and he prayed: "O Kṛṣṇa! Be merciful on these living entities. Forgive their offense of torturing me."[35] Haridāsa was more worried about the sinful reactions that were to be visited upon all those responsible for his mistreatment and torture, than he was for his own terrible (from the material perspective) situation. Haridāsa Ṭhākura knew that the Lord would be very angry at those responsible for the severe *Vaiṣṇava-aparādha* inflicted upon His sincere servant, so the Ṭhākura began to pray for the deliverance of his torturers and the Lord's forgiveness. Śrīla Bhaktisiddhānta Sarasvatī Ṭhākura comments: "Such characteristics are also seen in the lives of Jesus Christ and Prophet Mohammed."[36]

The guards continued to beat Haridāsa Ṭhākura attempting, with their best efforts, to kill him. However, not only were they unsuccessful in their endeavor, but Haridāsa was not even disturbed by their beating. Fear and astonishment entered the hearts of his tormentors. They began to wonder how any human being could survive such treatment.

"If we beat someone in two or three marketplaces, they die. But we've beaten him in twenty two marketplaces." They thought, "He has not died, and moreover we see that he is smiling! Is he a powerful saint [*pīr*]?"[37]

Śrīla Bhaktisiddhānta Sarasvatī Ṭhākura comments on the word *pīr* used by the guards. "The word *pīr* (a Farsi word) refers to a Mohammedan[38] saintly person who knows God or a widely respected great personality with extraordinary powers."[39]

Devotional Mysticism

The Muslim servants were very afraid and began to plead with Haridāsa Ṭhākura: "O Haridāsa, we'll be killed because of you! Although we've beaten you so much, you're still alive. Therefore, the *kazi* will kill us."[40]

Haridāsa simply smiled and replied with great compassion: "If my remaining alive creates a problem for you, then I will give up my body right now."[41] He then proceeded to enter a deep state of meditation on Kṛṣṇa.

Śrīla Bhaktisiddhānta Sarasvatī Ṭhākura explains: "Haridāsa entered into *samādhi* by meditating on the Supreme Lord within his heart, saturated with pure goodness, and thus enacted the pastime of dying. Due to being in deep *samādhi* on the Supreme Lord, his inhaling and exhaling could not be openly perceived."[42]

Haridāsa Ṭhākura was endowed with all mystic power. His life symptoms were suspended. He became completely motionless, and from all external signs appeared to be dead. The Muslim guards were astounded by this, but also grateful since it appeared that their lives would now be spared. They carried the apparently lifeless body of the Ṭhākura to the king. Immediately the king ordered that Haridāsa Ṭhākura be buried, since burial, and not cremation, is the custom in the Muslim community.

The *kazi*, however, disagreed: "Then he will achieve a higher destination. He was already born in a good Muslim family, but he engaged in degraded Hindu practices. Therefore, he does not deserve a higher destination. If we bury him, he will certainly attain a better destination in his next life. Better throw him in the Ganges, so that he'll suffer forever."[43]

It appears that the *kazi* was powerful, and the king felt bound to do whatever he advised in "religious matters." The guards grasped the body of Haridāsa Ṭhākura to throw it into the Ganges. However, as they were poised to do so, the body of the Ṭhākura became erect and immovable. Lord Viśvambhara, the Lord of the universe, had entered his body. Haridāsa Ṭhākura could not be moved. Professor Sanyal writes: "Mighty men pushed the body from every side. Lord Haridas remained immovable like a great tower."[44]

Haridāsa Ṭhākura did not know whether he was in the sky, on the land, or in the waters of the Ganges. He, like Prahlāda Mahārāja, was able to be perfectly fixed in remembrance of Lord Kṛṣṇa. Vṛndāvana dāsa Ṭhākura also cites another example of extreme tolerance: Hanumān in Lanka accepted immobilization by the *brahmāstra* weapon of Indrajit, along with very rough treatment by his captor Rākṣasas without complaint.

Śrīla Bhaktisiddhānta Sarasvatī Ṭhākura describes the tolerance exhibited by Haridāsa Ṭhākura: "Haridāsa also accepted the cruel, severe beating of the Muslims in order to set an example of the highest ideal of tolerance to the world."[45]

Vṛndāvana dāsa Ṭhākura writes: "What to speak of Haridāsa himself, even one who remembers his activities is immediately relieved of all material miseries. **Haridāsa, who had the power to control the universe [!], was certainly one of the topmost devotees of Sri Caitanya.**"[46]

Śrīla Bhaktisiddhānta Sarasvatī Ṭhākura comments on this rather extraordinary statement which refers to Haridāsa Ṭhākura as *jagat-īśvara*:

> "Another reading for *jagat-īśvara*, or 'the Lord of the universe,' is *pūrva-vipra-vara*, or 'the already qualified best *brāhmaṇa*.' Actually Ṭhākura Haridāsa was already the crest-jewel amongst the best of the *brāhmaṇas*. Although the materialists see that he was born in a Muslim family, he was the greatest Vaiṣṇava, servant of the Lord, most sober, and endowed with all brahminical qualifications from time immemorial. Only those who constantly serve the Supreme Lord are decorated with the eternal brahminical qualifications from time immemorial. Some people compose imitation literatures in which they claim that Haridāsa Ṭhākura was born in a seminal *brāhmaṇa* family, and thereby they attribute to him insignificant mundane social considerations born from their own ignorance. Such imaginary truth is always contrary to historical facts.
>
> "The phrase *jagat-īśvara* may also be an adjective for Caitanyacandra, or it may have been used to indicate the former position of Haridāsa as Lord Brahmā. Any *mahā-bhāgavata* who controls the six urges mentioned by Śrīla Rūpa Gosvāmī is qualified to be called Gosvāmī, Jagat-īśvara, or Vaiṣṇava."[47]

Rāghava Caitanya Prabhu comments on the lessons to be learned by Haridāsa Ṭhākura's extreme fortitude in preaching the holy name: "The firm faith and the constant chanting of the Holy Name in the face of all risks, sacrifices, and hardships are the important teachings that Haridas Thakur, out of his overflowing kindness, leaves to the world."[48]

Raised From the Dead: Repentance of King and Citizens

The Muslims exhausted themselves in the effort to move the body of Haridāsa Ṭhākura, but finally, by the Lord's supreme will, He allowed the body of Haridāsa Ṭhākura to be thrown into the sacred Ganges. Haridāsa Ṭhākura floated on the pure waters of the Ganges for some time, regained his external awareness by the will of the Lord, and came to the shore. He rose from the waters in great transcendental ecstasy and headed for Phuliyā while loudly chanting the holy names of Kṛṣṇa.

The Muslims who witnessed this were transformed and purified, and then gave up their envy and offered obeisances to the transcendental hero. They considered him to be a *pīr*, a powerful saint, and they were all delivered from material bondage. After some time, Haridāsa, smiling and laughing, met the Nawab, the King of Bengal, who stood before Haridāsa with folded hands, saying:

"Now I know for certain that you are a powerful saint (*mahā-pīr*), for you are firmly convinced that the Supreme Lord is one. All the so-called *yogis* and *jñānis* simply speak big words, but you have actually attained perfection. O sir, I have personally come to meet you, therefore, please, forgive all my offenses. You are equal to everyone—both friend and enemy—but there is no one in the three worlds who can understand you. You are free to go wherever you wish. You may stay in a cave on the bank of the Ganges or wherever you desire. Now you may stay wherever you like and do whatever you please."[49]

Although the king showed sincere repentance for his sinful behavior and was forgiven by Haridāsa Ṭhākura, his attempt to give a benediction indicates that he still imagined he had the power to offer Haridāsa Ṭhākura freedom. In fact, Haridāsa Ṭhākura was always free to stay where he liked and do as he liked. He accepted being captured and tortured as a means to deliver many sinful persons and set the most sterling example of forbearance and tolerance. Just as Christ allowed himself to be crucified and Hanumān allowed himself to be captured, Haridāsa Ṭhākura also underwent torture and apparent degradation in order to teach Śrī Caitanya Mahāprabhu's principle of *taror api sahiṣṇu,* of being more tolerant than a tree. Any of the above great souls could have utilized their mystic perfections to escape humiliation and torture, but they accepted such difficulty for the service of the Lord.

This is the qualification of a great preacher. Śrīla Bhaktisiddhānta Sarasvatī Ṭhākura exhibited tolerance when his *saṅkīrtana* party was stoned, and when his life was repeatedly threatened. Śrīla Prabhupāda exhibited tolerance when he was gored by a bull while trying to preach, when he fainted in the hot sun of Delhi while trying to distribute his *Back To Godhead* magazines, when he crossed the ocean on the Jaladuta suffering agonizing heart attacks, when he lived in the Bowery in a poverty-stricken condition, walking the frozen streets of New York City, and by tolerating the antics of his early followers. Preachers have to tolerate. Otherwise, without tolerance, it is not possible to preach. Because the king apologized with all the sincerity and humility at his command, and further rectified himself by granting Haridāsa Ṭhākura complete freedom to pursue his devotional activities wherever he liked in his kingdom, Haridāsa Ṭhākura whole-heartedly excused him and prayed for his deliverance. The Lord clearly agreed as the king was not destroyed for his offense. Therefore, both *kṣamā* (forgiveness) and *anugraha* (favor) were granted to the king by Haridāsa Ṭhākura.

After glancing mercifully upon the humbled Muslims, Haridāsa entered Phuliyā loudly chanting, and was greeted by an assembly of *brāhmaṇas*. When they saw him, they were filled with happiness, and they began to chant the holy name, as Haridasa danced in ecstasy. Haridāsa arrived in this way to benefit the *brāhmaṇa* community. Śrīla Bhaktisiddhānta Sarasvatī Ṭhākura explains:

> "Due to narrow-minded sectarianism and social aversion towards devotional service, some so-called *brāhmaṇas* did not previously consider it proper to accept Haridāsa as the spiritual master for awarding the holy names. But now after hearing about his extraordinary and unlimited prowess, all the prestigious *brāhmaṇas* accepted him as the giver of the holy names, which are non-different from the Lord Himself. All of them happily began to respect Haridāsa."[50]

Vṛndāvana dāsa Ṭhākura writes: "Haridāsa displayed endless ecstatic transformations like crying, shivering, laughing, falling unconscious, hairs standing on end, and roaring. Then in ecstatic love, Haridāsa crashed to the ground. Seeing this, the *brāhmaṇas* began to float in ecstasy. After a while, when Haridāsa became pacified, the *brāhmaṇas* sat around him."[51]

Valuable Lessons

"Haridāsa then said, 'O *brāhmaṇas*, please listen. Don't feel sorry for me. I've heard so much blasphemy of the Lord. That is why He has punished me. I'm satisfied, for whatever happened to me was for my benefit. The Lord has relieved me of my great offense by awarding me a token punishment. One who hears blasphemy of Lord Viṣṇu is sent to the hell known as Kumbhīpāka, and with my sinful ears I heard so much blasphemy of the Lord. Therefore, the Lord has given me an appropriate punishment so that I may not commit such sins in the future.'"[52]

In the commentary to the above verses Śrīla Bhaktisiddhānta Sarasvatī Ṭhākura gives an extensive analysis of these awe-inspiringly humble statements of Haridāsa Ṭhākura. He explains that Haridāsa Ṭhākura is presenting himself as an ordinary conditioned soul forced to suffer the results of sinful activity. By hearing blasphemy and not adequately protesting such harsh and offensive statements, he considers that he deserved much greater punishment, yet he received only a token of what he actually deserved.

Śrīla Bhaktisiddhānta Sarasvatī Ṭhākura explains that Haridāsa Ṭhākura was explaining his beating in this way to set an example for the *prākṛta-sahajiyās* (sentimental pseudo-Vaisnavas who take things very cheaply). Such persons attempt to imitate the sentiments of a *māha-bhāgavata*, while remaining on the fruitive platform. Thus, by Haridāsa Ṭhākura's behavior, he is informing them that by such imitation they will have to suffer the fruits of their activities since that mundane plane *is* their field of activities. However, in the case of Haridāsa:

"...the crest jewel among liberated souls and a chanter of the holy names of Hari, is certainly not forced to enjoy the fruits of his activities. Śrīla Rūpa Gosvāmīpāda has described this topic in his *Śrī Nāmāṣṭaka* (4) as follows: 'The seeds of sinful activities that cause rebirth for their fruition are not totally destroyed despite realization of oneness with Brahman through constant meditation. But, O Lord, as soon as Your holy names manifest on the tongue (even in the form of *nāmābhāsa*) all seeds of sinful activities are totally uprooted. This is elaborately glorified in the Vedas.'"[53]

Śrīla Bhaktisiddhānta Sarasvatī Ṭhākura, desiring to even more clearly explain the offense of the *prākṛta-sahajiyās* imitating the tolerance of Haridāsa Ṭhākura, speaks very sharply to such imitative devotees:

"Those who, even after hearing the blasphemy of Viṣṇu and the Vaiṣṇavas, display their 'cleverness' by posing as advanced and liberal on the pretext of artificial gentleness or tolerance without understanding the real purport of *taror api sahiṣṇu*[54]—'more tolerant than a tree' are understood to be enjoying the results of their grave offenses. One should not consider such grave offenses as trivial and advertise sense gratification aimed at accumulating mundane fame as worship of Hari. For this reason, in order to instruct the people of the world, *jagad-guru* Ṭhākura Haridāsa pointed out the great faults of the foolish *prākṛta-sahajiyās*, who display artificial humility..."[55]

Haridāsa Ṭhākura concludes his humble statements to the *brāhmaṇas* by stating that his punishment was appropriate and was designed so that he would not commit such sins in the future. Śrīla Bhaktisiddhānta Sarasvatī Ṭhākura, desiring to smash any lingering doubts about the position of those who take devotional principles cheaply, states:

"With the imitative *prākṛta-sahajiyās sampradāyas* in mind, Haridāsa spoke the following words of instruction: 'As a Vaiṣṇava, I will never again hear blasphemy against Viṣṇu and the Vaiṣṇavas under the shelter of *tṛṇād api sunīcena* or on the pretext of *taror api sahiṣṇuna*. I have had a sufficient lesson this time. The Lord is most merciful; He taught me by awarding a token punishment for a grave offense.' Due to misfortune, the *prākṛta-sahajiyā sampradāyas*, who are offenders of the holy names, cannot understand the actual purport and substance of these statements of Ṭhākura Haridāsa."[56]

The *brāhmaṇas* and Haridāsa Ṭhākura then happily chanted the holy names. The Yavanas who had beaten Haridāsa and their families were all destroyed by cholera or smallpox within a few days. Again, we see that those who do not sincerely repent for their *Vaiṣṇava-aparādha* by approaching and begging the offended devotee for forgiveness are not forgiven by the Lord. The king, though an offender, approached Haridāsa and asked for forgiveness and was excused, but those who beat Haridāsa, what to speak of the *kazi*, were utterly ruined. In the *Skanda Purāṇa* it is stated: "Whoever kills or blasphemes a Vaiṣṇava, whoever is envious of or angry with a Vaiṣṇava, and whoever does not offer obeisances or feel joy upon seeing a Vaiṣṇava certainly falls into a hellish condition."

Śrīla Bhaktisiddhānta Sarasvatī Ṭhākura calls the above verse "...an infallible scriptural decree."[57]

Endnotes

[1] *Śrī Caitanya-bhāgavata Ādi* 16.22—35, Vrajraj Press, 1999, by Vṛndāvana dāsa Ṭhākura, commentary by Śrīla Bhaktisiddhānta Sarasvatī Ṭhākura, translation by Bhumipati dāsa, edited by Puṇḍarika Vidyānidhi dāsa.

[2] *CB Ādi* 16.22 purport.

[3] *CB Ādi* 16.29 purport.

[4] One of the *kazi's* duties was to adjudicate based on the *Koran* and *Hadith*, which are the bases for *Shariya*, Islamic law. According to *Shariya*, an apostate, or one who converts from Islam to another religion, should be punished by death. Knowing this fact, devotees of Kṛṣṇa are not discouraged from preaching to Muslims, but they are careful not to

introduce sectarian attitudes. The *kaniṣṭha-adhikārī's* approach to preaching is characterized by religious competition (my religion is superior to yours), along with other aspects that are sometimes influenced by the bodily concept of life. Successful preaching requires expert judgment in regards to time, place, and circumstance. For example, when preaching that we are spirit soul, we can appeal to everyone, including non-Hindus. When preaching that we are part of the Hindu religion, we will appeal primarily to those of that religion. In Śrīla Prabhupāda's conversation with the Muslim Ali, cited later in this chapter, he quotes *nāmnām-akāri bahudhā* from *Śikṣāṣṭakam*. That is significant, because even the Gauḍīya translators, in the spirit of the Caitanya tradition, generally translate that verse by saying "names like, Krishna, Govinda." Śrīla Prabhupāda takes it a step further, in the spirit of Śrīla Bhaktivinoda Ṭhākura and Śrīla Bhaktisiddhānta Sarasvatī Ṭhākura, to represent that verse in a completely nonsectarian, universal way by saying that any authorized name of God from any religious culture or tradition may be chanted.

[5] *CB Ādi* 16.47.

[6] *CB Ādi* 16.50.

[7] Nisikanta Sanyal, *Sree Krishna Chaitanya*, p. 605.

[8] *CB Ādi* 16.53 purport.

[9] *CB Ādi* 16.53—67.

[10] *CB Ādi* 16.55 purport.

[11] *CB Ādi* 16.70—74.

[12] The spelling of the word *Kalmā* has been changed here to *Kalām*. Arabic or Persian words when translated from Bengali to English often suffer in the process. The above convention is found in a Persian dictionary.

[13] *CB Ādi* 16.74 purport.

[14] *CB Ādi* 16.75.

[15] *CB Ādi* 16.75—85.

[16] *CB Ādi* 16.76—77 purport.

[17] *The Bhagavat: Its Philosophy, Its Ethics & Its Theology (A Lecture Delivered in Dinajpore in 1869)*, by Śrīla Bhaktivinoda Ṭhākura, published by Gaudiya Mission, pp. 8, 9.

[18] Evening darshan with Śrīla Prabhupāda, Tehran, Iran, August 9, 1976.

[19] *CB Ādi* 16.88, 89.

[20] *CB Ādi* 16.89 purport.

[21] Nisikanta Sanyal, *Sree Krishna Chaitanya*, p. 618.

[22] *CB Ādi* 16.90, 91.

[23] *CB Ādi* 16.94.

[24] Rāghava Caitanya dāsa, *The Divine Name*, pp. 145, 146.
[25] Note that Śrīla Bhaktisiddhānta Sarasvatī Ṭhākura does not even mention Islam in this long paragraph. Pure devotees are not concerned with a particular ideology or religion. However, they are concerned with (or critical of) "manmade social behavior," which is not only found in Islam, but also in the broad domains of Hinduism, Buddhism, Christianity, Jeffersonian democracy, etc.
[26] *CB Ādi* 16.94 purport.
[27] *CB Ādi* 16.95.
[28] *CB Ādi* 16.96, 97.
[29] *CB Ādi* 16.98, 99.
[30] *CB Ādi* 16.103 purport.
[31] Sometimes neophyte Kṛṣṇa devotees feel hostility toward Muslims due to being contaminated by the tensions between modern Hindus and Muslims, or inflamed by the behavior of fanatical elements of the Islamic community. However, devotees are not fond of any materialist, materialistic attitudes, or materialistic culture. Śrīla Prabhupāda often had equal or greater disdain for British culture than he had for Islamic culture.
April 6, 1975, Mayapur Morning Walk: [Regarding slaughterhouses in India:] "...it is British contribution, the *mlecchas*. Before the British period, even in Mohammedan period, there was no slaughterhouse, neither the public used to take cow's flesh."
November 29, 1975, Delhi, Morning Walk: "When India was actually standing on its old culture, they were never defeated. Even the Mohammedans, they ruled over India for eight hundred years, but they could not defeat the Indian culture. But the British government is clever. They spoiled the Indian culture."
[32] *CB Ādi* 16.108, 109.
[33] *CB Ādi* 16.109 purport.
[34] *CB Ādi* 16.141.
[35] *CB Ādi* 16.113.
[36] *CB Ādi* 16.112 purport.
[37] *CB Ādi* 16.117, 118.
[38] The term "Mohammedan" is currently considered pejorative, being commonly used in the 19th and early 20th century by British Christians. "Moslem" or "Muslim" are considered the proper terms now. However, when Śrīla Bhaktisiddhānta Sarasvatī Ṭhākura and Śrīla Prabhupāda use the former term, they were simply following the English convention of their times.
[39] *CB Ādi* 16.118 purport.

[40] *CB Ādi* 16.119, 120.
[41] *CB Ādi* 16.121.
[42] *CB Ādi* 16.121, 122 purport.
[43] *CB Ādi* 16.125—127.
[44] Nisikanta Sanyal, *Sree Krishna Chaitanya*, p. 624.
[45] *CB Ādi* 16.138 purport.
[46] *CB Ādi* 16.142.
[47] *CB Ādi* 16.142 purport.
[48] Rāghava Caitanya dāsa, *The Divine Name*, p.152.
[49] *CB Ādi* 16.150—155.
[50] *CB Ādi* 16.159—161 purport.
[51] *CB Ādi* 16.162—164.
[52] *CB Ādi* 16.165—169.
[53] *CB Ādi* 16.166 purport.
[54] Śrīla Bhaktisiddhānta Sarasvatī Ṭhākura has introduced an interesting balance in this purport, and it may be taken as a caution to modern devotees not to display artificial humility or tolerance toward materialistic society. Śrīla Sarasvatī Ṭhākura's statements might also be taken as a caution in regards to devotees espousing the sentiments of elevated Vaiṣṇavas amongst themselves, simply to create a display of politically correct "humble" or "advanced" attitudes as a social convention or nicety. This is imitation and borders on the artifice exhibited by the *sahajiyās*. Śrīla Prabhupāda once responded to a devotee who claimed to be the "most fallen" that he (the devotee) was not the "most anything." Śrīla Prabhupāda was much more focused on what people did than what they said. Example is better than precept. He was practical. Talk is cheap. The cultivation of humility is not simply a matter of attitude or mental adjustment—it is the rendering of practical service to the Vaiṣṇavas, *guru*, and Kṛṣṇa, being conscious all the while of one's own defects and shortcomings, but striving always to improve.
[55] *CB Ādi* 16.167 purport.
[56] *CB Ādi* 16.169 purport.
[57] *CB Ādi* 16.171 purport.

trayo vedāḥ ṣaḍ-aṅgāni
chandāṁsi vividhāḥ surāḥ
sarvam aṣṭākṣarāntaḥsthaṁ
yac cānyad api vāṅ-mayam
sarva-vedānta-sārārthaḥ
saṁsārārṇava-tāraṇaḥ

THE ESSENCE OF ALL VEDIC KNOWLEDGE comprehending the three kinds of Vedic activity [*karma-kāṇḍa, jñāna-kāṇḍa and upāsanā-kāṇḍa*], the *chandaḥ* or Vedic hymns, and the processes for satisfying the demigods—is included in the eight syllables Hare Kṛṣṇa, Hare Kṛṣṇa. This is the reality of all *Vedānta*. The chanting of the holy name is the only means to cross the ocean of nescience."

Nārada-pañcarātra
[cited: *Śrī Caitanya-caritāmṛta Ādi-līlā* 7.76]

THE *PURĀṆAS* SAY THAT A PERSON WHO chants the Lord's name loudly is a hundred times more pious than the person who chants to himself. O *brāhmaṇa*, listen carefully to the reason behind this. One who softly chants the holy name liberates only himself. One who loudly chants the names of Govinda, however, liberates himself along with all living entities who hear him. Although all living entities have a tongue, only the human beings are able to chant the names of Kṛṣṇa. Tell me what is wrong with that activity by which living entities who have taken useless births will be delivered? One person may maintain himself, while another may maintain a thousand people. Of the two, consider carefully who is better. This is the superior characteristic of loud chanting."

Śrīla Haridāsa Ṭhākura,
Śrī Caitanya-bhāgavata Ādi-khaṇḍa 16.284–290

CHAPTER FIVE

Solitary Worship of the Lord

The Dangers

HARIDĀSA ṬHĀKURA AGAIN TOOK UP RESIDENCE in Phuliyā in the cave-like dwelling on the bank of the Ganges, and was always absorbed in the name and pastimes of the Lord. Śrīla Bhaktisiddhānta Sarasvatī Ṭhākura comments at some length on the *bhajana* of Haridāsa Ṭhākura, and explains that he never chanted silently only for his own benefit, but always loudly so that whoever overheard him was also benefited.

Śrīla Bhaktisiddhānta Sarasvatī Ṭhākura explains the dangers of both silent, solitary chanting and becoming a *guru* without following the perfect example of Haridāsa Ṭhākura:

"On the platform of *madhyama-adhikāra*, one may have to associate with worldly people while preaching the holy names in the course of *jīve-dāya*, showing compassion to the living entities, but since he preaches the holy names with utmost attention, he does not become affected by the sinful reactions of the audience, rather he distributes mercy by removing the contamination of their sinful reactions. If, while chanting the holy names of the Lord with his many disciples, a *madhyama-adhikārī* becomes more or less affected by the reactions of their *karma*, then his falldown is assured. According to the statement, *jīvan-muktā api punar yānti saṁsāra-vāsanām*—'A person considered liberated in this life can again fall down and desire the material atmosphere for material enjoyment,' even a *madhyama-adhikārī* chanter of the holy names can again fall into material existence. That is why mundane pride in the form of worldly association[1] and accepting many disciples simply produces *ku-phala*, or evil results.

"While describing the topics of Haridāsa Ṭhākura's devotional service, the injunction for loudly chanting and attentively hearing the holy names has been prescribed for practitioners who desire their own welfare in order to deliver from great inauspiciousness those who mistakenly consider satisfying their own senses as satisfying Hari while remaining busy in activities of sense gratification such as accepting many disciples like the immature yogis...

"Ṭhākura Mahāśaya, who is *jagad-guru*, Vaisnava *ācārya*, and best of the liberated souls, has taught people in general the process of remembering the pastimes of Kṛṣṇa in the course of realizing that Kṛṣṇa is nondifferent from His names, forms, qualities, associates, paraphernalia, and pastimes. Those who give up hearing and loud chanting of the holy names received from the mouths of devotees free from *nāma-aparādha* and in order to gratify their senses display artificial imitation of remembering the pastimes of the Lord in their impure, enjoyment prone hearts—their attempts to imitate remembrance of the Lord's pastimes in this way is simply thirst for material enjoyment born from aversion to the Lord."[2]

Śrīla Bhaktisiddhānta Sarasvatī Ṭhākura has enumerated some of the pitfalls for *gurus* who do not strictly follow in the footsteps of the Nāmācārya in the above excerpts. There are great dangers faced by preachers who accept disciples at an immature stage of spiritual development, unless such preachers follow the example of Haridāsa Ṭhākura by loudly and attentively chanting and hearing the glories of the Lord. Otherwise, it is very easy to become carried away by the attentions of neophyte disciples or to be overwhelmed by disciples' karmic reactions. These difficulties have also been discussed in Śrīla Prabhupāda's purports to *Śrī Caitanya-caritāmṛta*, in *Perfect Questions, Perfect Answers*, as well as *Śrī Upadeśāmṛta* (*Nectar of Instruction*). All preachers, what to speak of those with the specific service of being *dīkṣā-gurus*, should follow the example of the Ṭhākura and loudly chant and attentively hear the Lord's glories to ensure their rapid progress in Kṛṣṇa consciousness and to prevent their losing their way on the path of progressive enlightenment in Kṛṣṇa consciousness. The preaching of Kṛṣṇa consciousness cannot be avoided on the plea of the dangers of worldly association, but rather preachers must become absorbed in hearing and chanting the holy name, form, qualities, etc. of the Lord—that will save them in all circumstances without a doubt.

Vṛndāvana dāsa Ṭhākura states:

> "He would chant the holy name of the Lord three hundred thousand times a day, and his cave was thus transformed into Vaikuṇṭha."[3]

Śrīla Bhaktisiddhānta Sarasvatī Ṭhākura comments on the transformation of a devotee's dwelling into the spiritual world:

"...according to the purport of the following statement of a *mahājana: ye dina gṛhe bhajana dekhi, gṛhete goloka bhāya*—'One day while performing devotional practices, I saw my house transformed into Goloka Vṛndāvana.'"[4]

The *mahājana* referred to by Śrīla Bhaktisiddhānta Sarasvatī Ṭhākura is none other than his father and *guru*, the Seventh Gosvāmī, Śrīla Bhaktivinoda Ṭhākura!

Serpent in the Cave

A poisonous smell began to manifest in the cave of Haridāsa Ṭhākura, and the offensive odor created such a noxious atmosphere that no one seeking his association could tolerate it for more than a few moments. All of his visitors, finding the acrid smell and toxic fumes overwhelming, met together and tried to understand why the atmosphere appeared so polluted. Some learned physicians in the village (who were also experts in the treatment of snakebite) were able to ascertain the cause: a large serpent was dwelling in the cave-like dwelling with the saintly Vaiṣṇava!

Śrīla Bhaktisiddhānta Sarasvatī Ṭhākura comments: "Considering that it is never proper to live with a cruel, deceitful, fierce, poisonous snake, the visitors requested Haridāsa to shift to another place."[5]

Haridāsa Ṭhākura was surprised by their request, since he had not noticed any burning sensation, but replied:

"...since you are all suffering and unable to tolerate the burning of the poison, I will leave tomorrow for another place. If there is a snake in this cave and it doesn't leave by tomorrow, then I'll leave and go to some other place. Don't worry. Let us all chant Kṛṣṇa's names."[6]

As the *brāhmaṇas* chanted with the Ṭhākura, to their surprise, the large snake immediately left the cave. Vṛndāvana dāsa Ṭhākura writes:

> "The large wonderful snake looked most fearful, yet it was also very beautiful, being colored yellow, blue, and white. As the *brāhmaṇas* saw the brilliant jewel adorning its head, they fearfully remembered Kṛṣṇa. After that snake left that place, the *brāhmaṇas* were overjoyed to find that the burning sensation was gone. They all appreciated Haridāsa's marvelous potency and developed great devotion for him."[7]

Śrīla Bhaktisiddhānta Sarasvatī Ṭhākura explains that this incident had the effect of convincing "...many atheistic nondevotee *brāhmaṇas*, who were attached to yogic perfections..."[8] that Haridasa Ṭhākura was as exalted as others had claimed. They all developed special respect for Haridāsa on the strength of this incident. Previously they had considered that Haridāsa's birth in a Muslim family indicated a sinful background; however, seeing that the mere wish of the Ṭhākura was sufficient to cause a dangerous serpent to quit the cave out of respect, they considered that his mystic opulence was extraordinary, and thus they considered him the best of the *brāhmaṇas*.

The fact that the *brāhmaṇas* only considered Haridāsa Ṭhākura great upon his display of mysticism in the form of a materially inexplicable event shows clearly that such *brāhmaṇas* were *dvijabandhus* (unqualified descendants of *brāhmaṇas*). Such displays of mystic power are very impressive to those who require a mundane demonstration of extraordinary power to be relieved of doubt and cynicism. For the pious souls, the transforming example and behavior of the Ṭhākura convinced them of his divinity and melted their hearts. However, we see that in the life histories of great devotees they sometimes feel compelled to exhibit such mysticism for the benefit of cynics, atheists, and neophyte followers. There are many such examples of miraculous displays in the lives of Śrī Caitanya Mahāprabhu, Lord Jesus Christ, Śrī Madhvācārya, Śrī Rāmānujācārya, Lord Buddha, and other great saints. According to His followers, when Lord Buddha was asked about miracles and mystic power He identified three kinds of miraculous powers:

1. The power to appear as many persons, to pass through walls, to fly through the air, walk on water. These are physical actions that ordinary people cannot perform.
2. The power to read other people's minds.
3. The power to be able to guide people according to their mental development, for their own good, using suitable methods appropriate for each person.

He taught that a monk who displays the first two superhuman powers for his own sake in order to impress people, is no different than a shaman or a magician. Lord Buddha said that a monk who practices such worldly miracles (unless it is solely to convince them to take up the path of enlightenment) is a source of shame, humiliation, and disgust. This is because such actions may impress and win converts and followers, but they do not help them put an end to their suffering.

The third kind of superhuman power, which Lord Buddha calls "the miracle of instruction," helps people to get rid of suffering. This, in Lord Buddha's opinion, is the only power that is fit to be practiced and which He encouraged and practiced.[9]

In a similar vein, Śrīla Prabhupāda, when asked about his mystic powers, pointed to his disciples and remarked that they were the evidence of his mystic power: the hearts of those who had been addicted to meat-eating, illicit sex, many forms of intoxication, and gambling had been transformed, and they had become saintly persons Although pure Vaiṣṇavas and elevated saintly persons have all mystic perfections at their command by the grace of Yogeśvara, they do not generally bother with developing or exhibiting such powers, except in the rare instance that such displays will create faith in the hearts of doubting persons and inspire them to take up the path of devotional service.[10]

Vṛndāvana dāsa Ṭhākura explains that it is ***not*** so glorious that the snake left due to Haridasa Ṭhākura's request. Vṛndāvana dāsa Ṭhākura explains what ***is*** glorious:

> "Simply by his [Haridasa Thakura's] glance, one's bondage born of nescience is destroyed. Even Lord Kṛṣṇa does not transgress the words of Haridāsa."[11]

Śrīla Bhaktisiddhānta Sarasvatī Ṭhākura explains that:

> "Only one who is blessed by Haridāsa Ṭhākura is able to constantly chant the names of Hari and take shelter of the pure holy names without committing offenses, and thus his contamination of ignorance, which is the root of material enjoyment, is totally uprooted. As a result of serving Haridāsa Ṭhākura and receiving his mercy, the Supreme Lord becomes obliged."[12]

Let us all pray for the service and blessings of Nāmācārya Śrīla Haridāsa Ṭhākura! May he enable us to come to the platform of constant offenseless chanting of the holy name!

* * *

The Snake Charmer & The King of the Snakes

In another incident which involved the king of snakes and a snake charmer, the amazing qualities of Haridāsa Ṭhākura were again exhibited. While a snake charmer was practicing his art, Haridāsa Ṭhākura came to watch, and while the charmer chanted various *mantras*, Vāsuki (*nāga-rāja*)[13] appeared in the snake charmer's body and caused him to dance. As he danced, the Lord of Serpents began to sing about Kṛṣṇa's dancing on the hoods of Kālīya at Kālīya-daha Lake in the Yamunā. Vāsuki, through the body of the snake charmer, began to imitate that dancing of Kṛṣṇa.

As Haridāsa heard the wonderful pastimes of Kāliya-Kṛṣṇa, he became overwhelmed with ecstasy, falling unconscious to the ground, and his breathing stopped. He then regained consciousness, leapt to his feet, roaring loudly, and began to dance in great ecstasy.

Seeing the wonderful symptoms of ecstasy erupting on the body of Haridāsa, Ananta (Vāsuki), manifesting Himself in the body of the snake charmer, stood respectfully to one side and watched. Remembering the extraordinary mercy of the Lord to an envious being (Kālīya) who attempted to kill the inhabitants of Vṛndāvana and Kṛṣṇa Himself, Haridāsa Ṭhākura was absorbed in love of Kṛṣṇa, and all those who witnessed the scene began to chant the glories of the Lord.

After the Ṭhākura returned to external consciousness, the snake charmer again began to dance. Everyone eagerly began to take the dust from Haridāsa Ṭhākura's feet and smear it on their bodies.

An envious *brāhmaṇa,* who had observed the behavior of the Ṭhākura, thought that Haridāsa Ṭhākura was merely an illiterate and foolish person, who gained the respect of other ignorant persons by an artificial display of ecstasy. This is a clear example of *ātmavan manyate jagat*—one thinks that others think as he thinks. Thinking to take advantage of the situation, in a display of imitative behavior, the pseudo-*brāhmaṇa* crashed to the ground and became motionless.

Immediately the snake charmer, who was still possessed by Lord Anantadeva, began severely beating the *brāhmaṇa* very violently with a stick[14]. The anguished imitator ran away screaming. Then the snake charmer resumed his own dance. Later some members of the crowd cautiously approached the snake charmer and questioned him as to why he had so severely thrashed the apparently ecstatic *brāhmaṇa.*

In a scathing and humorous attack on the behavior of the envious *brāhmaṇa,* Śrīla Bhaktisiddhānta Sarasvatī Ṭhākura summarizes and voices the *brāhmaṇa's* foolish mentality:

> "Due to their blind faith, whenever ordinary foolish people see or hear any dancing or singing in a petty religious function, they offer abundant respect. Therefore, since people offered such respect to Haridasa Ṭhākura, who is an ordinary human being born in a non-Hindu family, while I am born in the topmost *varṇa* in Hindu society; if I can imitate the characteristics and eight ecstatic transformations of a Vaiṣṇava Ṭhākura's love, like an actor on a stage, then no one can estimate how much profit, adoration and distinction I will achieve. When people respect an ordinary human being and non-seminal *brāhmaṇa* like Haridasa Ṭhākura[15] so much just by seeing his display of petty ordinary emotions, then if I, the son of a seminal *brāhmaṇa*, can simply mimic his transcendental emotions, I can't imagine how much profit, adoration and distinction I will receive. If I exhibit artificial emotions, then my insignificant material fame will certainly surpass the fame of the transcendental Vaiṣṇava."[16]

The snake charmer (still possessed by Ananta) explained the artificial and offensive display of the pseudo-*brāhmaṇa*, contrasting it with the true ecstasy and greatness of Haridāsa. "Out of audacity, he tried to imitate Haridāsa, and therefore I punished him accordingly."[17]

Śrīla Bhaktisiddhānta Sarasvatī Ṭhākura then poetically paraphrases the words of the snake charmer/Ananta and comments further on this incident:

> "Haridasa Ṭhākura is a nonduplicitous, transcendental, spontaneous, pure devotee of the Lord, while this pseudo *brāhmaṇa* is an abominable *prākṛta-sahajiyā*. Artificial imitation born of false rivalry with non-duplicitous pure devotees is the fraudulent drama of hypocritical *sahajiyās*. Since this *prākṛta-sahajiyā* tried to artificially imitate the activities of a *mahā-bhāgavata* Vaiṣṇava Ṭhākura out of envy and hate, and with a desire to cheaply acquire mundane fame from the foolish persons ignorant of the truth, I have sufficiently punished him."[18]

Vāsuki in the form of a snake charmer further explained:

> "Actually that arrogant and deceitful *brāhmaṇa* has no love for Kṛṣṇa. To achieve the devotional service of Lord Kṛṣṇa one has to be free from duplicity. One who sees Haridāsa dancing is freed from all bondage. When Haridāsa dances, Lord Kṛṣṇa personally dances. Thus the whole universe can be purified by seeing his dance. His name 'Haridāsa' is appropriate, for Lord Kṛṣṇa constantly dwells in his heart. He is affectionate to all living entities, and he is always engaged in their welfare. He accompanies the Lord whenever He incarnates. He is never offensive to Viṣṇu or the Vaiṣṇavas, and even in a dream he does not deviate from the proper path. One who associates with Haridāsa for even a fraction of a moment will certainly attain shelter at the lotus feet of Kṛṣṇa. Lord Brahmā and Lord Śiva always desire to associate with a devotee like Haridāsa. On the order of the Lord, Haridāsa was born in a low-class family to show that birth in a high caste or good family is useless. If a devotee of the Lord is born in a

low-class family, he is still worthy of worship. This is the verdict of the scriptures. And if someone is born in a high-class family but does not worship the lotus feet of Śrī Kṛṣṇa, then his high birth is useless and he falls to hell. Haridāsa thus took birth in a low-class family to prove the words of the scriptures. Haridāsa was born in a low-class family just as Prahlāda was born in a demoniac family and Hanumān was born in a monkey family. The demigods desire the touch of Haridāsa, and even mother Gaṅgā desires that Haridāsa immerse in her waters. What to speak of his touch, just by seeing Haridāsa one is released from the bondage of fruitive activities. Indeed, even if one sees a person who has taken shelter of Haridāsa, he is freed from material bondage. If I glorify Haridāsa for a hundred years with a hundred mouths I would still not reach the end of his glories. You are all fortunate, for because of you I received an opportunity to glorify Haridāsa. I assure you that one who simply chants the name of Haridāsa without offense will certainly attain the abode of Kṛṣṇa."[19]

After glorifying Haridāsa Ṭhākura in this way, the Vaiṣṇava king of the snakes[20] became silent, and those who were pious were fully satisfied.

Opposition of the Faithless

Despite Haridāsa's repeated exhibitions of pure devotion, there were many atheistic and faithless persons who were opposed to his practice of loudly chanting the name of Kṛṣṇa. In the present era some persons strongly object to the public chanting of the holy name. Despite being bombarded by all kinds of obnoxious sounds from radios, televisions, and other sound-amplifying equipment, replete with foul language and false messages promising sense happiness, they cannot tolerate the congregational chanting of the holy names. Nevertheless, the devotees of the Lord, like the associates of Śrī Caitanya Mahāprabhu, take all opportunities and use all means to chant in spite of such objections.

The conventional wisdom of those objecting in Haridāsa Ṭhākura's era was that chanting should be done silently, especially during the four months of Cāturmāsya, the period in which the Lord enters a state of transcendental slumber called *yoga-nidrā*. The idea was that loud chanting would disturb the Lord's slumber, and the offense of disturbing Him with loud chanting might bring famine and other adverse reactions upon them.

Such an idea was clearly a pretext for demanding that the devotees not chant at all, for logically the same persons proposing the ban on loud chanting were habitually inviting actual inauspiciousness by vibrating volumes of rubbish sounds in the manner of croaking frogs and barking dogs.

Vṛndāvana dāsa Ṭhākura writes: "People throughout the world were devoid of devotional service to Lord Viṣṇu. They had no understanding of the meaning or goal of *kīrtana*."[21]

Śrīla Bhaktisiddhānta Sarasvatī Ṭhākura comments:

> "At that time people who were bewildered by *māyā* were fully engaged in gratifying their senses, and therefore they became devoid of devotion to Viṣṇu. No one could understand why Haridāsa Ṭhākura was performing *hari-nāma-saṅkīrtana* and what his motive was, because at that time Śrī Gaurasundara had not yet begun propagating love and devotion to Lord Kṛṣṇa."[22]

The situation prior to the advent of Śrī Caitanya Mahāprabhu was terrible—there were many atheistic and godless persons who opposed the Vaiṣṇavas who regularly met and chanted in Navadvīpa within the privacy of their homes. Such envious rascals became agitated even by this restrained and humble practice. Vṛndāvana dāsa Ṭhākura enumerates some of their more stupid remarks:

"If the Lord's sleep is disturbed, He'll become angry and create a famine in this country. There's no doubt about it.
"Someone said, 'If the price of rice increases, then I'll catch them and give them a punch.'
"Someone else said, 'On Ekādaśī, these devotees stay up all night and chant the name of Govinda. What is the need for chanting the Lord's name every day?' In this way, the atheists condemned the devotees in various ways.
"The devotees all felt aggrieved on hearing these things, yet none of them gave up chanting the names of Lord Hari. Haridāsa was particularly aggrieved to see the people's lack of interest in the process of devotional service. In spite of this, Haridāsa continued to loudly chant the holy names of the Lord. The most sinful miscreants were even unable to hear this loud chanting."[23]

Vṛndāvana dāsa Ṭhākura tells us that there was an "impious *brāhmaṇa*" from the village of Harinadī in Yaśohara district who became especially angry at the loud *nāma-kīrtana* of Haridāsa Ṭhākura and challenged him to justify it.

Of course the expression "impious *brāhmaṇa*" is an oxymoron since he was no *brāhmaṇa* at all, although from the consideration of birth he was considered as such. Moreover, from ancient times, there is a practice of referring to such persons as *brahma-bandhus:* indicating those born in *brāhmaṇa* families but incapable of exhibiting the proper character of *brāhmaṇas* or who do not perform the sacrifices required of *brāhmaṇas*.

Śrīla Bhaktisiddhānta Sarasvatī Ṭhākura describes him as "...foolish, ignorant, atheistic, fallen..." Out of blind faith and envy, he considered Haridāsa Ṭhākura, the giver of the holy names, unfit to act as a spiritual master due to the Ṭhākura's low birth, and, therefore, Śrīla Sarasvatī Ṭhākura explains: "...he feared that if Haridāsa loudly chanted the names of Hari he would have to automatically hear the holy names from the mouth of a pure devotee and thus naturally become his disciple, so he wanted Haridāsa to refrain from loudly chanting *hari-nāma*, which is the function of a *jagad-guru*."[24]

The spiritually blind fool angrily issued the following challenge:

"O Haridāsa, what is this behavior? Why are you loudly chanting the names of the Lord. The injunction is that one should chant in his mind. Which scripture says that one should chant loudly? Who has taught you to chant the name of Hari loudly? Please give your explanation before this assembly of learned scholars."[25]

Haridāsa Ṭhākura humbly replied that surely the members of the assembly and the "*brāhmaṇa*" knew the glories of the holy names and that he would repeat whatever he had heard from persons like them. He initially remarked that the scriptures repeatedly glorify loud chanting and that for one who does so, there is 100 times the benefit than for soft or silent chanting. In an ecstatic mood he began to offer evidences from the *Vedas* and the *Śrīmad-Bhāgavatam*:

"Anyone who chants Your name purifies all who hear this chanting, as well as himself. How much more beneficial, then is the touch of Your lotus feet." (*Śrīmad-Bhāgavatam* 10.34.17)

Haridāsa Ṭhākura further explained that even animals, birds, or insects will go to Vaikuṇṭha if they hear the holy name from the mouth of a pure devotee. Even though such creatures cannot chant the holy name, when they *hear* the holy names they will all be delivered. Silent chanting may deliver the hearer, but by loud chanting others can be delivered also. Haridāsa Thakura capped his argument by citing the words of Prahlāda Mahārāja in the *Nāradīya Purāṇa*:

japato hari-nāmāni sthāne sata guṇādhikaḥ
ātmānaṁ ca punāty uccair japan śrotṛn punāti ca

"One who loudly chants the holy names of the Lord is a hundred times greater than one who silently chants, because those who chant silently purify only themselves, while those who chant loudly purify themselves as well as those who hear them."

At this point Haridāsa Ṭhākura had completely defeated the so-called *brāhmaṇa*, supplying more than enough evidence for his activities, but with a final appeal to logic, he gave an additional line of argument:

"Tell me what is wrong with that activity by which living entities who have taken useless births will be delivered? One person may maintain himself, while another may maintain a thousand people. Of the two, consider carefully who is better. This is the superior characteristic of loud chanting[26]."
[27]

When characterless persons are defeated by pure logic and *śāstra* (scripture), rather than surrender to the person who has shattered their ignorance, such rascals will take shelter of the false tactic of *argumentum ad hominem*—attacking the speaker—i.e., give the dog a bad name and hang him.

Such persons will never address the speaker's philosophy; rather they will simply attempt to discredit the speaker, since they have no other means to uphold their confused ideas.

Such fools are condemned to suffer by resorting to such a fraudulent tactic due to their committing *Vaiṣṇava-aparādha*.

The *brāhmaṇa* scornfully remarked: "Now even Haridāsa has become a philosopher! I can see that Vedic culture is being destroyed by the course of time. It is stated that *śūdras* will explain the *Vedas* at the end of Kali-yuga. But why only at the end of the age? We can see it happening even now."[28]

In a lengthy purport Śrīla Bhaktisiddhānta Sarasvatī Ṭhākura discusses the fallacious idea that by birth one is a *brāhmaṇa*. *Saṁskāras* (purificatory activities) are no longer strictly observed and therefore birth is not much of an indicator in Kali-yuga. Therefore, *guṇa* (quality) and *karma* (activity) are stressed, not *janma* (birth). The so-called *brāhmaṇa* correctly stated that in Kali-yuga unqualified *śūdras* would attempt to explain the *Vedas*. What the envious *brāhmaṇa* didn't realize was that ***he*** was the unqualified *śūdra*! By exhibiting envy towards a *paramahaṁsa* Vaiṣṇava like Haridāsa Ṭhākura, he was exhibiting the very behavior he condemned with such contempt.

Compounding his offense and digging his grave even deeper, he spoke the following unfortunate words: "This is how you advertise yourself, so you can eat nicely at other's houses. If the explanation that you have made is not true, then I will cut off your nose and ears."[29]

Śrīla Bhaktisiddhānta Sarasvatī Ṭhākura remarks: "…the atheistic fallen *brāhmaṇa's* animalistic propensity became more prominent."[30]

Haridāsa Ṭhākura simply smiled and left that place, chanting the holy names very loudly. None of the members of an assembly in that place raised any objections to the nasty, offensive, and abominable remarks of the atheistic *brāhmaṇa.* Vṛndāvana dāsa Ṭhākura, quoting a verse from the *Varāha Purāṇa*, spoken by Lord Śiva, states:

"In Kali-yuga, demons will take birth in the families of *brāhmaṇas* to harass those rare persons who are conversant with the Vedic way of life."

Lord Śiva further states in the *Padma Purāṇa*:

"There is no need to speak further on this. Even by mistake one should not touch or speak to those *brāhmaṇas* who have no devotion for the Supreme Lord. If a person born in a *brāhmaṇa* family is an *avaiṣṇava* , a nondevotee, one should not see his face, exactly as one should not look upon the face of a *caṇḍāla*, or dog-eater. However, a Vaiṣṇava found in *varṇas* other than *brāhmaṇa* can purify the three worlds."

The above quote actually precedes modern social reforms by centuries. By personal transformation one can actually be elevated to a higher position in society. It is not by law, money, or mental adjustment that a person goes from a lowly position to a higher one. Rather by education, by training, by transformation, by purification, one is relieved of ignorance, bad habits, and suffering. Ultimately, there are no real material solutions to material problems, although some temporary relief may be offered by material adjustments. The real problems correctly identified by great sages like Haridāsa Ṭhākura are birth, disease, old age, and death. No amount of material adjustment or mundane attempts at social reform can solve these real problems which everyone must universally confront. The only way that such problems can be successfully confronted and social reform can be actually accomplished is through personal transformation by applying the practices of self-realization. In this age, the recommended means is the chanting of the *mahā-mantra*: Hare Kṛṣṇa, Hare Kṛṣṇa, Kṛṣṇa Kṛṣṇa, Hare Hare, Hare Rāma, Hare Rāma, Rāma Rāma Hare Hare. By this transcendental chanting and by following the nine-fold practices of *bhakti*, one can achieve the topmost position in human society, as well as become a fully liberated soul, free from all fear and distress.

In a few days the wretched and envious *brāhmaṇa* came down with small pox, and his nose melted and fell off. The very punishment he proposed for Haridāsa Ṭhākura was awarded to him. Haridāsa was depressed by such incidents. To see the whole world so absorbed in bodily consciousness and sense gratification gave him pain, and he would sigh deeply while chanting, lamenting the unfortunate situation.

Coming to Māyāpura

After some days Haridāsa Ṭhākura came to Śrī Māyāpura to associate with the Vaiṣṇavas there. All the devotees were overjoyed to see Haridāsa, considering him to be like a member of their family. Advaita Ācārya[31] considered Haridāsa Ṭhākura to be dearer than his own life and maintained him with utmost care. All of the Vaiṣṇavas showered their affection, and he reciprocated their feelings with great devotion. They discussed the offensive remarks of the atheists with great concern, lamenting their unfortunate condition, desiring the highest eternal benefit for the entire world.

Vṛndāvana dāsa Ṭhākura mercifully grants his readers this benediction: "One who reads or hears these topics will attain the lotus feet of the Supreme Lord, Śrī Gauracandra."[32]

ENDNOTES

[1] Mundane pride in worldly association is one danger for a preacher. Another danger is to think that avoiding the association of worldly people in an effort to remain pure while preaching is praiseworthy. Dayānanda Prabhu tells the following story, related to him by Tamāla Kṛṣṇa Mahārāja. In early 1969 Śrīla Prabhupāda wanted to organize a World Saṇkīrtana Party. Tamāla Kṛṣṇa Brahmacārī was making regular visits to Śrīla Prabhupāda's Los Angeles apartment on Melrose Avenue. During one such visit Śrīla Prabhupāda suggested to Tamāla Kṛṣṇa that he charter an airplane, sell tickets to non-devotees, and, with the profits, travel around the world on those chartered flights, chanting and dancing on the streets of major cities. At that time, street chanting had been established in only a few cities around the world, and even then within a very limited scope with sometimes only a few devotees participating. Śrīla Prabhupāda's suggestion was that Tamala Kṛṣṇa bring Viṣṇujana Brahmacārī and a dozen other *brahmacārīs* and *brahmacāriṇīs* with him. Tamāla Kṛṣṇa replied with some distaste that the *brahmacārīs* would have to sit next to the *karmīs* (materialistic persons) to whom they had sold tickets, implying that such association was unfavorable or forbidden. Śrīla Prabhupāda shot back, "Six months ago you were a *karmī*, Tamāla Kṛṣṇa!" Of course, Tamāla Kṛṣṇa's concern about materialistic association was not a fault; however, Śrīla Prabhupāda's concern was to preach at all costs or risks.

[2] *CB Ādi* 16.172 purport.

[3] *CB Ādi* 16.173.

[4] *CB Ādi* 16.173 purport.

[5] *CB Ādi* 16.180 purport.

[6] *CB Ādi* 16.186—188.

[7] *CB Ādi* 16.192—195.

[8] *CB Ādi* 16.195 purport.

[9] www.parami.org/buddhistanswers/what_about_miracles.htm.

[10] *SP lecture*, SB 1.2.6 Vṛndāvana, India, October 17, 1972 (721017SB. VRN). "So *bhukti, mukti*, that is also desire. *Bhukti, mukti and siddhi. Siddhi-kāmī, yogis, aṣṭāṅga-yoga*, and *aṣṭa-siddhi*: *aṇimā, laghimā, prāpti-siddhi, īśitā, vaśitā* like that. *Aṇimā, aṇu*, you can become very small...Actually those who are in perfectional yoga, they can become like that, smaller than the smallest. So *aṇimā, laghimā*, you can become lighter than the lightest. You can fly in the air. They go, by touching the beam of sun, moon, they can go. They are trying to go to the moon planet by artificial, material means, but those who are *yogīs*, they can

catch up the beam of the moon and go... *Mahimā*. You can become very big, heavy. *Mahimā*. Just like Hanumān, he jumped over this ocean. That means he assumed a big body so that one leg here, one leg there. He can jump. That is called *mahimā-siddhi*. *Prāpti*: you can get anything you like at any time. *Prāpti-siddhi*. So many things. Sometimes they do not like the devotees because the devotees...within four years, five years, the whole world should be chanting Hare Kṛṣṇa mantra. That is not magic. But if he can jump over a river, that is the magic. That is magic. The other side of the magic they have no eyes to see.

"So the *yoga-siddhi*, that is magic. But devotee can show better magic, but they do not bother their time for *yoga* practice. That is *bhakta*. Because he's under the care of the supreme magician, Kṛṣṇa. So if there is need of magic, Kṛṣṇa will show. Why he should bother? Just like a small child is dependent on his father. Father is a rich man. So he says to his father, 'Father, I want this.' That is very costly. So he doesn't require to get the money. The father is there. He'll get the money. 'All right, take it.' So that is the facility for the devotees. A devotee is under the care of the Yogeśvara. *Yatra yogeśvara hariḥ*. If you can catch up the hand of Yogeśvara Hari, then you can show wonderful magic, which no magician, no *yogīs* can display. That is the position of devotee. They do not care for practicing *yoga* to show some magical feats. Neither they require it. Neither they want it. Because devotee's position is *āśliṣya vā pāda-ratāṁ pinaṣṭu mām adarśanān marma-hatāṁ karotu vā* [Cc. Antya 20.47]. 'Whatever You like, You can do.' That's all. He has no desire."

[11] *CB Ādi* 16.197.

[12] *CB Ādi* 16.197 purport.

[13] In the eighth canto of *Śrīmad-Bhāgavatam* there is a description of Vāsuki taking the role of an immense rope wrapped around the Mandara Mountain in order to churn an ocean of milk. The great mountain was situated on the back of Kurma-*avatāra*, the great tortoise incarnation of the Lord, and the *devas* and the *daityas* did the churning.

[14] Generally the great Vaiṣṇava followers of Lord Caitanya corrected by means of verbal rather than physical chastisement. This is the procedure followed by great personalities like Śrīla Svarūpa Dāmodara Gosvāmī, Śrīla Bhaktisiddhānta Sarasvatī Ṭhākura, and Śrīla Prabhupāda. However, in certain instances other devotees like Abhirama Ṭhākura used physical chastisement with amazing effects. When the great devotee Śrīnivāsa

Ācārya stopped at the well-known Abhirāma Ṭhākura's house in Khanakul Krishnanagar to deliver a letter from Jāhnavā Devī, the Ṭhākura greeted him with three loving lashes from an extraordinary whip. However, this unusual greeting was a benediction. The whip, known as Jai Maṅgala, would bestow love of God on anyone it touched.

[15] The fact that Śrīla Bhaktisiddhānta Sarasvatī Ṭhākura refers to Haridāsa Ṭhākura as a non-seminal *brāhmaṇa* is significant. By birth, Haridāsa Ṭhākura had no qualifications, but by quality and activity (*guṇa* and *karma*—BG 4.13) he was much more than a *brāhmaṇa*. Advaita Ācārya confirmed the exalted position of the Ṭhākura by offering the *śrāddha-pātra* (*prasādam* offered to Lord Viṣṇu) to Haridāsa, thereby establishing that Haridāsa Ṭhākura was the best of the *brāhmaṇas*, or those who know the Supreme Brahman, Kṛṣṇa. Haridāsa Ṭhākura was the topmost Vaiṣṇava, a position far above even the position of a *brāhmaṇa*. This has been elaborately established in the writings of Śrīla Bhaktisiddhānta Sarasvatī Ṭhākura.

[16] *CB Ādi* 16.213—218 purport.

[17] *CB Ādi* 16.227.

[18] *CB Ādi* 16.227 purport.

[19] *CB Ādi* 16.229—247.

[20] The Lord does not limit His appearances to a particular species or caste of humans. Furthermore, His devotees are found amongst all sorts of humans, as well as animals.

[21] *CB Ādi* 16.252.

[22] *CB Ādi* 16.252 purport.

[23] *CB Ādi* 16.259—266.

[24] *CB Ādi* 16.268 purport.

[25] *CB Ādi* 16,268—270.

[26] Here is another important reason why devotees are interested in propagation of the *Bhāgavata* culture, or the culture of the Holy Name, even more than in temple worship or home worship.

[27] *CB Adi* 16.288—290.

[28] *CB Ādi* 16.292, 293.

[29] *CB Ādi* 16.294, 295.

[30] *CB Ādi* 16.295 purport.

[31] Śrī Advaita Ācārya was a *brāhmaṇa* and professor (*ācārya*) and thus well respected in Navadvīpa society. He set the example for those of his

time, and indeed for all times. Real devotees who have been awarded titles like *ācārya*, swami, guru, Ph.D., etc. still deeply respect other devotees without any titles.

[32] *CB Ādi* 16.315.

āpannaḥ saṁsṛtiṁ ghorāṁ
yan-nāma vivaśo gṛṇan
tataḥ sadyo vimucyeta
yad bibheti svayaṁ bhayam

LIVING BEINGS WHO ARE ENTANGLED IN the complicated meshes of birth and death can be freed immediately by even unconsciously chanting the holy name of Kṛṣṇa, which is feared by fear personified."

Śrīmad-Bhāgavatam 1.1.14
[The sages at Naimiṣāraṇya to Sūta Gosvāmī]

śuna śuna nityānanda, śuna haridāsa
sarvatra āmāra ājñā karaha prakāśa

prati ghare ghare giyā kara ei bhikṣā
'bala krsna, bhaja krsna, kara krsna-sikṣā'

ihā baiā āra nā balibā, balāibā
dina-avasāne āsi' āmāre kahibā

tomarā karile bhikṣā, yei nā baliba
tabe āmi cakra-haste sabāre kāṭiba

LISTEN, NITYĀNANDA! LISTEN, HARIDĀSA! Go out and preach My order everywhere. Go to every house and beg in this way, 'Chant the names of Kṛṣṇa, worship Kṛṣṇa, follow Kṛṣṇa's instructions.' Apart from this, you should not speak or have others speak anything else. At the end of the day come and give Me your report. I will take up My *cakra* and cut off the heads of those who will not chant after being requested by you."

Śrī Caitanya-bhāgavata Madhya 13.8—11

CHAPTER SIX

The Lord's Saṅkīrtana

Prior to the Lord's Manifestation

UPON THE BIRTH OF ŚRĪ CAITANYA Mahāprabhu, Advaita Ācārya and Haridāsa Ṭhākura were at the house of Advaita Ācārya in Śāntipura. Both of these great Vaiṣṇavas danced in jubilation at the time of the Lord's appearance. However, no one else could understand why those two saintly persons were dancing and loudly chanting the holy names.[1] Perceptions differ from person to person according to physical, mental, intellectual, or spiritual development. For example, a miser's mentality is different than a philanthropist's; a child's perception is different than an adult's; and a genius will see things differently than a person of ordinary or less than ordinary intelligence. Amongst devotees, spiritual perceptions will vary according to purity, desire, spiritual attainment, sincerity, and bestowed mercy. Śrīla Bhaktisiddhānta Sarasvatī Ṭhākura describes five planes of perception: *pratyakṣa, parokṣa, aparokṣa, adhokṣaja*, and *aprākṛta*. *Pratyakṣa* refers to direct perception (literally "against the eye"); *parokṣa* means *jñāna-* or *śāstra-cakṣuṣa* ("through the eye of another") or with the eye of knowledge or scripture; *aparokṣa* (direct spiritual perception or revelation) refers to perception not dependent on the perception of others or one's own material senses; *adhokṣaja* perception refers to the level of perception of the inhabitants of Vaikuṇṭha; and *aprākṛta* perception refers to the level of perception of the inhabitants of Goloka Vṛndāvana[2]. Advaita Ācārya and Haridāsa Ṭhākura are Mahā-Viṣṇu (Sadāśiva) and Lord Brahmā (Prahlāda), respectively, and, by the arrangement of Śrī Caitanya Mahāprabhu, they were favored with acute spiritual vision in regard to Mahāprabhu's identity which was not initially bestowed on others. Furthermore, it was by the pleas of these two great personalities that the Lord had agreed to appear. When their prayers were answered, they were notified by the ecstatic condition of their hearts and the supreme arrangement of Śrī Caitanya Mahāprabhu.

Haridāsa Ṭhākura, seeking the association of pure Vaiṣṇavas, came to stay in Navadvīpa-Māyāpura where Śrī Advaita Ācārya had established a *tol* (school) in the neighborhood of the house of Śrīvāsa Paṇḍita. Unfortunately, during the period before Lord Caitanya manifested Himself as the greatest Vaiṣṇava, the Vaiṣṇavas were relentlessly criticized by atheistic persons. During this dark period, Nimāi Paṇḍita exhibited His pastimes as a young boy always engaged in naughtiness. Yet whenever He appeared in the midst of the Vaiṣṇavas, they felt unaccountably blissful in His association.

Advaita Ācārya knew who the boy was, but to others Nimāi's identity remained hidden. Haridāsa Ṭhākura continued to associate with Advaita Ācārya and the other Vaiṣṇavas of Māyāpura, and incessantly glorified the name, form, qualities and pastimes of the Lord, despite all criticism, threats and opposition, which were almost constant.

Gayā

When Nimāi Paṇḍita was a teenager and became a renowned scholar and teacher, he noted how distressed the Vaiṣṇavas were. He witnessed how the Vaiṣṇavas were being subjected to almost constant blasphemy and harassment, and He became increasingly concerned for His sincere servants. Vṛndāvana dāsa Ṭhākura writes:

"The Lord thus desired to manifest Himself, but He thought He should first visit Gayā. The supremely independent Lord Gaurasundara desired to see the holy place of Gayā."[3]

Śrīla Bhaktisiddhānta Sarasvatī Ṭhākura explains: "The purport of the Lord's visit to Gayā is as follows: Śrī Gaurasundara desired to visit Gayā in order to personally enact the pastime of accepting the dress of a devotee prior to exhibiting the opulence of being the only shelter of His devotees."[4]

Nimāi, after performing the *śrāddha* ceremony for His father, departed for Gayā with many of His students. There He saw the lotus feet of Lord Viṣṇu and experienced overwhelming happiness accompanied by ecstatic symptoms. By His own divine arrangement, He met with Īśvara Purī, the great pure Vaiṣṇava, the disciple of Mādhavendra Purī, who came in the lineage of the Mādhva-*sampradāya*. In Īśvara

Purī's association Nimāi experienced an intense transformation of consciousness. The Lord ascribed this transformation to the influence of Īśvara Purī, whereas Īśvara Purī ascribed Nimāi's transformations to the influence of His own divinity.

Śrī Caitanya Mahāprabhu began to manifest Himself as an elevated devotee, brimming with spiritual emotion and all the sentiments and symptoms of an exalted pure Vaiṣṇava. After taking initiation from Īśvara Purī, He came back to Māyāpura in a completely altered state. Mother Śacī, the Lord's former students, and the other Vaiṣṇavas did not know what to make of this new Nimāi Paṇḍita.

The Lord exhibited all kinds of spiritual perturbations, and Mother Śacī started to believe that He had gone mad. Śrīvāsa Ṭhākura gave assurances to Mother Śacī, to her great relief, that it was not madness but love of God that Nimāi was experiencing, one drop of which he wished he could attain. *Laulyam,* the intense eagerness, greed, or covetousness to serve Kṛṣṇa is sometimes characterized as a form of madness. In a conversation with Allen Ginsberg, the American Beat poet, Śrīla Prabhupāda stated that madness was a qualification for a great devotee or poet:

> **Prabhupāda:** What is it called? Lunatic...compact in thought. (chuckles) So a Kṛṣṇa lover is also another kind of lunatic effect.
> **Allen Ginsberg:** I'm slowly developing all qualities except sanity. (laughter)
> **Prabhupāda:** Insanity for seeking Kṛṣṇa, that is required. Yes. Unless you become insane after Kṛṣṇa just like Lord Caitanya became... Yes. His worship is to become insane after Kṛṣṇa.[5]

In a lecture in Mumbai (Bombay) in 1972, Śrīla Prabhupāda remarked: "Also, *laulyam* means...we become very much greedy in achieving some success or receiving something sometimes. We become *mad*. That is required. *Laulyam eka mālyan*. To achieve Kṛṣṇa consciousness perfectly, this ecstatic eagerness or greediness to serve Kṛṣṇa is the only price to achieve success in devotional service."[6]

The Lord has descended to taste the love that Śrīmatī Rādhārāṇī feels for Him. Her love in serving Kṛṣṇa unconditionally is the pinnacle of emotion, far beyond the experience of other living beings:

eta cinti' rahe kṛṣṇa parama-kautukī
hṛdaye bāḍaye prema-lobha dhakdhaki

"Thinking in this way, Lord Kṛṣṇa was curious to taste that love. His eager desire for that love increasingly blazed in His heart."[7]

Inauguration of Saṅkīrtana

Advaita Ācārya immediately acknowledged the identity of the Lord to all the Vaiṣṇavas and worshipped Him. Soon after that, all the Vaiṣṇavas were able to understand the actual identity of the Lord, and the inauguration of the *saṅkīrtana* movement took place. Nocturnal *kīrtanas* were held nightly in the houses of Śrīvāsa Ṭhākura or Candraśekhara Prabhu. Locana dāsa Ṭhākura describes one of the first meetings of Śrī Caitanya Mahāprabhu (in his revealed identity as the Lord of the Vaiṣṇavas) with Haridāsa Ṭhākura in his *Śrī Caitanya-mangala*.

Haridāsa had come to Navadvīpa to see the Lord, Who had been chanting all night in the company of Advaita Ācārya, Nityānanda Prabhu, and other intimate associates.

> "The great soul Haridāsa arrived, continuously chanting the holy name of Kṛṣṇa with great delight in his heart. He was like an intoxicated bee around the sweet lotus feet of Kṛṣṇa. In his absorption in *kīrtana-rasa*, he was like a young lion. Mahāprabhu beckoned him closer with a smile of satisfaction, saying, 'Come here! Come here!' Mahāprabhu tightly embraced him with profound affection and ordered him to be seated. Haridāsa remained on the veranda offering Him obeisances, but the Lord lifted him up with His own hands. Śrī Caitanya Mahāprabhu smeared fragrant sandalwood paste upon his limbs and adorned him with His own flower garland. The Lord ordered Haridāsa to take *prasāda*, and Haridāsa partook of the ample *mahā-prasādam* with great satisfaction."[8]

Vṛndāvana dāsa Ṭhākura writes: "Every night *kīrtana* was held at the house of Śrīvāsa, except some nights it was held at the house of Candraśekhara...Haridāsa Ṭhākura...and innumerable other servants of Lord Caitanya were present in those *kīrtanas*."[9]

Atheistic persons were infuriated by the tumultuous sounds of the nocturnal *saṅkīrtana* and made many threats and complaints, but the Vaiṣṇavas and Śrī Caitanya Mahāprabhu ignored them. In the sixth chapter of the *Madhya-khaṇḍa* of *Śrī Caitanya-maṅgala* the blissful *saṅkīrtana* of Nityānanda Prabhu and Lord Caitanya and other intimate associates is described. After an especially emotional meeting between Lord Nityānanda and Lord Caitanya took place, Haridāsa Ṭhākura arrived on the scene in a state of extreme ecstasy. His body became covered with horripilation, tears fell in streams, and he roared like a lion. It was impossible for the universe to contain the bliss that Haridāsa relished at that moment...while Haridāsa danced, he manifested the four-headed form of Lord Brahmā. He fell at the feet of Viśvambhara to offer his respects and used his four mouths to chant Vedic hymns. Gaurāṅga embraced him and requested him to again take the form of Haridāsa and honor the *prasāda* He had arranged for him. Haridāsa then peacefully honored the *prasāda.*[10]

Preaching Door to Door

Śrī Caitanya Mahāprabhu, desiring to deliver all unfortunate persons, began to organize the door to door distribution of the holy names. One day He called for Nityānanda Prabhu and Haridāsa Ṭhākura and instructed them as follows:

śuna śuna nityānanda, śuna haridāsa
sarvatra āmāra ājñā karaha prakāśa

prati ghare ghare giyā kara ei bhikṣā
'bala krsna, bhaja krsna, kara krsna-sikṣā'

ihā baiā āra nā balibā, balāibā
dina-avasāne āsi' āmāre kahibā

tomarā karile bhikṣā, yei nā baliba
tabe āmi cakra-haste sabāre kāṭiba

"Listen, Nityānanda! Listen, Haridāsa! Go out and preach My order everywhere. Go to every house and beg in this way, 'Chant the names of Kṛṣṇa, worship Kṛṣṇa, follow Kṛṣṇa's instructions.' Apart from this, you should not speak or have others speak anything else. At the end of the day come and give Me your report.[11] I will take up My *cakra* and cut off the heads of those who will not chant after being requested by you."[12]

This all-important order of Śrī Caitanya Mahāprabhu was made to Haridāsa Ṭhākura and Nityānanda Prabhu, but the order is a standing order meant for all preachers of Kṛṣṇa consciousness, indeed for all living beings. At the San Francisco Rathayatra in 1975, Śrīla Prabhupāda called the Hare Kṛṣṇa Movement, "...a movement for the living entity." The *yuga-dharma* for the present age of Kali is *nāma-saṅkīrtana*, the *Kali-yuga-avatāra* is Śrī Caitanya Mahāprabhu, and His right and left arms, the generals of Śrī Caitanya Mahāprabhu's *saṅkīrtana* army, are Nityānanda Prabhu, the original spiritual master, and Nāmācārya Haridāsa Ṭhākura, the incarnation of Lord Brahmā, through whom Mahāprabhu's order was initially executed. Śrīla Bhaktisiddhānta Sarasvatī Ṭhākura expansively declares that the order is for: "...those who are outside *varṇāśrama*, those who follow *varṇāśrama*, those who are beyond *varṇāśrama*, all living entities, all plants, the animate, and the inanimate. Individually and collectively, according to their ability, all should accept Mahāprabhu's orders."[13]

The remarks by the Lord about cutting off the heads of those who will not chant the holy names cited in the paragraph before the previous one presents an apparent contradiction, since we shall see that the Lord's mission and practice in Kali-yuga was to deliver souls by transforming their hearts, not removing their heads. Nonetheless, His statement may certainly be taken literally in another way: Eternal time, as represented by the *cakra* of the Lord, is bringing about the unfortunate deaths of all those who waste their time in this world by not practicing Kṛṣṇa consciousness. Examining the Lord's statement from another angle of vision, He can be seen to foreshadow His willingness to behead Jagāi and Mādhāi for their offense to Nityānanda Prabhu. It was only by Nityānanda Prabhu's intercession that the two offenders were saved.

Those who practice Kṛṣṇa consciousness, following the order of the Lord, are able to step on the head of death as Dhruva Mahārāja did at the end of his life, due to their absorption in Kṛṣṇa consciousness which enables them to achieve the perfection of the human form of life.

Śrīla Bhaktisiddhānta Sarasvatī Ṭhākura also discusses the transcendental tactic of adopting the role of a beggar, or *bhikṣuka,* by exalted persons like Lord Nityānanda and Haridāsa Ṭhākura:

> "A *bhikṣuka* is dependent on the donor, therefore, knowing that the *bhikṣuka* is situated on a lower platform, the higher placed donor becomes compassionate on him. To beg for someone's favor is called *bhikṣā*. The higher placed donor comes down from his platform and uplifts the needy *bhikṣuka*. Realizing that when Nityānanda Prabhu, the Lord of the fourteen worlds, and Nāmācārya Ṭhākura Haridāsa, the grandfather of everyone and the best of the pure devotees, would go begging alms in the dress of *bhikṣukas*, wealthy people would have no alms suitable to offer them, Gaurasundara employed the act of begging alms to bring those people to the transcendental kingdom...The Lord's instruction—'Chant the name of Kṛṣṇa'—is the prime example of the Lord's magnanimity. The name of Kṛṣṇa is nondifferent than Kṛṣṇa—only Kṛṣṇa in the form of *guru* can teach this. Becoming initiated into this teaching and eagerly preaching such teachings is service to Śrī Caitanya—in order to make this known, Śrī Nityānanda Prabhu and Śrī Nāmācārya Haridāsa followed the order of the Lord. One who knows Śrī Nityānanda Prabhu as the origin of *guru-tattva* and who after being freed from the bondage of material existence chants Kṛṣṇa's name, which appeared in the form of address from the mouth of Nāmācārya Haridāsa, will be delivered from all material obstacles and attain *kṛṣṇa-prema*, which is the goal of all living entities."[14]

Śrīla Bhaktisiddhānta Sarasvatī Ṭhākura further reveals the magnificent potency of this standing order for all preachers of Kṛṣṇa consciousness:

"...although this order was given to the original Śrī Jagad-gurudeva and Śrī Nāmācārya, since these two *ācāryas* carried out this order of the Lord, all pious persons who follow this order will also certainly become qualified to act as *ācāryas*, who alone are able to fully engage in the service of Śrī Caitanya. In the language of a *bhikṣuka, bala kṛṣṇa*—'Chant the name of Kṛṣṇa,' indicates the deliverance of the living entities. When this is received by a listener, he follows the order of Caitanyadeva, becomes freed from material conceptions, and acts as an *ācārya*, who is a manifestation of the Lord. Defeating the concept of only one *jagad-guru*, the exalted spiritual masters who are manifestations of *guru-tattva* engage in delivering the living entities."[15]

Certain devotees think that there can only be one *ācārya*. Śrīla Bhaktisiddhānta Sarasvatī Ṭhākura, however, makes it very clear in this commentary that anyone who sincerely follows the order of Śrī Caitanya Mahāprabhu to induce others to chant the name of Kṛṣṇa can become qualified to be an *ācārya*. This order of Śrī Caitanya Mahāprabhu to approach others and convince them to chant carries the full purifying potency to successfully transform the lives of such preachers as well as the lives of those they approach. As Lord Caitanya states in *CC Madhya* 7.128: *yāre dekha, tāre kaha 'kṛṣṇa'-upadeśa āmāra ājñāya guru hañā tāra' ei deśa*—"Instruct everyone to follow the orders of Lord Śrī Kṛṣṇa as they are given in the *Bhagavad-gītā* and *Śrīmad-Bhāgavatam*. In this way become a spiritual master and try to liberate everyone in this land." Certain preachers who exhibit an especially deep level of commitment and sincerity may become more prominent, but there is no barrier blocking any sincere devotee from becoming a liberated soul and liberating others by following this powerful order of the Lord as one's life and soul.

The two *saṅkīrtana* preachers immediately took the order of the Lord on their heads and went out on the street.

On March 18, 1933, Śrīla Bhaktisiddhānta Sarasvatī Ṭhākura ordered his preachers to go to the Western countries. In a part of his remarks he spoke the following powerful words in the mood of Śrī Caitanya Mahāprabhu:

> "We have not been actuated by any attempt of rivalry or hostility in undertaking this propaganda. This should always be borne in mind. We should call at the door of each and every seeker of the Truth, **bearing on our heads the baggage of the Real Truth to be offered to them**. It is no business of ours to be elated or discouraged by the praise or neglect of any person. We must be constantly alive to the duty of enhancing the pleasure of our Master by serving Him with perfect sincerity."[16]

Going door to door, Haridāsa Ṭhākura and Nityānanda Prabhu, the fearless *saṅkīrtana* warriors, requested everyone: *bala kṛṣṇa, gāo kṛṣṇa, bhajaha kṛṣnere*: Chant the name of Kṛṣṇa, sing the glories of Kṛṣṇa, and engage in the worship of Kṛṣṇa.

kṛṣṇa prāṇa, kṛṣṇa dhana, kṛṣṇa se jīvana
hena kṛṣṇa bala bhāi hai' eka-mana

"Kṛṣṇa is your life, Kṛṣṇa is your wealth, Kṛṣṇa is your very life and soul. O brothers, chant the name of that Kṛṣṇa with full attention."[17]

As the two effulgent renunciants went from door to door, they received many invitations to take their meals with those pious householders who were very pleased to receive them. However, following the Lord's order, the two exalted personalities would reply: "Our only request is that you chant the names of Kṛṣṇa, worship Kṛṣṇa, and follow the teachings of Kṛṣṇa."[18] Pious persons were very pleased by the two mendicants, and many became supremely fortunate by accepting the perfect advice of the Lord delivered by the two *saṅkīrtana* warriors.

Śrīla Bhaktisiddhānta Sarasvatī Ṭhākura, while ordering his preachers to spread Kṛṣṇa consciousness to the Western world, further remarked:

> "Those nations to whom you are going for the propagation of the chant of Hari are mounted on the summit of proficiency in all affairs of this world. They are practiced in the exercise of their rational judgment, are endowed with the quality of good manners and are superior and glorious in many respects. Therefore, we should maintain our hope unshaken that they will prove to be the worthiest recipients of the heard transcendental Voice if we unlock to them the gates of the natural exhibition of abiding argument and enduring judgment. If we unpack our baggage of the genuine discourse of Hari by relying on the qualities of forbearance it will certainly receive the garland of welcome from the hearts of nations gifted with keen intelligence."[19]

However, there were those in Navadvīpa who thought Haridāsa Ṭhākura and Nityananda Prabhu were crazy and considered that the intelligence of the *saṅkīrtana* partners had been polluted by Nimāi Paṇḍita. Some people even threatened to beat them or turn them over to the king.

"These two are crazy because of bad advice...You have become mad on account of bad association. Why have you come to make us mad? Many sober and civilized persons have become mad in this way. Nimāi Paṇḍita has spoiled them all...Beat them! Beat them!"[20]

Śrīla Bhaktisiddhānta Sarasvatī Ṭhākura comments: "While following the order of Śrī Caitanyadeva, the preachers of Śrī Caitanya Maṭha face similar behavior even today. A former doctor of Sealdah, the society of caste *brāhmaṇas*, the community of pseudo renunciants, the *sakhī-bekīs* [pseudo devotees who imagine they are intimate associates of the *gopīs* and dress like the *gopīs*] and the twelve other unauthorized Māyāvādi *sampradāyas* are prime examples of such people."[21]

Others said, "Perhaps these two are the spies of a thief. They are wandering door to door on the pretext of preaching. Why would good people act in that way? If they come again, we will take them to the king."[22]

We see that the modern day Kṛṣṇa consciousness movement is similarly harassed by aggressive, unfortunate persons who are fully absorbed in a false conception of life, i.e. that life and consciousness is no more than an exhibition of chance chemical combinations. Also some narrow-minded, sectarian religionists, who suffer from the disease of party spirit and do not understand the universal, non-sectarian philosophy of Kṛṣṇa consciousness, attempt to discredit the Kṛṣṇa consciousness movement as a dangerous cult, often resorting to verbal attacks, or even physical violence. Despite the opposition and scorn of such confused persons, members of the Kṛṣṇa consciousness society approach those persons who are confused by such unfortunate offenders and attempt to convince such innocent persons of the eternal, spiritual nature of consciousness, presenting them with a conception of the self that is non-material, eternal and full of bliss.

Nityānanda Prabhu and Haridāsa simply laughed at the threats and scornful words. On the strength of Lord Caitanya's order, they were not at all frightened. At the end of the day, they would submit the report of their activities to Lord Caitanya. This fearless transcendental attitude must be adopted by all preachers who wish to successfully follow the order of Śrī Caitanya Mahāprabhu.

Jagāi and Mādhāi

One day, however, Nityānanda Prabhu and Haridāsa Ṭhākura saw two drunkards carrying on in the street. The inebriated duo was locally infamous for engaging in drunken debauchery, meat-eating, assault, robbery, and arson. It was said that there was no sin they had not committed. Typically, they were almost continuously in an intoxicated condition and would punch and pummel whoever crossed their path. The local people tried to stay clear of them, not always successfully, and there were many stories about their heinous activities. Practically the only offense they had not committed was the blasphemy of Vaiṣṇavas. At the time of Lord Caitanya, there were many sinful persons who were opposed to the *saṅkīrtana* movement. Many of them practiced a degraded form of dark arts *tantra* or worshipped the demigods for material benedictions. Still others were meat-eaters, drunkards, and atheists. Sometimes the supposed pristine nature of the past is idealized; however, Kali-yuga culture is filled with degradation and vicious social attitudes which also afflicted the Vaiṣṇava followers of Śrī Caitanya Mahāprabhu. In the social climate faced by 20th and 21st century preachers there is likewise a society composed of many Jagāis and Mādhāis. Jagāi and Mādhāi were supposed to be leaders in their society (*brāhmaṇas*), and yet we see that they were drunkards, meat-eaters, and indulged in unlimited forms of degradation and exploitation. Similarly, many people in the modern era may have fortunate births, education, and social backgrounds, and yet they also indulge in nasty habits, degraded practices, and exploitation. Despite the fortunate circumstances of their birth and education, such two-legged animals never bother to examine themselves for faults or consider that any of their activities require rectification or atonement. Their callous and ignorant arrogance is the emblem of their misfortune; they are incapable of perceiving the long-term effects of their misbehavior. Without the compassionate intervention of the Vaiṣṇava preachers, there is little hope for such impious creatures. Inspiration for exhibiting compassion can be drawn from the tolerant and merciful behavior exhibited by Nityānanda Prabhu and Haridāsa Ṭhākura toward the Kali-yuga population represented in its extremity by Jagāi and Mādhāi.

Nityānanda Prabhu and Haridāsa Ṭhākura watched the brothers from a distance and questioned the local people about the particulars of the caste and antecedents of the bestial brothers. They were surprised to learn that they were born in a respectable family of *brāhmaṇas*. From an early age the brothers had engaged in sinful activities and had been rejected by their relatives. They kept association with other drunkards and demonic persons. The residents of Nadia were in constant fear that their houses might be burned to the ground for any perceived insult to the two madmen, and thus scrupulously avoided them.

After hearing all of this, Nityānanda Prabhu began to consider how they might be delivered:

"The Lord has incarnated to deliver the sinful. Where will He find such sinners as these?"[23]

In a lengthy purport to this verse, Śrīla Bhaktisiddhānta Sarasvatī Ṭhākura has discussed the varieties of sinful activities, including sexual offenses, murder, arson, meat-eating, theft, vile speech, lies, etc. Almost every conceivable sort of sinful act is detailed, and there were very few that the brothers had not committed.

Nityānanda Prabhu continued: "If the Lord bestows His mercy on these two, then the whole world will know His glories. If I can reveal Lord Caitanya to them, then I, Nityānanda, will be known as Lord Caitanya's servant. Now they are fully intoxicated and do not know themselves. If only they could become intoxicated like this under the influence of Kṛṣṇa's names.[24] If the two cry as they say, 'O my Lord!' then My wandering will be successful. If persons who previously took bath in the Ganges with their clothes on when they touched the shadow of these two consider themselves as purified as having taken bath in the Ganges by seeing them, then My name will be remembered."[25]

Nityānanda Prabhu then turned to Haridāsa and out of unlimited compassion for Jagāi and Mādhāi's miserable condition made a plea to Haridāsa Ṭhākura for their deliverance:

"When you were beat practically to death by the Yavanas, you thought about even their welfare. If you think about the welfare of these two, then they will certainly be delivered. The Lord never neglects to fulfill your desire. This truth was personally disclosed by the Lord. Let the entire world see Lord Caitanya's influence when He delivers these two."[26]

Haridāsa Ṭhākura smiled at these statements of Nityānanda Prabhu. He knew very well that the two brothers were as good as delivered just by Nityānanda Prabhu's wish. The Ṭhākura pointed out to Nityānanda Prabhu that He was guilty of deceiving him as one would an animal.[27] Haridāsa Ṭhākura reasoned that if he took Nityānanda Prabhu's declaration seriously and thought of himself as a Vaiṣṇava whose request would cause the Lord to act, then he was no better than a bewildered animal. In fact, he responded, it was the desire of Nityānanda Prabhu, who was personally the Supreme Lord, which would be the cause of the brothers' deliverance, since Nityānanda Prabhu was the original spiritual master.

Nityānanda Prabhu smiled at this wonderful analysis of Haridāsa Ṭhākura. He embraced Haridāsa Ṭhākura and softly spoke, "Let us go and inform these two drunkards of the Lord's order that we are carrying around. The Lord's order is for everyone to worship Kṛṣṇa, but this is especially meant for the most sinful. Our responsibility is to simply repeat the Lord's order. If people do not follow, that is His responsibility."[28]

This is an important instruction for all preachers. Their only business is to carry the order of the Lord and request people to chant the holy name and take a book or magazine filled with transcendental instruction; if the people do not take it up, even after very sincerely and humbly being requested to do so, then it must be considered that it is the will of the Lord that those requested do not take it up. Such persons have thus invited inauspiciousness upon themselves. Therefore, Mahāprabhu, the order-giver, takes part in such a result.[29]

The above statement, paraphrased from the purport by Śrīla Bhaktisiddhānta Sarasvatī Ṭhākura in *Caitanya-bhāgavata Madhya-khaṇḍa* 13.76, may strike the reader as mysterious. If a living being, in the exercise of free will, decides not to accept the advice of a saintly person, how is it in any way the Lord's responsibility? The answer is that the Lord is all-powerful in His influence. As the Paramātmā, the Lord in the heart, He can influence the living being to act as He likes. Ordinarily He does not interfere with the minute free will of the living being. However, out of loving feeling for His devotees, He feels obligated, at times, to intercede on behalf of His devotees to benedict others, out of affection for the preachers' sincere effort to please Him. Out of love, He may fulfill the desires of the Vaiṣṇavas that conditioned souls be freed from the shackles of the illusory energy. When the preacher executes the order of the Lord to approach people to take up the path of devotional service and chant the holy name, the Lord sometimes intercedes on behalf of his devotees and inspires a conditioned soul to take up His order, due to the very intense desire of the pure Vaiṣṇavas that such persons be delivered (as expressed by Haridāsa Ṭhākura and Nityānanda Prabhu). Therefore, the preacher's only responsibility is to sincerely attempt (with intelligence and humility) to convince people to take up the Lord's order; the rest is between the Lord and the living being who has been approached.

Still, the point may be raised that such dealings of love between the Lord and His followers overrides the free will of the materially conditioned living beings. This is so; however, it is on the platform of loving compassion that all these loving dealings take place. Out of intense loving compassion, Vāsudeva Datta prayed that all living beings in the universe be delivered, and that he would remain behind to accept their load of sinful reactions. Lord Caitanya assured Vāsudeva Datta that, by his desire, all the souls in the universe would certainly be delivered. The Lord agreed to give the highest benediction to all the souls in the universe, both human and otherwise, to reciprocate the loving desires of His exalted servant. Divine love is thus the highest principle and transcends all other considerations or rules. The minute free will of the living being who foolishly chooses to go on suffering in illusion can be overturned by the desire of a pure soul and the response of the Lord to such sincere desire. This exchange of love between the preacher and the Lord constitutes the wonderful spiritual politics and freedom of divine love. The result of such loving exchanges is that a living being can be delivered by the mercy of the preacher and the Lord, despite the mule-headed obstinacy of the conditioned soul.

The important point is that preachers should desire nothing but the greatest benediction for all those they approach. If the preachers of Kṛṣṇa consciousness can intensify their prayers and entreaties to the Lord that He award the supreme benediction of love of God to all those they approach, this will do inestimable good to all the inmates of the material universe. In 1935 in Dacca, Śrīla Bhaktisiddhānta Sarasvatī Ṭhākura stated: "To transform the adverse desires of the *jīvas* is the supreme duty of the most merciful. To rescue one person from the stronghold of Mahāmāyā is an act of superb benevolence, far superior to opening innumerable hospitals." Śrīla Sarasvatī Ṭhākura also movingly stated at that time, "I wish that every selfless, tender-hearted person of Gauḍīya Maṭha will be prepared to shed two hundred gallons of blood for the nourishment of the spiritual corpus of every individual of this world." In this connection, Śrīla Prabhupāda comments: "I have received one complaint from [an]Indian devotee at Mayapur...that he is maltreated by our American devotees. Kindly inquire into this matter and do the needful. Either Indian or foreign, who ever joins us they are not under any obligation, our only tie is Love of Godhead. It should be our definite policy that nobody is ill treated that he may go away. We recruit a person to join us after spending gallons of blood. Everyone comes for reformation, you cannot expect everyone to be perfect, rather it is our duty to make everyone perfect as far as possible. So we shall be very much cautious and careful in this connection."[30]

The townspeople, seeing the intention of the saintly pair to attempt the deliverance of Jagāi and Mādhāi, tried to stop them, warning them that the brothers had killed *brāhmaṇas* and cows in the past. However, Nityānanda Prabhu and Haridāsa Ṭhākura joyfully approached the sinful brothers and loudly announced the order of the Lord:

"Say, 'Kṛṣṇa,' worship Kṛṣṇa, and chant the names of Kṛṣṇa. Kṛṣṇa is your mother, Kṛṣṇa is your father, and Kṛṣṇa is your life and wealth. Kṛṣṇa has incarnated for your benefit. Therefore, give up all sinful activities and worship Kṛṣṇa."[31]

Śrīla Bhaktisiddhānta Sarasvatī Ṭhākura comments at length on the ontological position of *Viṣṇu-tattva, jīva-tattva*, etc. in the purport to the above verses, but in a portion of such remarks he explains the behavior of Nityānanda Prabhu and Haridāsa Ṭhākura:

> "Having received the direct order of Mahāprabhu, Jagad-guru Sri Nityānanda and Jagad-guru Ṭhākura Haridāsa, as specific manifestations of Jagad-guru, preach the topics of Kṛṣṇa's munificent incarnation to the people of the world...Knowing themselves as nondifferent from participants in Kṛṣṇa's pastimes, Śrī Baladeva-Nityānanda Prabhu, the original source of the *viṣṇu-tattvas* and the chief of all devotees, and Nāmācārya Ādi-guru Brahmā, the chief of all devotees [Haridāsa Ṭhākura], vigorously concealed this fact from unfortunate persons while revealing real knowledge during the manifested pastimes of the covered incarnation [Lord Caitanya]..."[32]

On hearing this loud declaration by Haridāsa Ṭhākura and Nityānanda Prabhu, the two brothers, turned their heads, their eyes reddening with anger, and began to run towards the merciful Vaiṣṇavas with evil intent. They shouted for

Nityānanda Prabhu and Haridāsa Ṭhākura to stop, as the preachers quickly took to their heels. The townspeople engaged in reassuring each other that they had warned the foolhardy preachers, and the atheists smugly thought that justice was being served. As the devotees were running away, being pursued by the animalistic and vicious brothers, the preachers laughed and joked about their own situation. Vṛndāvana dāsa Ṭhākura refers to their exchanges as "blissful quarrels."

Even though Jagāi and Mādhāi were quite fat, they still ran very quickly and seemed about to overtake the preachers.

Haridāsa remarked: "I cannot go further. Why did I knowingly come with this restless person [Nityānanda Prabhu]? Kṛṣṇa just saved me from the wrath of the Yavanas, and now today I will lose my life due to Your mischievous nature."[33]

Nityānanda Prabhu protested Haridāsa Ṭhākura's allegation, saying that it was due to the restless nature of Lord Caitanya, who gives difficult orders like a king, which was the cause of their difficulty. "If we disobey His order, we'll be ruined, and if we follow His order, this is the result. You do not admit your Lord's fault. Although we both spoke to them, you accuse Me of being at fault!"[34] This humorous statement, stemming from deep love for Lord Caitanya and and manifested as a joking complaint, embodies simultaneously some of the fears, doubts, humiliations, embarrassments, etc. that the modern day preacher regularly experiences. Some neophyte preachers only like to give lectures to large, receptive audiences; however, advanced preachers are prepared to undergo considerable difficulties and adversities in planning, strategizing, and executing their programs for fulfilling the mission of Lord Caitanya. We have only to look at the adversities faced by Śrīla Prabhupāda in the first years of his preaching in America as vivid evidence of his painstaking and revolutionary efforts.

The preachers ran towards the Lord's house, and the drunken louts following them became confused and rolled on the ground, intoxicated with wine. Being intoxicated, they began to push and shove one another. Seeing that they were no longer pursued, Haridāsa Ṭhākura and Nityānanda Prabhu felt pacified, and, embracing one another and laughing, they went to see Viśvambhara to give Him their report.

"Today we have seen two strange persons—they were great drunkards, yet they called themselves *brāhmaṇas*. We nicely requested them to chant the names of Kṛṣṇa. In response they chased us, yet fortunately we survived."[35]

Lord Caitanya was very surprised to hear this, but Gaṅgādāsa and Śrīvāsa then began to tell Sri Caitanya Mahaprabhu the sordid history of the two brothers. Lord Caitanya then remarked: "I know these two fellows. If they come here I will cut them to pieces."[36]

Nityānanda Prabhu began to joke with the Lord, saying:

"You may cut them to pieces, but I will not go out as long as they are there. Why do You brag so much? First, get these two to chant the name of Govinda. A pious person naturally chants the name of Kṛṣṇa, but these two do not know anything other than sinful activities. If You deliver these two by awarding them devotional service, then I will know that You are Patita-pāvana, the deliverer of the fallen! The deliverance of these two will certainly be more glorious than the deliverance of Me."[37]

Viśvambhara smiled at the humorous exasperation of Nityānanda Prabhu, stating:

"They were delivered the moment they got your *darśana*. You are so concerned for their benefit that Kṛṣṇa will soon arrange for their well-being."[38]

All the devotees who heard the Lord's statements immediately chanted, "Jaya! Jaya! Hari! Hari!"

This exchange between Śrī Caitanya Mahāprabhu and Śrī Nityānanda Prabhu is quite wonderful. At first glance, it may appear that Nityānanda Prabhu is being critical of the Lord, accusing Him of bragging, inciting Lord Caitanya to deliver Jagāi and Mādhāi, and implying that if Śrī Caitanya Mahāprabhu was really the deliverer of the most fallen, then why had He not delivered them immediately! He also states that the Lord's delivering Him (Nityānanda) was a minor feat, but that if He could deliver Jagāi and Mādhāi, then Nityānanda Prabhu would be impressed. His statements are apparently riddled with criticism, sarcasm, and scorn. In fact, Nitāi Prabhu is simply expressing intense love for the Lord, fraternal affection, eagerness for the deliverance of the sinful brothers, humility, and glorification of Lord Caitanya as Patita-pāvana, the deliverer of the fallen. The Lord immediately understood all of this, and stated that simply by the degraded brothers receiving the glance of Lord Nityānanda they were already as good as delivered. He suggested further that Kṛṣṇa (Lord Caitanya) would soon arrange for their well-being. When great spiritual personalities, united in love, converse in a mysterious manner, neophyte devotees should suppress the brash impulse to interject opinions or comments into such an exchange.

Learning from the associates of the Lord, a wise and circumspect person, who appreciates the opportunity to listen to the words of the Lord or elevated Vaiṣṇavas, would do best to listen without judgment or opinion and try to relish such extraordinary exchanges which are always actuated by affection and love.

Haridāsa's Complaints

Haridāsa Ṭhākura then approached his old friend Advaita Ācārya and lodged his ecstatic complaints against Nityānanda Prabhu:

"The Lord sends me with this restless person. He leaves me behind and who knows where He goes? During the rainy season there are many crocodiles in the Ganges, and He goes swimming in the waters to catch them. In great anxiety I call Him loudly from the riverbank, but He continually floats around in the waters of the Ganges. If He sees some boys, He comes out of the water and chases them to beat them. When their parents come back with sticks in their hands, I fall at their feet and send them back. He steals butter and yogurt from the cowherd men and flees, and they catch me and want to beat me. Whatever He does is unreasonable. When He sees an unmarried girl He tells her, 'Marry Me.' He rides on the back of an ox and declares that He is Maheśa. He takes milk from other's cows and drinks it. When I try to teach Him something, He abuses me and says, 'What can your Advaita do to Me? And Śrī Caitanya, whom you consider the Lord, what can He do to Me?' I have not said anything about this to the Lord, but today my life has been saved by providence. There were two great drunkards lying in the street, and He went before them to preach Kṛṣṇa's instructions. In great anger they rushed to kill us. It is Your mercy that our lives have been saved."[39]

Śrī Advaita Prabhu heard all of these loving complaints with amusement and then replied:

"This is not at all astonishing, for drunkards should associate with other drunkards. It is befitting that the three drunkards[40] were together. But, being a celibate, why were you there?"[41]

Śrīla Bhaktisiddhānta Sarasvatī Ṭhākura comments by paraphrasing Advaita Acarya's statement and purporting it simultaneously: "O Haridāsa, Śrīla Nityānanda Prabhu is intoxicated from drinking the liquor of love for Kṛṣṇa, whereas Jagāi and Mādhāi are intoxicated from drinking ordinary wine. Therefore, it is befitting that the three associate together. Since you are attached to the Supreme Lord, you should not go near them."[42]

Advaita Ācārya continued: "Nityānanda will make everyone intoxicated. I know His character very well. Just wait and see, within two or three days He will bring those drunkards into our assembly."[43]

Advaita is then described by Vṛndāvana dāsa Ṭhākura as both without clothing (!) and angry, and the Ācārya declared very emphatically:

"Everyone will hear about Lord Caitanya's devotional service to Kṛṣṇa. And they will see His potency—how He dances and chants. You will see tomorrow how Nimāi and Nitāi will bring the two drunkards and dance with them."[44]

Haridāsa Ṭhākura smiled upon hearing Advaita Ācārya's declarations and was convinced that the drunkards would be delivered. Vṛndāvana dāsa Ṭhākura comments that no one but Haridāsa Ṭhākura can understand Advaita Ācārya's words.

Jagāi and Mādhāi continued their wanderings and came to the place where Lord Caitanya took bath in the Ganges. By divine arrangement, they made that place the base of their raiding expeditions. The inhabitants of that area were very fearful, and no one went to take bath there at night except in groups of ten or twenty.

Thus, the brothers were camped near the Lord's house, and at night they could hear the Lord's *kīrtana*. Upon hearing the chanting, they mistook it for Maṅgalacaṇḍī, glorification of the goddess Durgā-devī, and, upon hearing it, they sang and danced in an intoxicated condition. The goddess Durgā-devī is worthy of worship even by Vaiṣṇavas; however, Jagāi and Mādhāi provide an example of the quality of some of her followers. Throughout history, less intelligent persons have revered the divine energy and neglected the energetic source: the Lord. To worship the energy and not the energetic source is a symptom of impaired discrimination. Those who become obsessed with material goods sometimes find success by worshipping the Mother Goddess with the blood of animals and human beings. Similarly, millions of people currently pride themselves in being educated and sophisticated; however, in practice they are devoted to the worship and enjoyment of the energy of the creation. They revere the womb, or the field, into which the Lord plants His seed. Ironically, like the worshippers of Durgā, modern materialists have no qualms about killing animals, plants, and humans, almost indiscriminately, in order to achieve their goals. All the while, like the worshippers of Devī, they insist that their killing is proper according to their relationship with the energies and laws of the universe, or in the case of the Durgā worshippers themselves, the Mother of Creation.

Deliverance

One evening as Lord Nityānanda headed for the house of Mahāprabhu, He was spotted by the drunken brothers, who demanded to know who He was.

"My name is Avadhūta[45]," was the reply.[46]

On hearing the name "Avadhūta," Mādhāi became angry. He picked up a broken clay pot and hit the Lord in the head with it. The Lord was cut and blood flowed from the wound, yet He simply remembered Govinda. Jagāi felt compassionate and tried to stop Mādhāi and said,

"Why did you do that? You are very cruel. What will you gain by beating an outsider. Leave Avadhūta alone. Do not beat Him again. What will you gain by beating a *sannyāsī*?"[47]

Lord Caitanya was quickly informed, and the Lord immediately appeared on the scene, along with His associates. Even though the body of Nityananda Prabhu was covered with blood, He simply stood there smiling. When the Lord saw what had happened, He became infuriated and began to call out: "*Cakra! Cakra! Cakra!*"[48]

Jagāi and Mādhāi both saw the shimmering *cakra* in the hand of Śrī Caitanya Mahāprabhu and realized that He was ready to destroy them both. At that point Nityānanda Prabhu interceded and cited Jagāi's intervention on His behalf and asked the Lord to give Him the two brothers in charity.

Hearing this recommendation of Nitāi, Lord Caitanya became very happy and embraced Jagāi and told him:

"May Kṛṣṇa bestow mercy on you. By protecting Nityānanda, you have purchased Me. Ask Me for any benediction you desire. May you attain pure devotional service from this day on."[49]

All the Vaiṣṇavas were pleased to hear this benediction bestowed upon Jagāi, and Jagāi lost consciousness due to ecstatic love. The Lord commanded him to awake and showed him His four-armed form. The Lord placed His foot on Jagāi's chest, and Jagāi tightly grasped the lotus feet of the Lord and shed tears of happiness.

When Mādhāi witnessed all of this, he let go of Nityānanda Prabhu's cloth, fell flat, and held on to the Lord's lotus feet, begging for equal mercy. However, the Lord did not agree, since the offense had been to Nityānanda Prabhu, saying: "...you have drawn blood from the body of Nityānanda. The body of Nityānanda is superior to Mine. I emphatically tell you this truth."[50]

Śrīla Bhaktisiddhānta Sarasvatī Ṭhākura comments: "It is a greater offense to hit the body of Nityānanda, who is the servant of Viṣṇu, than to become envious of Viṣṇu. To harm Śrī Nityānanda is more offensive than attacking the body of the Lord."[51]

Mādhāi continued to plead for deliverance and the Lord told him: "You have committed a grave offense. Go and grab hold of Nityānanda's lotus feet."[52]

Mādhāi did what he was told, and the Lord asked Nityānanda Prabhu to show him mercy. Nityānanda Prabhu replied: "I declare emphatically that if I have ever accumulated piety in any lifetime, I give it all to Mādhāi. He is relieved of any offense committed against Me. Do not bewilder him, bestow mercy on Your Mādhāi."[53]

Śrī Caitanya Mahāprabhu then ordered Nityānanda Prabhu: "If You have actually forgiven Mādhāi, then embrace him and make his life successful."[54]

The embrace of Nityānanda Prabhu freed Mādhāi from all material bondage and invested him with Nityānanda Prabhu's energies. He was filled with good qualities and was empowered to be a servant of the Lord. The brothers both began to offer prayers to the two Lords. Śrī Caitanya Mahāprabhu ordered them to not commit any further sins, and they promised: "Never again, O Lord."[55] The illusion of the two brothers was destroyed, and they were plunged into an ocean of ecstasy.

The Lord ordered: "Pick these two up and bring them to My house. Today we will perform *kīrtana* with these two. Today I will award them that which is rare for even Lord Brahmā. I will place them in the topmost position in this world. Those who took bath in the Ganges after bing touched by these two will now say that these two are equal to the Ganges. The determination of Nityānanda is never baffled. Know for certain that this was the desire of Nityānanda."[56]

The brothers were brought into the house of Śrī Caitanya Mahāprabhu, and they all sat down together in great happiness. The two brothers, being still situated in the throes of ecstasy, rolled on the ground and exhibited all kinds of

of ecstasy, rolled on the ground and exhibited all kinds of ecstatic symptoms. Vṛndāvana dāsa Ṭhākura states that anyone who has faith in these pastimes attains Kṛṣṇa, while those who have doubts will fall down.

The purified brothers began to offer many wonderful prayers, being empowered by Śuddhā Sarasvatī (the goddess of learning) by the Lord's request. The brothers were crying, and all of the Vaiṣṇavas present, including Haridāsa Ṭhākura, offered prayers glorifying the Lord's wonderful mercy to the two previously demonic *brāhmaṇas*.

Śrī Caitanya Mahāprabhu declared: "These two are no longer drunkards. From today on, these two are My servants. All of you bestow your mercy on these two, so that birth after birth they do not forget Me. Forgive whatever offenses they have committed against you and show compassion upon them."[57]

All of the devotees gave their blessings, and the brothers were freed from all offenses. After ecstatic *kīrtana*, all of the Vaiṣṇavas and the transformed brothers went to the Ganges and engaged in blissful water sports in which the devotees all witnessed the ecstatic quarrels and water fights between Nityānanda Prabhu and Advaita Ācārya.

Rescue of the Lord & Chastisement of Advaita Ācārya

Wandering throughout Navadvīpa in the association of His Vaiṣṇava associates, Nimāi Paṇḍita kept His identity concealed. Most of the atheists were intimidated by His reputation as a great scholar and left Him alone. But some of the more foolhardy and atheistic persons warned Him that He should soon expect an order from the king prohibiting his nocturnal *kīrtana*. Śrī Caitanya Mahāprabhu was unconcerned and stated that there was no one who could challenge Him in any case. The atheists then sarcastically remarked, "The king will listen to Your *kīrtana*. Because he is a Muslim he does not care for scriptural debate."[58]

The Lord thought very little of such foolish taunts, but upon arriving at His home asked His associates to perform *kīrtana* and relieve Him of the misery He felt by having the association of faithless persons. Somehow the Lord's ecstasy did not manifest despite the *kīrtana*. He thought perhaps it was due to having associated with atheists. Then He addressed the assembled devotees and pleaded:

"If I have insulted you in any way, then please forgive My offenses and save My life."[59]

Advaita Ācārya then began to speak in a mysterious and apparently mad fashion. He claimed that He had drained the Lord of ecstatic love; that He and Śrīvāsa were not the recipients of the Lord's ecstatic love, because the Lord shared it with oil millers and gardeners. He claimed that Avadhūta (Nityānanda Prabhu) was the storekeeper of the Lord's love, and if the Lord would not bestow such love upon Him (Advaita Ācārya), then He would dry it up.

The Lord did not reply to these peculiar declarations, and Advaita Ācārya danced in ecstasy. Suddenly, the Lord leapt up, opened the door, and ran out, with Haridāsa Ṭhākura and Nityānanda Prabhu close behind Him. Thinking that there was no point in remaining in the world in a body devoid of love of Godhead, the Lord jumped into the Ganges. As He jumped, Haridāsa Ṭhākura and Nityānanda Prabhu jumped in behind Him. Lord Nityānanda grabbed the Lord by the hair and Haridāsa Ṭhākura grabbed the Lord's feet. The two carried Him from the water, and the Lord demanded to know why they had restrained Him.

"For what purpose should I maintain this life, which is devoid of love of God? Why did you two hold Me back?"

Looking at Nityānanda Prabhu, the Lord demanded: "Why did You grab My hair?

Nityānanda Prabhu replied: "Why did You try to kill Yourself?"

Śrī Caitanya Mahāprabhu said: "I know You are most restless."

Nityānanda Prabhu humbly responded: "O Lord, please forgive Me. Do You want to give up Your body because of someone that You can easily punish? If servants speak something out of pride, does their master take their lives?"

Nityānanda Prabhu began to cry because Lord Caitanya was His life, His wealth, and His friend.

The Lord then ordered Haridāsa Ṭhākura and Nityānanda Prabhu: "Do not tell anyone that you have seen Me."[60]

The Lord then went to the house of Nandana Ācārya, and the two *saṅkīrtana ācāryas* were forced to keep His whereabouts a secret. All of the devotees became filled with distress at the absence of the Lord and began to cry from feelings of separation.

Advaita Ācārya considered that the incident was due to His offenses and began to fast. The Lord passed the night at the home of Nandana Ācārya, and in the morning He met with Advaita Ācārya and forgave him in the mood of master to servant. This treatment made Advaita Ācārya ecstatic, for it was his constant ambition to be treated as a servant of Lord Caitanya. He laughed and began to dance ecstatically and exclaimed, "Now I can say You are My Lord!"[61] Upon seeing the Lord's favor bestowed upon Advaita Ācārya, both Nityānanda Prabhu and Haridāsa began to laugh in great happiness. Sometimes the Lord or His devotees appear to be displeased with their followers so that the followers will increase the quality and quantity of their service. There are many documented examples of Śrīla Prabhupāda's exchanges with his leaders and with the managers of the BBT which illustrate this principle.

Transcendental Trickery

Lord Caitanya generally treated Advaita Ācārya with great respect as one would a *guru*. As shown by the previous pastime, Advaita Ācārya did not like this because in the core of His heart He considered Mahāprabhu His Lord, and He always desired to be treated like a servant.

"Śrīla Advaita Ācārya Prabhu appeared as an incarnation of a devotee. He is in the category of Kṛṣṇa, but He descended to this earth to propagate devotional service. His natural emotions were always on the platform of fraternity and servitude, but the Lord sometimes treated Him as His spiritual master."[62]

Advaita Ācārya was very frustrated by the formal respect of Lord Gaurāṅga, and so He devised a plan to force Śrī Caitanya Mahāprabhu to treat Him as a servant. Advaita Ācārya was living in Śāntipura, along with Haridāsa Ṭhākura, and one day He began extolling the glories of *jñāna* (impersonal monism) very loudly.

Some distance away, Lord Caitanya and Lord Nityānanda had just leapt into the Ganges to purify Themselves after being offered the "benediction" of wine from a bogus renunciant. As they floated down the Ganges, They gradually came to Śāntipura, and the omniscient Lord proceeded quickly towards the house of Advaita Ācārya in an angry mood.

When Haridāsa Ṭhākura and Acyuta, the son of Advaita Ācārya, saw the two effulgent Lords, they offered their obeisances. Haridāsa Ṭhākura was a regular fixture in the home of Advaita Ācārya at Śāntipura. Śrī Advaita and Haridāsa were intimate friends, and although Haridāsa was not a member of the Pañca-tattva, he was a favorite associate of these five exalted personalities. As practicing devotees, it is not possible to directly associate with the Supreme Lord, nor should we ever imitate Him; however, if we have the opportunity to serve or follow in the footsteps of His exalted servants like Haridāsa Ṭhākura, Śrīla Prabhupāda, or other great souls, we should not miss the opportunity, either in person (*vapuḥ*) or by instruction (*vāṇī*).

Lord Caitanya approached Advaita Ācārya in a furious mood and demanded to know which was superior, *jñāna* (knowledge leading to impersonal liberation) or *bhakti* (de-

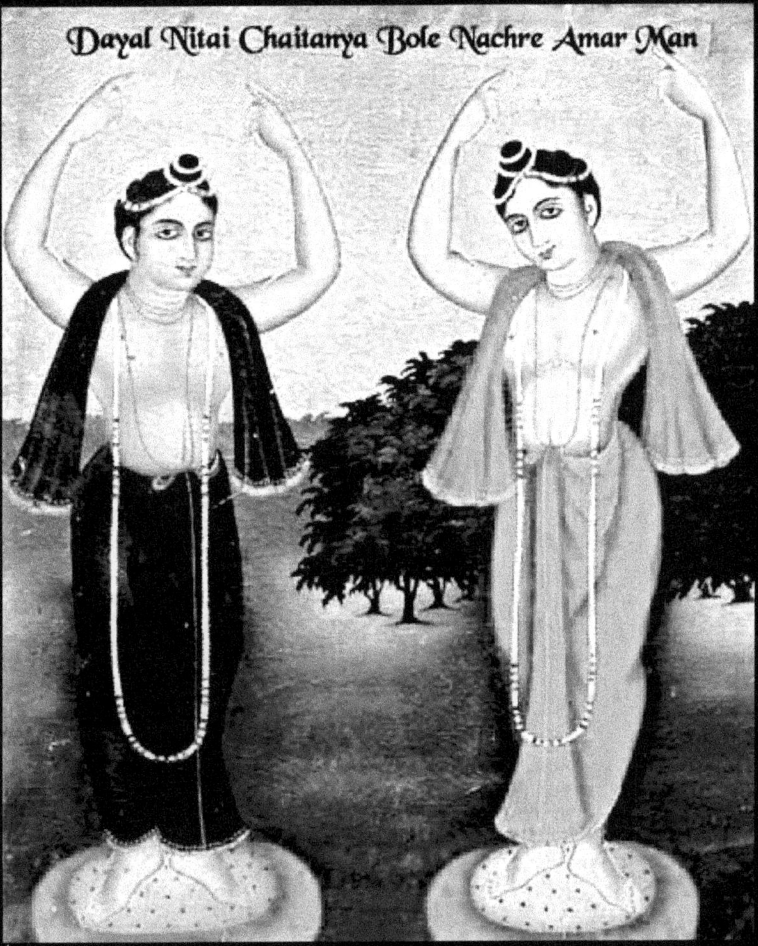
Dayal Nitai Chaitanya Bole Nachre Amar Man
1

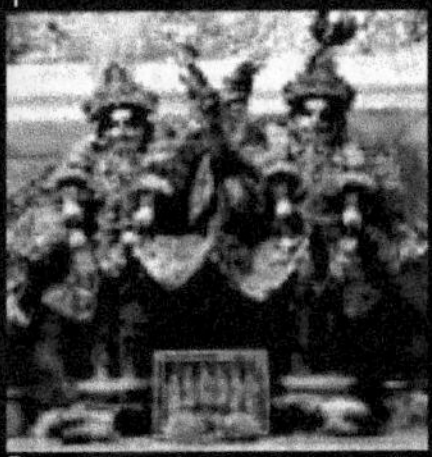
2

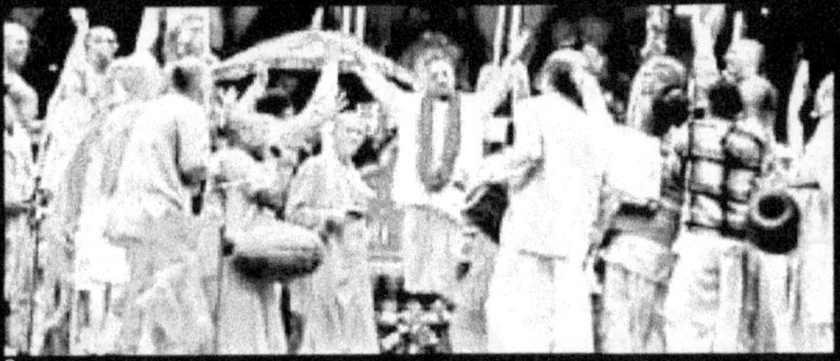
3

PLATE I

Plate II

PLATE III

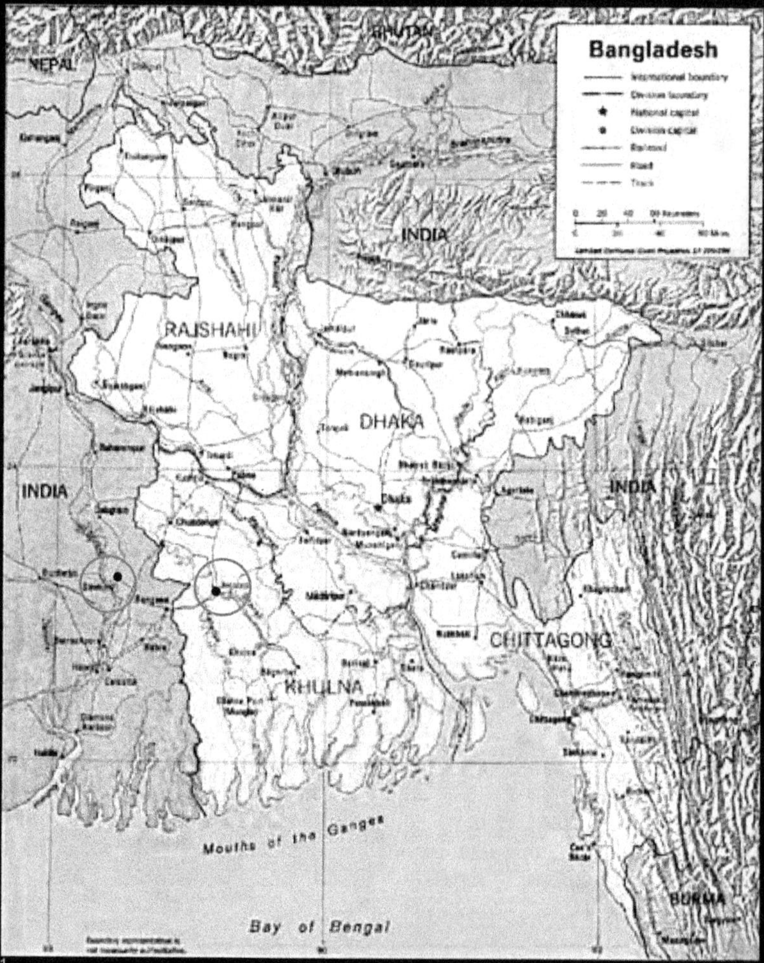

1

2

3

4

5

PLATE IV

1

2

PLATE V

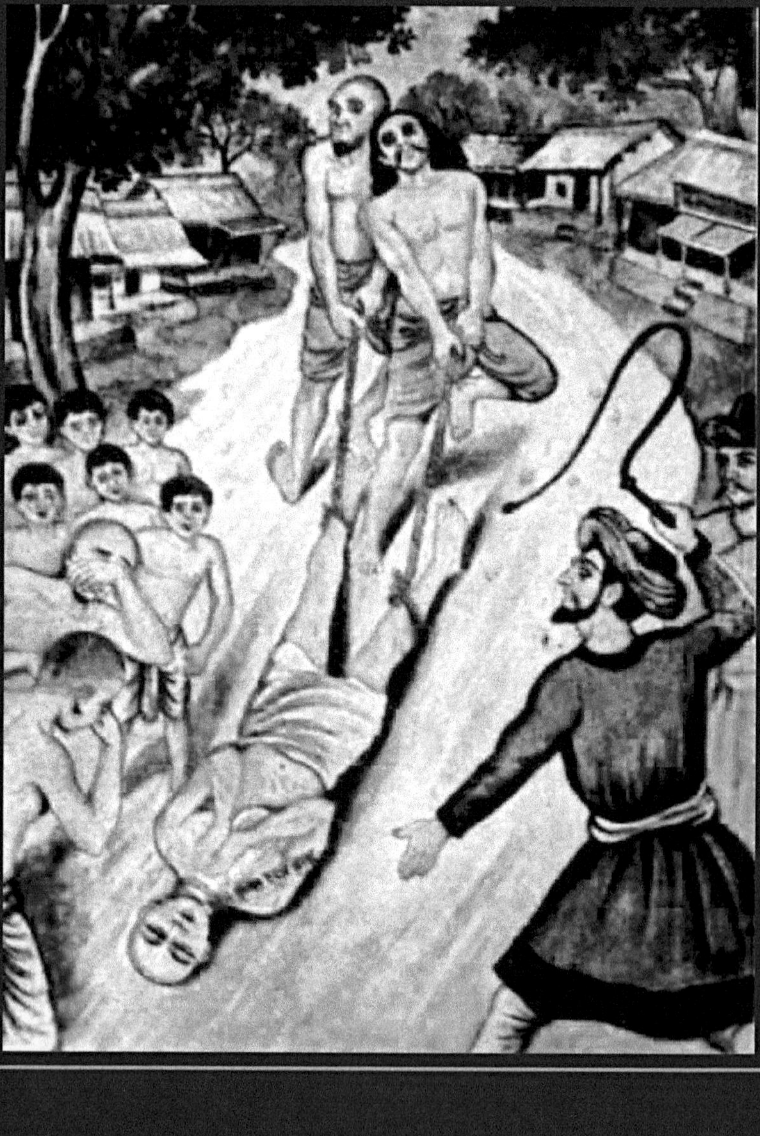

Plate VI

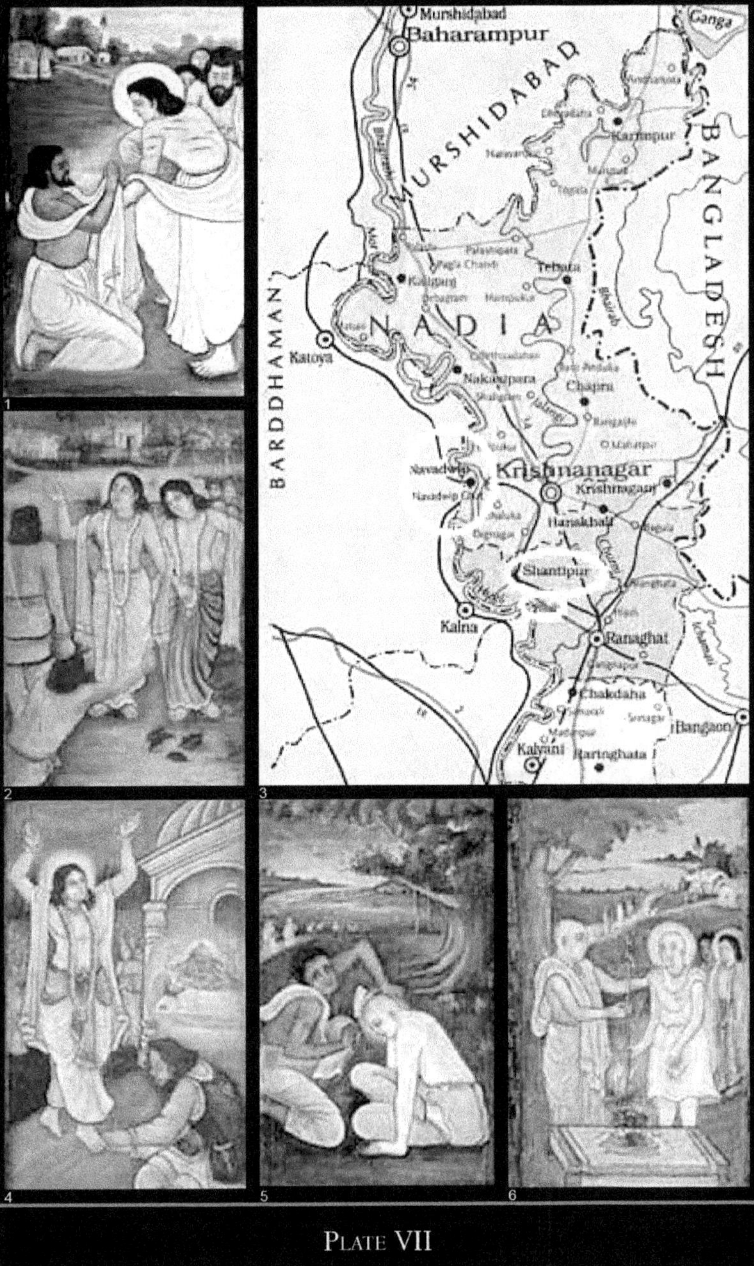

1
2
3
4
5
6
Murshidabad
Baharampur
MURSHIDABAD
Ganga
Karimpur
BANGLADESH
Tehatta
NADIA
Katoya
BARDDHAMAN
Nakashipara
Chapra
Krishnanagar
Shantipur
Kalna
Ranaghat
Chakdaha
Bangaon
Kalyani
Haringhata

Plate VII

Plate VIII

PLATE IX

PLATE X

PLATE XI

Plate XII

1

2

3
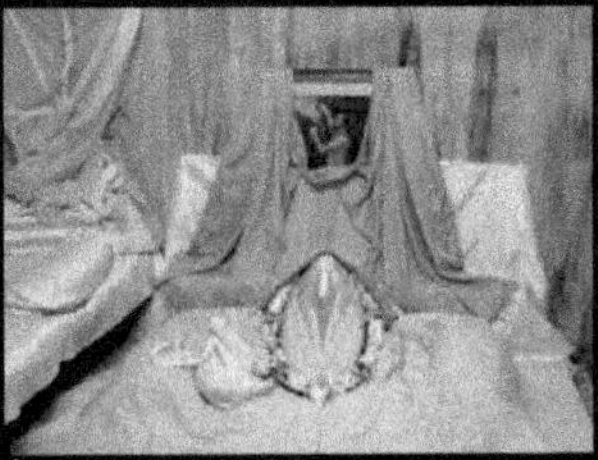
4

5

PLATE XIII

1

2

PLATE XIV

1

2

ALL GLORIS TO SRI GURU & GOURANGA
HARE KRISHNA
THIS MEMORIAL BUILT BY
BHAKTI VEDANTA SWAMI
CHARITY TRUST ISKCON
FOUNDER ACARYA-H.D.G.
A.C.BHAKTIVEDANTA SWAMI PRABHUPAD
YEAR-1994 GOURABDA-507

3

4

PLATE XV

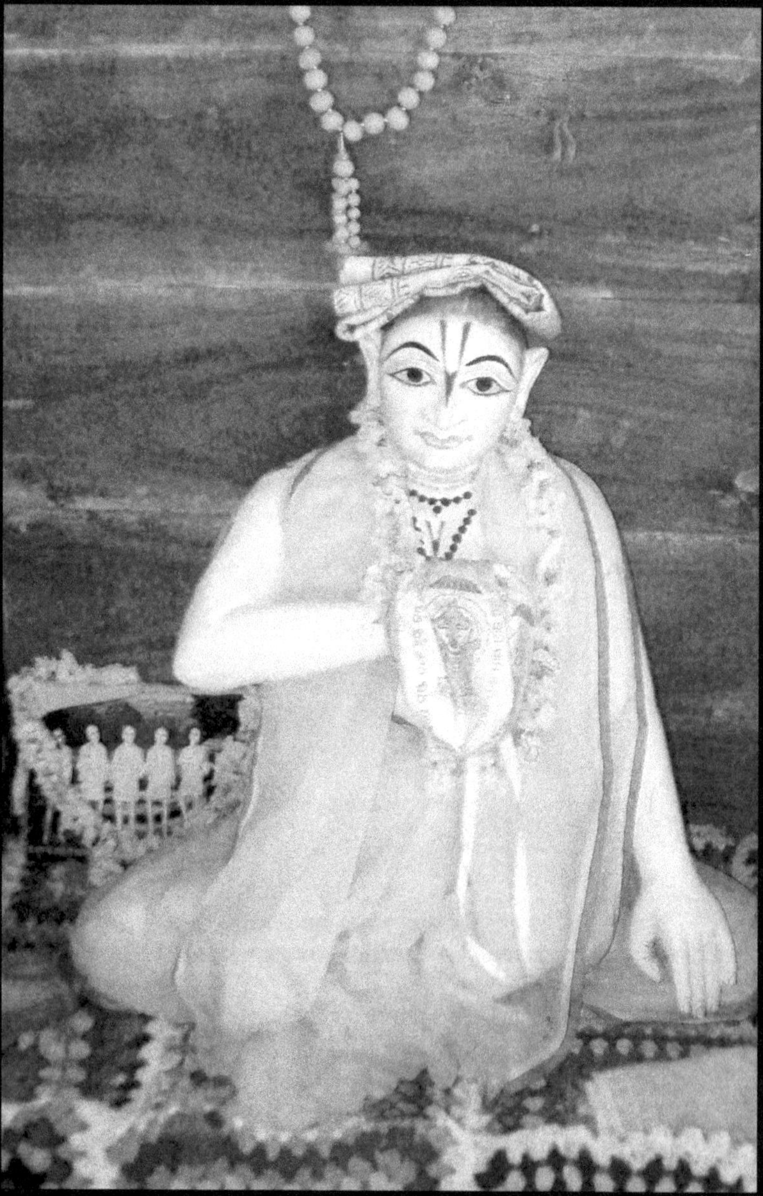

PLATE XVI

votion which leads to love of God). Advaita Ācārya asserted that *jñāna* was always superior.

Hearing this outrageous statement by Śrī Advaita Prabhu whom the Lord had always treated as His *guru* and elder, Śrī Caitanya Mahāprabhu dragged Him from His seat into the courtyard and began to profusely beat Him.[63] Advaita Ācārya's wife, Sītā devī, began to plead for her husband's life, as Nityānanda Prabhu smiled, and Haridāsa Ṭhākura chanted in fear.

Śrī Caitanya Mahāprabhu then angrily demanded to know if *jñāna* was superior, then why had Advaita Ācārya beseeched Him to descend to propagate *bhakti*. Śrī Caitanya Mahāprabhu began to loudly proclaim His own supremacy and glories. Advaita Ācārya was filled with ecstasy and danced in humility, feeling He had been properly chastised as a servant.

Then Advaita Ācārya frowned and with great emotion demanded:

"Where has Your glorification of Me gone now? Where has all Your deceitful behavior gone now? I am not Durvāsā Muni, whom You insulted by smearing his remnants all over Your body. I am not Bhṛgu Muni, whose foot-dust You happily accepted on Your chest as Śrīvatsa. My name is Advaita, and I am Your unalloyed servant. My only wish is to honor Your remnants birth after birth. By the influence of Your remnants I am unaffected by Your illusory energy. You have punished Me, now give Me the shelter of Your lotus feet."[64]

The Lord of Śāntipura then devotedly fell down and placed His head at Lord Caitanya's feet. At this point,

Śrī Caitanya Mahāprabhu picked up Advaita, embraced Him and cried profusely. Haridāsa Ṭhākura also fell to the ground and cried, along with Sītā devī and all the servants of Advaita Ācārya and Sītā devī. In this way Advaita Ācārya achieved His divine objective.

Kṛṣṇadāsa Kavirāja Gosvāmī summarily recounts this incident in his *Śrī Caitanya-caritāmṛta*, citing Advaita Ācārya's retelling of his chastisement to Kāmalākanta Viśvāsa who had been banished by Śrī Caitanya Mahāprabhu:

"Formerly, Lord Caitanya Mahāprabhu always respected Me as His senior, but I did not like such respect. Therefore, My mind being afflicted with unhappiness, I made a plan. Thus I expounded the *Yoga-vāśiṣṭha*, which considers liberation the ultimate goal of life. For this, the Lord became angry with Me and treated Me with apparent disrespect. When chastised by Lord Caitanya, I was very happy to receive a punishment similar to that awarded Śrī Mukunda[65]. A similar punishment was awarded to Mother Śacīdevī[66]. Who could be more fortunate than she to receive such punishment?"[67]

Drama

On another occasion, the Lord wished to enact a drama in which He would dance in the mood of Lakṣmī, the goddess of fortune. Costumes were arranged, and the Lord assigned parts: Gadādhara would play Rukmiṇī; Brahmānanda would be an elderly female companion named Suprabhā; Nityānanda would play Paurṇamāsī, Rādhārāṇī's grandmother who is also Yogamāyā, the arranging instrument of Rādhā and Kṛṣṇa's meetings; Haridāsa Ṭhākura would play a guard who would keep everyone alert; and Śrīvāsa would dress as Nārada.

Other roles were also assigned. However, the Lord declared that only those who had control of their senses would be allowed to watch. Advaita Ācārya and Śrīvāsa then excused themselves from participation, declaring that they did not have sufficient qualification, but Śrī Caitanya Mahāprabhu said, "Do not worry. Today you will all become great mystic *yogīs*. None of you will be bewildered while seeing Me dance."[68]

All of this took place in the house of Candraśekhara, and for him this was the summit of his good fortune. Advaita Ācārya inaugurated the proceedings by dancing and there was ecstatic *kīrtana*. Then Haridāsa Ṭhākura appeared first on the stage with a long handlebar moustache, dressed in a loincloth, and his head decorated with a turban. With a stick in his hand, he cautioned everyone:

"O brothers, get ready! The life and soul of the universe will now dance in the dress of Lakṣmī.

"As he ran about with a stick in his hand alerting everyone, the hairs of his body stood on end out of love for Kṛṣṇa. Haridāsa proudly[69] invited everyone, 'Worship Kṛṣṇa, serve Kṛṣṇa, chant Kṛṣṇa's names!'

"Everyone laughed as they watched Haridāsa. They inquired, 'Who are you, and why are you here?'

"Haridāsa replied, 'I am a watchman of Vaikuṇṭha. I always wander around awakening people to Kṛṣṇa consciousness. The Lord has left Vaikuṇṭha and come here. He will distribute pure love of God everywhere. Today He will per sonally dance in the dress of Lakṣmī. Therefore carefully plunder that ecstatic love today.'"[70]

After delivering the above lines, Haridāsa Ṭhākura began curling his moustache and running about with Murāri Gupta, the incarnation of Hanumān, in tremendous happiness and to the joy of all the Vaiṣṇavas.

Mahā-prakāśa Benediction

During the Lord's exhibition of 21 hours of ecstasy (*mahā-prakāśa*) at the house of Śrīvāsa Ṭhākura, He called for Haridāsa Ṭhākura and said:

"O Haridāsa, behold My form! You are dearer to Me than My own body. I certainly belong to the same caste as You[71]. Listen, Haridāsa. When the Yavanas beat you in the various villages, I saw your distress and descended from Vaikuṇṭha with the disc in My hand in order to cut everyone to pieces.

"Yet you desired the well-being of those who almost tortured you to death. You ignored how severely you were beaten and desired their well-being. When you desired their benefit, I was unable to use My power against them. My disc became powerless because of you. Due to your resolve, I could not sever their heads.

"When I saw how severely they were beating you, I covered your back. I then took the beating on My own body. Here are the marks. I am not speaking a lie. Besides the other indirect reasons that made Me appear, I came quickly because I could not tolerate your distress. My Nāḍā[72] [Advaita Ācārya] properly recognized you, for Advaita has completely bound Me with His love."[73]

From this statement of Lord Caitanya, we can get an even clearer picture how dear Haridāsa Ṭhākura was to Him. The activities of Haridāsa Ṭhākura and Advaita Ācārya expedited the Lord's descent. Lord Caitanya could not bear the suffering of those who loved Him so sincerely.

Upon hearing such compassionate statements from the Lord, Haridāsa Ṭhākura was overwhelmed and fell unconscious to the ground. Śrī Caitanya Mahāprabhu demanded, "Get up! Get up! My dear Haridāsa. See My manifestation to the satisfaction of your heart."[74]

Haridāsa Ṭhākura tried to see the form of the Lord, but was blinded by his tears. The Lord attempted to pacify him without much success, and Haridāsa Ṭhākura began to pray:

"My dear Viśvambhara, O Lord of the universe, please be merciful to this sinful person. I fall at Your feet. I have no good qualities. I am a fallen outcaste. How can I possibly describe Your glories? If one sees me, he becomes sinful. If one touches me, he should take bath.

"How then can I glorify Your topics? You have personally declared that You will never forsake anyone who remembers Your lotus feet, even if he is as insignificant as an insect. But you forsake the greatest kings if they do not remember Your lotus feet. These words do not apply to me, however, for I do not remember You. You protect even a fallen soul if he simply remembers You.

"Once, the sinful brothers Duryodhana and Duḥśāsana brought Draupadī to disrobe her in the royal assembly. Finding herself in that dangerous condition, she remembered You. By the influence of her remembrance, You entered into her cloth. As a result of her remembrance, the cloth became unlimited, yet those miscreants did not understand why.

"One time, when Parvatī was surrounded by witches, she remembered You as they were about to devour her. By the influence of her remembrance, You appeared to chastise those witches and deliver that great Vaiṣṇavī. But I am so sinful that I cannot remember You, therefore, My dear Lord, please give me shelter at Your lotus feet.

"Although the sinful Hiraṇyakaśipu tortured Prahlāda by giving him poison, throwing him to the snakes, throwing him into the fire, and throwing him bound to a rock into the water, Prahlāda simply remembered Your lotus feet and was delivered from all those calamities by the influence of that remembrance. Some lost their teeth and some lost their prowess when You manifested by the influence of his remembrance.

"In fear of Durvāsā, the sons of Pāṇḍu remembered You in the forest, and You appeared before them out of compassion. You then said, 'Do not worry, Yudhiṣṭhira, for I am here. I will give alms to the sages. You sit and watch.' In order to protect Your servants, You happily ate the last piece of vegetable from the pot. As a result, the sages' stomachs became filled as they took bath, so they immediately ran away out of fear.

"The sons of Pāṇḍu were thereby delivered by the influence of remembering You. All these wonderful incidents were the result of remembering You. The characteristic of these personalities was to constantly remember You. Therefore, it is not at all wonderful that they were delivered.

"The glories of Ajāmila's remembrance are unlimited, even though he did not engage in any religious duties. In fear of the Yamadūtas, he affectionately looked at the face of his son and remembered the form of Nārāyaṇa while calling out the name of his son. By that remembrance, all of his sinful reactions were vanquished. Therefore, remembrance of You is the wealth of Your devotees.

"I am fully devoid of the remembrance of Your lotus feet, yet nevertheless, O Lord, do not forsake me. What qualification do I have to see You? O Lord, I will ask You for only one thing, not more."[75]

After the extreme humility of these prayers[76], the Lord was more anxious than ever to please his sold-out servant, and He said:

"Speak, speak. Everything is yours. There is nothing that I will not give you."[77]

Folding his hands, Haridāsa Ṭhākura prayed:

"Although I am less fortunate, I have a great desire. May the remnants of the servants who worship Your lotus feet be my foodstuffs. Let this be my devotional service birth after birth. Let honoring these remnants be my only occupation and religious duty. My life is sinful because I am devoid of remembrance of You.

"Please make my life successful by allowing me to eat the remnants of Your servants. I think this an offense on my part, for I have no qualification to ask for such an exalted position. O my Lord, O master, O my dear Viśvambhara. I am like a dead person. Please forgive my offense. O son of Śaci, O dear Lord, please be merciful to me. Kindly keep me in the house of a devotee as a dog."[78]

Despite all his humble pleadings, Haridāsa Ṭhākura's desires were still not satisfied, because Śrī Caitanya Mahāprabhu began to glorify Haridāsa Ṭhākura to make certain that Haridāsa Ṭhākura's humble prayers would not be misunderstood by anyone before He fulfilled the innermost desire of Haridāsa Ṭhākura for eternal service.

"Listen, My dear Haridāsa. Anyone who resides with you for even a day or speaks with you for even a moment will certainly achieve Me. There is no doubt about it. One who respects you, respects Me, for I constantly reside within Your body. My glories are increased by a servant like you. You have eternally bound Me within your heart. You have not committed any offense to Me or to any Vaiṣṇava, therefore I am awarding you devotional service."[79]

What constitutes service is determined by the master, not the servant. True devotional service is not cheap. We may call our work "devotional service," and even though we may give much of ourselves to the Lord, it is up to Their Lordships to accept that service. The Masters are the ones Who decide what is service and what is something other than service.

All the devotees present expressed their joy at the benedictory words of the Lord and the good fortune of His surrendered servant. In Haridāsa's prayers he asks to always be allowed to eat the remnants of Vaisnavas, and in Jagannātha Purī the Lord used to bring him the remnants of Lord Jagannātha every day! No desire of such a pure soul ever remains unfulfilled. Whenever the Vaiṣṇavas in Purī took *prasādam*, Haridāsa Ṭhākura would also take the remnants which were delivered to him by Lord Caitanya's servant, Govinda. To emphasize the glories of Haridāsa Ṭhākura still further, Vṛndāvana dāsa Ṭhākura grants a series of benedictions to those who hear the prayers of Haridāsa Ṭhākura and the benedictions granted to him by Lord Caitanya.

"Anyone who hears the prayers of Haridāsa and the benediction he received will certainly obtain the treasure of *kṛṣṇa-prema*. This is not my statement, this is the verdict of all the scriptures. Simply by hearing topics about the devotees, one develops devotion for Kṛṣṇa. All glories to the great devotee, Haridāsa Ṭhākura! By remembering Haridāsa, all one's sinful reactions are vanquished."[80]

Civil Disobedience

Śrī Caitanya Mahāprabhu later enacted a civil disobedience pastime in which He chastised Chand Kazi (the *phaujadarā* or city magistrate of Nadia) for trying to stop the *saṅkīrtana* movement. The Lord had ordered all the citizens of Navadvīpa to perform *saṅkīrtana*, and it was going on with great force all over the city.

Because of the complaints of the Muslims and atheistic persons, Chand Kazi demanded that *saṅkīrtana* be stopped and even broke a *mṛdaṅga*. Lord Caitanya was very angry upon hearing this, and He ordered that a mass torchlight *saṅkīrtana* procession be taken to the home of the Kazi. In the lead party He very significantly placed the Nāmācārya Haridāsa Ṭhākura, who had been born in a Muslim family. Here again Mahāprabhu's placement of Haridāsa Ṭhākura in the lead party shows that the Lord was not simply absorbed in ecstasy and oblivious of His surroundings. He designed and orchestrated many aspects of His fledgling movement, as Śrīla Prabhupāda, following in his footsteps and in the footsteps of Śrīla Sarasvati Ṭhākura, did as well.

The Lord's *Sannyāsa*; Haridāsa's Plea

Towards the end of the Lord's Navadvīpa pastimes, Śrī Caitanya Mahāprabhu decided to take *sannyāsa* due to the disrespect and even threats of violence offered to Him by His own students. The threats offered by his students came about by an incident in which one of his students dared to criticize the Lord, not understanding the ecstatic mellows of devotional service. The incident is described in *Sri Caitanya-caritāmṛta*:

"One day the Lord, in the ecstasy of the *gopīs*, was sitting in His house. Very morose in separation, He was calling, 'Gopī! Gopī!' A student who came to see the Lord was astonished that the Lord was chanting 'Gopī! Gopī!' Thus he spoke as follows:

"'Why are You chanting the names '*gopī gopī*' instead of the holy name of Lord Kṛṣṇa, which is so glorious? What pious result will You achieve by such chanting?'"

"Hearing the foolish student, the Lord became greatly angry and rebuked Lord Kṛṣṇa[81] in various ways. Taking up a stick, He rose to strike the student. The student ran away in fear, and the Lord followed him. But somehow or other the devotees checked the Lord. The devotees pacified the Lord and brought Him home, and the student ran away to an assembly of other students.

"The *brāhmaṇa* student ran to a place where a thousand students were studying together. There he described the incident to them. Hearing of the incident, all the students became greatly angry and joined together in criticizing the Lord.

"'Nimāi Paṇḍita alone has spoiled the entire country,' they accused. 'He wants to strike a caste *brāhmaṇa*. He has no fear of religious principles. If He again performs such an atrocious act, certainly we shall retaliate and strike Him in turn. What kind of important person is He, that He can check us in this way?'

"When all the students thus resolved, to criticize Śrī Caitanya Mahāprabhu, their intelligence was spoiled. Thus although they were learned scholars, because of this offense the essence of knowledge was not manifested in them. But the proud student community did not become submissive. On the contrary, the students spoke of the incident anywhere and everywhere. In a laughing manner they criticized the Lord.

"Lord Śrī Caitanya Mahāprabhu, being omniscient, could understand the degradation of these students. Thus He sat at home, contemplating how to rescue them.

"'All the so-called professors and scientists and their students generally follow the regulative principles of religion, fruitive activities and austerities,' the Lord thought, 'yet at the same time they are blasphemers and rogues. If I do not induce them to take to devotional service, because of committing the offense of blasphemy none of these people will be able to take to it. I have come to deliver all the fallen souls, but now just the opposite has happened. How can these rogues be delivered? How may they be benefited?'

"'If these rogues offer Me obeisances, the reactions of their sinful activities will be nullified. Then, if I induce them, they will take to devotional service. I must certainly deliver all these fallen souls who blaspheme Me and do not offer Me obeisances. I shall accept the *sannyāsa* order of life, for thus people will offer Me their obeisances, thinking of Me as a member of the renounced order. Offering obeisances will relieve them of all the reactions to their offenses. Then, by My grace, devotional service [*bhakti*] will awaken in their pure hearts. All the unfaithful rogues of this world can be delivered by this process. There is no alternative. This is the essence of the argument.'"[82]

As a householder, even though so exalted, He was not taken as seriously as was required for the propagation of the *saṅkīrtana* movement. The Lord revealed His plan to Nityānanda Prabhu, saying:

"As soon as they decided to beat Me, they were immediately entangled in unlimited bondage. I incarnated to deliver the people of the world, but it appears that I am destroying them. Soon You will see Me shave My head and give up My *brāhmaṇa* thread.[83] I will wander about begging as a *sannyāsī*. I will soon become a beggar at the door of those who have decided to beat Me. Then they will fall at My feet when they see Me, and in this way I will deliver the entire world. Everyone offers obeisances to a *sannyāsī*; no one dares to beat one.

"As a *sannyāsī*, I will soon wander from door to door begging. Let Me see then who beats Me. I have thus revealed My heart to You. I will certainly give up household life. Do not feel distressed because of this. Give Me Your permission to take *sannyāsa*. I will do whatever You want, but You know the purpose of My incarnation. If You want the world delivered, I hope You will not forbid Me from taking *sannyāsa*. Do not feel unhappy for even a moment, for You know the purpose of My incarnation."[84]

Vṛndāvana dāsa Ṭhākura very elaborately describes the pathetic scenes of unhappiness felt by the Lord's associates when the Lord accepted *sannyāsa* from Keśava Bhāratī Mahārāja at the end of the month of January, 1510 A.D. (1432 śakābda). According to *Gaura-gaṇoddeśa-dīpikā*, Keśava Bhāratī Mahārāja was either an incarnation of Sāndīpani Muni or Akrūra. Opinions on Keśava Bhāratī Mahārāja's identity vary according to the author, Kavi-karṇapūra. Following His *sannyāsa*, the Lord wished to proceed to Vṛndāvana, but somehow was diverted by Nityānanda Prabhu to the bank of the Ganges. There the Lord offered many prayers for the Yamunā, thinking He had arrived in Vṛndāvana.

Advaita Ācārya then appeared in a boat and a change of clothing for the Lord. Śrī Caitanya Mahāprabhu then thought He had been duped by Nityānanda Prabhu into thinking He was bathing in the Yamunā, but Advaita Ācārya explained that the Gaṅgā and Yamunā were both present at that spot and that wherever the Lord was present was Vṛndāvana, and then invited the Lord to His home.

Lord Caitanya spent some time feasting, chanting, and dancing at the home of Advaita Ācārya in Śāntipura just to assuage the grief of His mother and all of His devotees. The period was repeatedly extended by the pleas of the devotees, but after some time the Lord became firm in His determination to go. Mother Śacī requested that He make His camp in Jagannātha Purī, and the Lord happily agreed. He then requested all of His followers to go back to their homes and chant the holy names, worship Kṛṣṇa, and discuss Kṛṣṇa's pastimes.

At this time Haridāsa Ṭhākura began to cry, feeling lost.

"You are going to Jagannātha Purī, and that is all right, but what will be my destination? I am not able to go to Jagannātha Purī. Because I am the lowest among men, I shall not be able to see You. How shall I maintain my sinful life?"[85]

Śrīla Prabhupāda explains:

> "Although Śrīla Haridāsa Ṭhākura was born in a Mohammedan family, he was accepted as a properly initiated *brāhmaṇa*. As such, he had every right to enter the temple of Jagannātha Purī, but because there were some rules and regulations stipulating that only *brāhmaṇas, kṣatriyas, vaiśyas* and *śūdras* (members of the *varnasrama-dharma* system) could enter, Haridāsa Ṭhākura, out of his deep humility, did not want to violate these existing rules. He therefore said that he did not have the strength to enter into the temple, and he pointed out that if Lord Śrī Caitanya Mahāprabhu lived within the temple, there would be no way for Haridāsa Ṭhākura to see Him."[86]

The Lord replied to Haridāsa Ṭhākura: "Please check your humility. Just by seeing your humility, My mind becomes very much agitated."[87]

Śrī Caitanya Mahāprabhu assured Haridāsa Ṭhākura that He would place a petition before Lord Jagannātha and that He would take Haridāsa Ṭhākura to Jagannātha Purī. In the next chapter, we will see how Śrī Caitanya Mahāprabhu fulfilled all of Haridāsa Ṭhākura's desires.

Endnotes

1 *CC Ādi* 13.99.

2 Śrīla Prabhupāda also describes the different planes of perception in a *Bhagavad-gītā* lecture given in London on August 8, 1973 (730808LON.BG): "In the gross bodily platform we demand *pratyakṣa-jñānam. Pratyakṣa* means direct perception. There are different stages of knowledge. *Pratyakṣa, aparokṣa... pratyakṣa, parokṣa, aparokṣa, adhokṣaja, aprakṛta.* These are different stages of knowledge. So knowledge acquired in the

bodily platform, direct perception, is not real knowledge. Therefore, we can challenge these scientists, so-called scientists. Their basic principle of knowledge is on the bodily concept of life, *pratyakṣa*, experimental knowledge. Experimental knowledge means this gross sense perception. That is experimental. *Pratyakṣa*. Everyone says: 'We do not see God.' God is not such a subject matter that you can see with this *pratyakṣa*, direct perception. God's another name is Anubhāva. Anubhāva. Just like in this room we do not see the sun directly. But we know that there is sun. It is daytime. How do you know it? You do not see. But there are other processes by which you can experience. That is called *aparokṣa*. *Pratyakṣa parokṣa aparokṣa*. In this way, Kṛṣṇa consciousness means *adhokṣaja* and *aprakṛta*, beyond the senses. Therefore, in the *Bhagavad-gītā* it is said: *adhokṣaja*. Where direct perception cannot reach. So where direct perception cannot reach, then how you can perceive *anubhāva*? That is *śrota-panthā*. That is *śruti*. You have to take knowledge from the *Vedas*. And the Vedic knowledge is explained by *guru*. Therefore one has to take shelter of Kṛṣṇa as the Supreme *guru*, or His representative. Then all these troubles, means ignorance, can be dissipated. *Yac chokam ucchoṣaṇam indriyāṇām* [Bg. 2.8]."

"So that is explained here: *sa vai puṁsāṁ paro dharma yato bhaktir adhokṣaje* [SB 1.2.6]. *Adhokṣaje*. Beyond the sense perception. We have got different stages of knowledge: direct perception... *Pratyakṣa, parokṣa, aparokṣa, adhokṣaja, aprakṛta*—these are five stages of knowledge. Direct perception, knowledge received from others, then realization, then *anubhūti*, understanding what is the position of God and His situation. That is called *aprakṛta*. *Aprakṛta* means not within this material world but above that. Śaṅkarācārya, he has described, *nārāyaṇaḥ paraḥ avyaktāt*..." SB 1.2.6 Mauritius, October 5, 1975 (751005SB.MAU)

"There are different stages of knowledge: *pratyakṣa, parokṣa, aparokṣa, adhokṣaja, aprākṛta*. One has to go step by step. General knowledge means *pratyakṣa*, whatever you perceive by the senses. That is called *pratyakṣa*. And the knowledge which you receive from authorities, that is *parokṣa*. Then *aparokṣa*, realization. Then *adhokṣaja*. *Adhokṣaja* means knowledge which is beyond your perception. But there is source of knowledge, *adhokṣaja*. Therefore God's another name is Adhokṣaja... So any knowledge within the alphabets, ABCD, that is called *akṣaja*. And the knowledge which is beyond that, that is called *adhokṣaja*. And be yond the *adhokṣaja* knowledge there is *aprākṛta*. *Aprākṛta* knowledge." Śrīla Prabhupāda lecture, SB 3.26.21 Bombay (741213BOM.SB)

[3] *CB Ādi* 17.10.
[4] *CB Adi* 17.10 purport.
[5] SP Room conversation with Allen Ginsberg, May 13, 1969, Columbus, Ohio 690513RC.COL.
[6] SP lecture, December 26, 1972, Bombay, India, lecture on *Nectar of Devotion* (721226ND.BOM.) **Prabhupāda**: So here the point is that Sanātana Gosvāmī, Dabira Khāsa, he was so *mad* after meeting Caitanya Mahāprabhu that whatever money he had with the banker, the village banker, and even though it was sinful to bribe, he didn't care for it. He wanted...He resigned his service as a minister. Therefore, he was imprisoned. Now to get out of the prison house, he bribed [the jailer]. He was so much ecstatic. There is a verse about this *laulyam*:

kṛṣṇa-bhakti-rasa-bhāvitā matiḥ
krīyatāṁ yadi kuto 'pi labhyate
tatra laulyam api mūlyam ekalaṁ
janma-koṭi-sukṛtair na labhyate

"Pure devotional service in Kṛṣṇa consciousness cannot be had even by pious activity in hundreds and thousands of lives. It can be attained only by paying one price—that is, intense greed to obtain it. If it is available somewhere, one must purchase it without delay." (*Padyāvalī* by Śrīla Rūpa Gosvāmī, text 14, cited in *CC Madhya* 8.70)
"This is called *laulyam. Laulyam* means that we become very much greedy in achieving some success or receiving something sometimes. We become *mad.* That is required. *Laulyam eka mūlyam.* To achieve Kṛṣṇa consciousness perfectly, this ecstatic eagerness or greediness, to serve Kṛṣṇa, that is the only price to achieve success in devotional service. That is the only price. Not money, not anything. Not prestige, not good parentage, not beauty—nothing. Simply this ecstatic, intense desire, 'How I shall get Kṛṣṇa?' Then you'll get Kṛṣṇa. He'll take you. That is the example of the *gopīs*, intense desire. *Tatra laulyam eka mūlyam.* Now, *janma-koṭi, na labhyate janma-koṭibhiḥ sukṛtinaḥ.* This ecstatic desire, that 'I, in this life, I shall get recognition by Kṛṣṇa, that I have sacrificed everything for Kṛṣṇa,' this is required."
[7] *CC Adi* 4.136.
[8] *Śrī Caitanya-maṅgala, Madhya-khaṇḍa*, ch.5, texts 59—65, from the chapter concerning pastimes with Nityananda and Advaita.
[9] *CB Madhya* 8.111—116.
[10] *Śrī Caitanya-maṅgala, Madhya-khaṇḍa*, ch. 6, texts 26—33, from the

chapter concerning the deliverance of Jagāi and Mādhāi.

[11] This is an indication that the Lord's followers may have an intense interest or attachment to the results of their service to Kṛṣṇa. Such attachment stems from the joy of pleasing Kṛṣṇa. The servant knows how to make arrangements which are very pleasing to the master, and when the master is pleased, the servant also feels pleasure. Śrī Caitanya Mahāprabhu, in the mood of a devotee, was engaging Haridāsa Ṭhākura and Nityananda Prabhu in service, and as such He relished the daily report of the results of the preaching of Haridāsa Ṭhākura and Nityānanda Prabhu. Similarly, Śrīla Prabhupāda wanted to know the results of book distribution. There are a number of quantitative goals in Kṛṣṇa consciousness like the chanting of 16 rounds. (Of course chanting of rounds should include both quality *and* quantity; however, quantity cannot be ignored.) The Gosvāmīs themselves set the example of quantitative goals: *saṅkhyā-pūrvaka-nāma-gāna-natibhiḥ*—"chanting the holy names and bowing down in a scheduled measurement." In addition, many devotees recite the ten offenses to the holy name (quantitative) before chanting in order to remind themselves to be attentive to the quality of their chanting (qualitative). Judging from the lives of the *ācāryas*, it seems that sincere devotees try not to neglect either quality or quantity in regard to *bhakti*.

[12] *CB Madhya* 13.8—11. This statement of the Lord exhibits His readiness to protect His devotees. Just as Kṛṣṇa, during the battle of Kurukṣetra, was prepared to break His promise not to fight to protect Arjuna and the Pāṇḍavas, similarly, Śrī Caitanya Mahāprabhu was prepared to protect His preachers with violence even though His mission was to deliver with the Holy Name and not His *cakra*.

[13] *CB Madhya* 13.8 purport.

[14] *CB Madhya* 13.9 purport.

[15] *CB Madhya* 13.9 purport.

[16] *Shri Chaitanya's Teachings, L'Envoi*, Śrīla Bhaktisiddhānta Sarasvatī Ṭhākura, Sree Gaudiya Math, 1975, p. 383.

[17] *CB Madhya* 13.17

[18] *CB Madhya* 13.20.

[19] *Shri Chaitanya's Teachings, L'Envoi*, Śrīla Bhaktisiddhānta Sarasvatī Ṭhākura, Sree Gaudiya Math, 1975, p. 383.

[20] *CB Madhya* 13.23—26.

[21] *CB Madhya* 13.26 purport.

[22] *CB Madhya* 13.27, 28.

[23] *CB Madhya* 13.54

[24] Nityānanda Prabhu was an extraordinary preacher. While Śrī Caitanya Mahāprabhu was in Purī, He sent Nityānanda Prabhu to Bengal in order to increase the preaching. This was a brilliant strategy, since Nityānanda Prabhu's humility and tolerance were so developed that He melted the hearts of everyone He met. Sometimes it is thought that Śrī Caitanya Mahāprabhu was oblivious to the practical affairs of the world. The fact is, however, that the strategy of sending Nityānanda Avadhūta to Bengal resulted in the conversion of many people from all classes and statuses of life. In Śrīla Prabhupāda's preaching we see the parallel to this, as he cultivated Vaiṣṇavas from all classes—laborers, business people, administrators, and intellectuals. His followers continue to follow his example, although some of them specialize with certain segments of society. The point is that Nityānanda Prabhu saw potential in places where other devotees might not see it. That is the example also that Śrīla Prabhupāda set, and he did not limit himself to "the most fallen" or degraded persons, but recruited many ladies and gentlemen as well.

[25] *CB Madhya* 13.56—61.

[26] *CB Madhya* 13.65—68.

[27] *CB Madhya* 13.72 and purport.

[28] *CB Madhya* 13.74—76.

[29] *CB Madhya* 13.76 purport: "If by the will of the Lord the audience does not listen to their humble presentation, and thus invites inauspiciousness on themselves, then Mahaprabhu, the order-giver, takes part in the result."

[30] Letter to Tamal Krishna, 73-08-23.

[31] *CB Madhya* 13.83, 84

[32] *CB Madhya* 13.84 purport.

[33] *CB Madhya* 13.101, 102.

[34] *CB Madhya* 13.106, 107.

[35] *CB Madhya* 13.118, 119.

[36] *CB Madhya* 13.126.

[37] *CB Madhya* 13.127—131.

[38] *CB Madhya* 13.132, 133.

[39] *CB Madhya* 13.136—148.

[40] It is especially interesting that Vṛndāvana dāsa Ṭhākura, a disciple of Lord Nityānanda, has included this comment. Some scholars claim that a rivalry existed between Nityānanda and Śrī Advaita Ācārya. However, it is clear that the apparent tension was transcendental. Why would a disciple repeat a pejorative statement against his guru? These are jokes between preachers—not only preachers, but expansions of the Lord who

were playing parts as preachers. In fact, Vṛndāvana dāsa Ṭhākura has explained that anyone who misunderstands the transcendental loving exchanges between Advaita Ācārya and Nityānanda Prabhu, accepting one and not the other is doomed. In *CB Madhya-khaṇḍa* 13.358—360, the author of *Śrī Caitanya-bhāgavata* states: "Without understanding the purport of such loving quarrels if someone, considering Them different from each other, criticizes one and glorifies the other, he will be burned to death. Only one who is favored by Nityānanda and Gauracandra can understand the words of the Vaiṣṇavas. After Nityānanda and Advaita engaged in ecstatic pastimes for some time, They embraced each other."

[41] *CB Madhya* 13.149, 150.

[42] *CB Madhya* 13.149, 150 purport.

[43] *CB Madhya* 13.151, 152.

[44] *CB Madhya* 13.154, 155.

[45] This is a sublime name. It means one who has no worldly sense or obligation. One might say that Nityānanda Prabhu introduced Himself to Jagāi and Mādhāi by indicating, "Brothers, I am also unconcerned with social convention." When Gauḍīya devotees recite the Maṅgalācaraṇa, they glorify all the associates of Mahāprabhu and say "*sa-avadhūta*," meaning "along with Avadhūta (Nityānanda Prabhu)."

[46] *CB Madhya* 13.175.

[47] *CB Madhya* 13.181, 182.

[48] *CB Madhya* 13.183—189.

[49] *CB Madhya* 13.190—192.

[50] *CB Madhya* 13.205—209.

[51] *CB Madhya* 13.205—209 purport.

[52] *CB Madhya* 13.213.

[53] *CB Madhya* 13.219, 220.

[54] *CB Madhya* 13.221.

[55] *CB Madhya* 13.225

[56] *CB Madhya* 13.234. When Nityānanda Prabhu first thought of delivering Jagāi and Madhāi, He wished that the sight of the brothers would be as purifying as the Ganges, rather than their contact provoking others to bathe in the Ganges. Lord Caitanya thus fulfilled the desire of Lord Nityānanda.

[57] *CB Madhya* 13.290—292.

[58] *CB Madhya* 17.14.

[59] *CB Madhya* 17.20.

[60] *CB Madhya* 17.36—44.

[61] *CB Madhya* 17.100.

[62] *CC Ādi* 17.298, 299.

[63] The beating of Advaita Ācārya by Lord Caitanya is an exhibition of intimacy between master and servant on the spiritual platform. According to mundane vision, such an act would constitute criminal assault: a young man beating an older gentleman—it would appear to be strange at best, and brutal and inexcusable at worst. However, the entire pastime is simply a loving exchange between the Lord and Advaita, who always hankered to be treated as a servant, and was prepared to provoke the Lord in any number of ways in order to be treated as such, even to the extent of being physically chastised. No one was hurt, and both experienced ecstatic spiritual happiness—Advaita Prabhu considered it His good fortune to be treated in this way by the Lord.

[64] *CB Madhya* 19.157—160.

[65] Mukunda, the great devotional singer and eternal associate of Śrī Caitanya Mahāprabhu, was punished by Śrī Caitanya Mahāprabhu by being rejected from His association. Śrī Caitanya Mahāprabhu declared that because Mukunda associated with Māyāvādīs and at times extolled the glories of *Yoga-vāśiṣṭha* in the company of Śrī Advaita Prabhu, he would only get His association again after millions of births. When Mukunda heard that he would get the Lord's association after millions of births, he began to dance in jubilation, feeling ecstatic that some day he would again have the Lord's association. Upon seeing the dancing and jubilation of Mukunda, the Lord immediately forgave him and gave him the benediction that in each of His incarnations Mukunda would be the Lord's singer.

[66] Śrī Caitanya Mahāprabhu declared that His mother Śacīdevī was not a fit candidate for His mercy during His exhibition of the *mahā-prakāśa*, because of her committing offenses to Śrī Advaita Ācārya. Mother Śacī had lost her eldest son, Viśvarūpa, to *sannyāsa* due to the preaching of Advaita Ācārya, and it appeared she would soon lose the other (Śrī Caitanya Mahāprabhu) for the same reason, so she made some critical remarks about Advaita Ācārya. On account of these remarks, Lord Caitanya explained that she could never achieve love of God as long as she was an offender, and that He was unable to rectify matters. Only by Śrī Advaita Ācārya's mercy could she be forgiven. By the Lord's arrangement Advaita Ācārya arrived on the scene in an ecstatic state, and Mother Saci took the dust from his feet, accepting that she had committed an offense. This pastime was a demonstration by the Lord about the seriousness of *vaiṣṇava-aparādha*, and how a devotee debilitated by offenses one cannot achieve the goal of human life, love of God.

Chapter Six : The Lord's Saṅkīrtana

[67] *CC Ādi* 12.39—42.
[68] *CB Madhya* 18.26.
[69] One should not be proud in relationship to the body, but one can be proud of one's service to the Lord.
[70] *CB Madhya* 18.41—47.
[71] In the *CC Antya* 4.192, 193, it is stated: "At the time of initiation, when a devotee fully surrenders unto the service of the Lord, Kṛṣṇa accepts him to be as good as Himself. When the devotee's body is thus transformed into spiritual existence, the devotee, in that transcendental body, renders service to the lotus feet of the Lord."

In the *Sārārtha-darśinī* commentary of *SB* 5.12.11, it is stated: "Just as a piece of iron becomes gold by contact with a touchstone, the material body and senses of a person become spiritual in the association of devotional service...In order to exhibit the glories of devotional service, the Supreme Lord, by His inconceivable potencies, mysteriously manifests the transcendental body, senses, and mind of a devotee and mysteriously destroys his false body and senses. The purport of saying 'mysteriously' is that people who are blind to the truth identify a Vaiṣṇava with his previous material designations without realizing his actual identity and consider his body as a mortal bag of bones and flesh and thus commit offenses at his feet."

Śrīla Bhaktisiddhānta Sarasvatī Ṭhākura explains in the purport of *CB Madhya* 10.36 that the *sac-cid-ānanda* body of a devotee is "spontaneously manifest" which is appropriate for the Lord's service. He goes on to say: "Those who consider the appearance and disappearance of the devotees and the Supreme Lord to be like the birth and death of conditioned souls, who are forced to accept the fruits of their *karma*, repeatedly suffer material miseries rather than obtain liberation." Therefore, the caste of the Lord and Haridāsa is the same: both are *sac-cid-ānanda* inhabitants of the spiritual world, where everyone and everything are pure, full of knowledge, eternal, and full of bliss.
[72] Śrī Caitanya Mahāprabhu's referral to Advaita Ācārya as Nāḍā is discussed by Śrīla Bhaktisiddhānta Sarasvatī Ṭhākura in a purport to *CB Madhya* 2.264. Śrī Caitanya Mahāprabhu, in the ecstasy of the *mahā-prakāśa*, addresses Haridāsa Ṭhākura: "By your loud chanting and Nāḍā's roaring I left Vaikuṇṭha and came here with My associates." (*CB Madhya* 2.264). In the purport Śrīla Sarasvatī Ṭhākura states: "The editor of *Śrī Sajjana-toṣaṇī*, Śrīmad Bhaktivinoda Ṭhākura, has written in Volume 7, Part 11, as follows:

'Sriman Mahaprabhu often addressed Śrīla Advaita Ācārya as Nāḍā. I have heard a number of meanings of the word *nāḍā*. Some Vaiṣṇava scholar has said that the word *nārā* refers to Mahā-Viṣṇu because *nārā*, the total aggregate of all living entities, is situated within Him. Is the word *nāḍā* a corruption of the word *nārā*? The people of Rāḍha-deśa often use *ḍa* in place of *ra*. Is this the reason that the word *nārā* has been written as *nāḍā*?'"

In *CB Madhya* 5.50—55, Vṛndāvana dāsa Ṭhākura reports this exchange: "O Lord, who is this Nāḍā You are calling?" The Lord replied, "He by whose loud cries I came. This incarnation of Mine was induced by Nāḍā, whom you all call Advaita Ācārya. Nāḍā has brought Me from Vaikuntha, but now He is living free from all cares with Haridāsa. I have descended to inaugurate the *saṅkīrtana* movement, by which I will preach the chanting of the holy names in each and every house. I will not award love of God to those fallen souls who have offended My devotees because they are proud of their education, wealth, high birth, knowledge, and austerities. Otherwise, I will give everyone that which persons like Lord Brahmā enjoy."

[73] *CB Madhya* 10.35—46.

[74] *CB Madhya* 10.52—55.

[75] *CB Madhya* 10.58—83.

[76] These prayers contain many themes from the *Bhāgavata Purāṇa* and *Mahābhārata* which are significant to devotees today. One reason that Śrī Caitanya Mahāprabhu appeared (incarnated) was to establish the *Bhāgavata* culture. Vaiṣṇavas try to become absorbed in the various *līlās* of the Lord mentioned throughout the *Śrīmad-Bhāgavatam* and relate incidents in their everyday life to incidents contained in the spotless *Purāṇa*. Śrīla Prabhupāda would attend to managerial matters with his leaders during the day, and while discussing a particular problem he would often put the problem, or something related to the problem, in the context of the *Bhāgavatam* verse on which he had lectured that morning. Another reason these prayers are relevant is that they provide a model for devotees of Lord Caitanya. In his prayers, Haridāsa Ṭhākura does not ask for anything material for himself, and he does not make himself or his life the center of the prayers. Rather he makes the Lord the center of his prayers.

[77] *CB Madhya* 10.84.

[78] *CB Madhya* 10.85—91.

[79] *CB Madhya* 10.93—97.

Chapter Six : The Lord's Saṅkīrtana

[80] *CB Madhya* 10.103—105.

[81] Śrī Caitanya Mahāprabhu rebuked Kṛṣṇa as He was absorbed in the mood of the *gopīs*.

[82] *CC Adi* 17.247—267.

[83] The most prestigious and recognized form of *sannyāsa* during the time of Lord Caitanya's appearance was in the line of the Śaṅkarācārya. In that tradition, at the time of *sannyāsa*, a *brāhmaṇa* would give up the sacred thread.

[84] *CB Madhya* 26.130—141.

[85] *CC Madhya* 3.194, 195.

[86] *CC Madhya* 3.194 purport.

[87] *CC Madhya* 3.196.

tuṇḍe tāṇḍavinī ratiṁ vitanute tuṇḍāvalī-labdhaye
karṇa-kroḍa-kaḍambinī ghaṭayate /
karṇārbudebhyaḥ spṛhām
cetaḥ-prāṅgaṇa-saṅginī vijayate /
sarvendriyāṇāṁ kṛtiṁ
no jāne janitā kiyadbhir amṛtaiḥ kṛṣṇeti varṇa-dvayī

I DO NOT KNOW HOW MUCH NECTAR THE two syllables 'Kṛṣ-ṇa' have produced. When the holy name of Kṛṣṇa is chanted, it appears to dance within the mouth. We then desire many, many mouths. When that name enters the holes of the ears, we desire many millions of ears. And when the holy name dances in the courtyard of the heart, it conquers the activities of the mind, and therefore all the senses become inert."

Vidagdha-mādhava 1.15
by Rūpa Gosvāmī
[cited: *Śrī Caitanya-caritāmṛta Antya-līlā* 1.99]

tāra madhye sarva-śreṣṭha nāma-saṅkīrtana
niraparādhe nāma laile pāya prema-dhana

OF THE NINE PROCESSES OF DEVOTIONAL service, the most important is to always chant the holy name of the Lord. If one does so, avoiding the ten kinds of offenses, one very easily obtains the most valuable love of Godhead."

Śrī Caitanya-caritāmṛta Antya-līlā 4.71
[Lord Caitanya to Sanātana Gosvāmī]

I CANNOT GO NEAR THE TEMPLE BECAUSE I am a low-caste abominable person. I have no authority to go there. If I could just get to a solitary place near the temple, I could stay there alone and pass my time. I do not wish the servants of Lord Jagannātha to touch me. I would remain there in the garden alone. That is my desire."

Śrī Caitanya-caritāmṛta Madhya-līlā 11.165–167

Chapter Seven

Jagannātha Purī

Arrival

HAVING ACCEPTED THE RENOUNCED ORDER of life at the age of 24 in 1510 A.D., Lord Caitanya went to Jagannātha Purī in the month of Phālguna (February-March). There in Purī He observed the Dola-yātrā festival, and He shortly thereafter liberated the great scholar Sārvabhauma Bhaṭṭācārya who became a celebrated Vaiṣṇava and intimate associate of Śrī Caitanya Mahāprabhu. After this, He began an extensive tour of all the important holy places in South India which lasted for two years. He traveled from village to village liberating all the inhabitants by engaging them in *nāma-saṅkīrtana*. Many amazing events took place on this tour, including His momentous meeting with

His eternal associate, Rāmānanda Rāya, and, after visiting all the major *tīrthas*, He finally decided to return to Jagannātha Purī. This was Śrī Caitanya Mahāprabhu's pattern: "The Lord traveled all over India for six years. He was sometimes here and sometimes there, performing His transcendental pastimes, and sometimes He remained at Jagannātha Purī."[1]

The inhabitants of Navadvīpa-Māyāpura were experiencing intense separation from the Lord, and when they heard that the Lord was returning to Jagannātha Purī, they set out to meet the Lord, headed by Advaita Ācārya, Haridāsa Ṭhākura, and many other devotees. In fact, upon hearing the news of Śrī Caitanya Mahāprabhu's return, devotees began to come from many different areas, as rivers come from many places to finally flow into the sea. Devotees like Paramānanda Purī, Brahmānanda Bhāratī, Svarūpa Dāmodara (who had previously been known as Puruṣottama Bhaṭṭācārya), Īśvara Purī's servant (Govinda) who had come to serve Śrī Caitanya Mahāprabhu, and Kāśīśvara Gosvāmī, along with many others, were attracted by the promise of the Lord's imminent return to Nīlācala.

King Pratāparudra agreed to provide residences and *prasāda* for all of the Vaiṣṇavas who were traveling so far to be with the Lord. The Lord had been staying in Ālālanātha due to His feelings of separation from Lord Jagannātha during Anavasara, the period in which Lord Jagannātha remains indisposed after the bathing ceremony (*snāna-yātrā*).

Hearing that the Vaiṣṇavas from Bengal were coming to Jagannātha Purī, Lord Caitanya returned in great anticipation. Almost two hundred devotees had arrived from Bengal and were staying by the bank of Lake Narendra. Initially all of the devotees were presented with garlands and the *prasāda* of Lord Jagannātha by Svarūpa Dāmodara and Govinda. Then all the Vaiṣṇavas began to run toward the residence of Śrī Caitanya Mahāprabhu. King Pratāparudra observed the meeting of the Lord and His followers from the top of his palace in the company of Sārvabhauma Bhāṭṭācārya and Gopīnātha Ācārya, and each devotee in that great assembly was described and identified for the king. In the description given by Gopīnātha Ācārya to the king, Haridāsa Ṭhākura was described as "...the deliverer of the whole universe."[2]

When the devotees proceeded toward the house of Kāśī Miśra, Śrī Caitanya Mahāprabhu, along with His associates, met all of the Vaiṣṇavas on the road with great jubilation. All of the devotees crowded into the house of Śrī Caitanya Mahāprabhu, but there was insufficient room. After many affectionate exchanges with devotees like Advaita Ācārya, Śrīvāsa Ṭhākura (and his brothers), Murāri Gupta, Vāsudeva Datta, Dāmodara Paṇḍita, Śivānanda Sena, and others, the Lord asked, "Where is Haridāsa?"[3] He then saw that Haridāsa Ṭhākura was lying flat on the road at a distance offering obeisances without making any attempt to come closer. Many devotees immediately went to Haridāsa and told him that the Lord wanted to meet him and to come immediately.

Out of Vaiṣṇava humility Haridāsa Ṭhākura replied, "I cannot go near the temple because I am a low-caste abominable person. I have no authority to go there. If I could just get to a solitary place near the temple, I could stay there alone and pass my time. I do not wish the servants of Lord Jagannātha to touch me. I would remain there in the garden alone. That is my desire."[4]

After making arrangements for the lodging, bathing and feeding of all of the devotees, the Lord went to meet Haridāsa Ṭhākura, and saw him engaged in chanting the *mahā-mantra* in ecstasy. As soon as the Ṭhākura saw Śrī Caitanya Mahāprabhu, he fell down like a stick. The Lord raised him up and embraced him, and both began to cry out of transcendental happiness. Both were transformed by their love for each other, both servant and master.

A Solitary Place

Haridāsa Ṭhākura said, "My dear Lord, please do not touch me, for I am most fallen and untouchable and am lowest among men."

Śrī Caitanya Mahāprabhu replied, "I wish to touch you just to be purified, for your purified activities do not exist in Me."[5]

Śrīla Prabhupāda explains in the purport to the Lord's statement above:

> "The servant thinks that he is most impure and that the master should not touch him, and the master thinks that because He has become impure by associating with so many impure living entities, He should touch a pure devotee like Haridāsa Ṭhākura just to purify Himself. Actually both the servant and the master are already purified because neither of them is in touch with the impurities of material existence. They are already equal in quality because both of them are the purest. There is a difference in quantity, however, because the master is unlimited and the servant is limited. Consequently, the servant always remains subordinate to the master, and this relationship is eternal and undisturbed. As soon as the servant feels like becoming the master, he falls into *māyā*. Thus, it is by misuse of free will that one falls under the influence of *māyā*."[6]

The Lord glorified Haridāsa Ṭhākura, saying that he was better than any *brāhmaṇa* or *sannyāsī*, and then He took him within the secluded flower garden called Siddha-bakula[7] near

His own residence at the house of Kāśī Miśra and requested him: "Remain here and chant the Hare Kṛṣṇa *mahā-mantra.* I shall personally come here to meet you daily. Remain here peacefully and look at the *cakra* on the top of the temple and offer obeisances. As far as your *prasāda* is concerned, I shall arrange to have that sent here."[8]

Śrīla Prabhupāda points out in the purport to the above verses that although Haridāsa Ṭhākura was born in a Mohammedan family, Śrī Caitanya Mahāprabhu could have personally brought him before Lord Jagannātha. However, neither the Lord nor Haridāsa Ṭhākura wanted to disturb the local custom. Therefore, by requesting Haridāsa Ṭhākura to meditate on the *cakra* of the Jagannātha temple, the Lord indicated that this was equal to seeing the Deity within. By promising to see him daily, He indicated that although, by custom, he was not considered qualified to enter the temple, Haridāsa Ṭhākura was so elevated that the Lord would come personally to see him and arrange for his *prasādam.* Śrīla Prabhupāda also discusses the practice of chanting the holy name in seclusion. He points out that such a practice should only be initiated after receiving the direct order of Śrī Caitanya Mahāprabhu or his representative. Imitating a *mahā-bhāgavata* like Haridāsa Ṭhākura is not recommended. In fact, Śrīla Bhaktisiddhānta Sarasvatī Ṭhākura condemns such imitation as follows:

duṣṭa mana! tumi kisera vaiṣṇava?
pratiṣṭhara tare, nirjanera ghare,
tava hari-nāma kevala kaitava[9]

"My dear mind, you are trying to imitate Haridāsa Ṭhākura and chant the Hare Kṛṣṇa *mantra* in a secluded place, but you are not worthy of being called a Vaiṣṇava because what you want is cheap popularity and not the actual qualifications of Haridāsa Ṭhākura. If you try to imitate him you will fall down, for your neophyte position will cause you to think of women and money. Thus you will fall into the clutches of *māyā*, and your so-called chanting in a secluded place will bring about your downfall."[10]

After all of the Vaiṣṇavas had bathed in the ocean, they gathered in the presence of the Lord and took their lunch. Afterwards, Śrī Caitanya Mahāprabhu carefully delivered *prasāda* into the hands of Govinda to be given to Haridāsa Ṭhākura. Every day without fail, the Lord arranged for *prasādam* for Haridāsa Ṭhākura and personally went to visit him. We can only try to imagine the exalted position of the Nāmācārya Haridāsa Ṭhākura. It can be understood from this incident that trying to enter the Jagannātha temple is not very important for Vaisnavas born outside of India, despite their having sufficient brahminical qualifications. What is important is to become purified by humbly chanting the holy name and serving the Vaiṣṇavas. Śrīla Bhaktisiddhānta Sarasvatī Ṭhākura has often been quoted by Śrīla Prabhupāda as saying, "Don't try to see Kṛṣṇa, but act in such a way that Kṛṣṇa will want to see you." This was Haridāsa Ṭhākura's personal example and glory—he didn't attempt to contravene social convention; rather, he simply behaved purely, and the Lord came to see Him every day. This incident is very instructive for all those whose birth in meat-eating families or families outside the boundaries of India is viewed as a disqualification by persons whose vision is afflicted by the three modes of nature.

It is described in the *Caitanya-caritāmṛta Madhya-līlā* how Haridāsa Ṭhākura used to often keep company with

Govinda, the former servant of Īśvara Purī, Śrī Caitanya Mahāprabhu's spiritual master. Govinda had been ordered at the time of Īśvara Purī's disappearance to go to Nilācala and render personal service to the Lord. Lord Caitanya had been reluctant to accept service from Govinda, who was His God-brother, but Sāravabhauma Bhaṭṭācārya pointed out that the order of the spiritual master could not be ignored. Thus, Govinda began his service to the Lord. Since Govinda was from the *śūdra* caste, Haridāsa Ṭhākura, Junior Haridāsa, as well as the devotees Rāmāi and Nandāi used to stay with Govinda since such association did not go against the social practices of the time. Govinda constantly served all of the Vaiṣṇavas and saw to their needs. Haridāsa Ṭhākura and the devotees mentioned above used to stay with Govinda to be in the best possible position to offer service to Śrī Caitanya Mahāprabhu and His associates. Thus, the good fortune of Govinda and those who served with him was unlimited.

On one occasion, out of affection, Śrī Caitanya Mahāprabhu summoned Haridāsa Ṭhākura to come and take lunch with the other Vaiṣṇavas, but Haridāsa Ṭhākura kept himself at a distance. He answered the Lord's summons:

"Let Lord Śrī Caitanya Mahāprabhu take His lunch with the devotees. Since I am abominable, I cannot sit down among you. Govinda will give me *prasāda* later, outside the door."[11]

The behavior of Haridāsa Ṭhākura is most instructive. When a human being is born into circumstances that place him in a socially disadvantaged position in human society, he will tend to resent his situation and burn inwardly for the day when he can retaliate against those who have disparaged or maltreated him. If such a person, by endeavor and good fortune, rises above his former position in society, he finds ways to strike back at those who formerly oppressed him, or at least to remind them of their former wrongs. This tendency to "lord over" or seek vengeance upon others is very strong in conditional life. However, Haridāsa Ṭhākura not only had no such retaliatory mood, despite his being recognized as the greatest Vaiṣṇava by the Supreme Lord Himself and His associates. He continued to possess the mood of a person without position or status in human society. Even within Vaiṣṇava society, which judges the status of a person by spiritual development, he kept himself in the most humble position, considering himself to have no qualifications in any societal realm whatsoever. He had no scent of a desire for profit, adoration, or distinction. Therefore, he fully met the qualifications for constant chanting mentioned in the verse composed by Śrī Caitanya Mahāprabhu:

tṛṇād api sunīcena
taror api sahiṣṇunā
amāninā mānadena
kīrtanīyaḥ sadā hariḥ

"One should chant the holy name of the Lord in a humble state of mind, thinking oneself lower than the straw in the street; one should be more tolerant than the tree, devoid of all sense of false prestige, and should be ready to offer all respect to others. In such a state of mind one can chant the holy name of the Lord constantly."[12]

Sometimes real humility is misunderstood to be an inactive or passive state. This is not the case. In fact, the active preacher is a superb example of humility. A preacher who humbly takes up the difficult order of Śrī Caitanya Mahāprabhu and the spiritual master to approach conditioned souls and to try to convince them to begin spiritual life, and, in the process, endures endless rejection, condescension, dismissal, and sometimes even physical violence, is certainly showing a wonderful example of humility. Elevated humility may be defined as the selfless action that one takes to satisfy Lord Caitanya and the spiritual master. Even if one is not free from selfish desires, his sincere effort to distribute Kṛṣṇa consciousness on the order of the Lord and the *guru* is a practical demonstration of surrender and humility. "Kṛṣṇa says in the *Bhagavad-gita, na ca tasmād manuṣyeṣu kaścin me priya-kṛttamaḥ*: 'One who is doing this humble service of preaching work, Kṛṣṇa consciousness, nobody is dearer than him to Me.'"[13]

Although actual humility is preaching on behalf of the Lord, still a demonstration of humility is important in relation to the public:

> "So you have to become very humble, *tṛṇād api sunīcena*, humbler than the grass. Just like everyone is trampling over the grass. It doesn't protest, 'Why you are going, keeping your leg on my head?' But that is the... *Tṛṇād api sunīcena.* Go on trampling. Hundreds and hundreds of people are trampling over the grass; they [the grass] don't protest. *Tṛṇād api sunīcena taror api sahiṣṇunā.* The tree is standing. You sit down. When there is scorching heat, you take pleasure by sitting down under the shade. But the reward is that you cut the branches. That is their reward. He gives you shelter, and you cut the branch. You cut the whole tree. This is your gratitude. You see? Because we are rascals, we do not know what gratitude is. They are taking milk from the cow and killing... So Caitanya Mahāprabhu advises, *taror api sahiṣṇunā*—tolerant, humbler than the grass. *Amāninā mānadena.* Don't expect any honor for your person, but to the others give honor: 'Oh, you are most exalted person,' although he's a rascal. What can be done? Otherwise you cannot preach.

> If you call a rascal a rascal, immediately your preaching will be stopped. So you have to say that 'You are the greatest intelligent man, *sādhu*, most honored. The only request is that you forget what you have learned. That's all. And take this.' In this way, practical preaching. Otherwise it is not possible. Everyone is thinking he is the most exalted personality, scientist, philosopher, great man. That is the material disease. Actually he is being kicked every moment by the urges of the senses, and he is thinking he is a very great man. *Go-dāsa. Go* means senses. He is always curbed down by the sense urges, and he is thinking, 'independent.' 'Independent' means servant of the senses. This is going on. So you have to understand the real position of the world, and if you want to preach, then you have to (be) humbler than the tree, humbler than the grass, more tolerant than the tree...Then it will be possible to say something. Otherwise it is very difficult. We have to deal with all rascals, fools, rogues, ruffians...You must know these things. You are dealing with all rascals. So if we call them directly 'rascal,' they will be angry. Your preaching will not be successful. So follow the principles enunciated by Prabodhānanda Sarasvatī and Caitanya Mahāprabhu."[14]

Some pseudo-Vaiṣṇavas demonstrate the attitude of humility, but fail to translate their "humility" into practical service. Sometimes they spend their time criticizing the folly of those who try to preach. They talk a great deal about Vaiṣṇava humility but tend to see the practical service of preaching as something for the neophytes, and thus their neglect is the cause of many conditioned souls' continued suffering in material existence. "They [the *sahajiyās*] should better consider His [Mahaprabhu's] instructions and, instead of seeking to be considered humble and meek, should refrain from criticizing the followers of Śrī Caitanya Mahāprabhu who engage in preaching."[15]

Haridāsa Ṭhākura was the personification of the *tṛṇād api* verse. His whole life was the living example of a humble Vaiṣṇava situated in love of God, without a tinge of false egotism. In the course of his life he was spurned by so-called *brāhmaṇas*, taunted and tortured by Muslim tyrants, insulted by village leaders, and reviled by many other kinds of ignorant people. Despite all of this, he never deviated from the principle of humility while attempting to deliver the message of Sri Caitanya Mahaprabhu, considering himself unqualified in every respect, despite his having achieved the ultimate goal of human life, love of God. His humility was not a social mask to gain respect, not a hypocritical convention, not a mental adjustment, and not low self-esteem. His sincere conviction was that all the devotees were more sincere and worthy than he was in their service to Kṛṣṇa, and that all the non-devotees were actually better devotees due to their sincere service of the pure devotee Māyā, who is the illusory energy of the Lord and the Lord's surrendered servant. This is the consciousness of an *uttama-adhikārī* (a topmost devotee), a genuine *mahā-bhāgavata*. At the same time, Haridāsa Ṭhākura was always daring and active in chanting and trying to influence others to take it up.

Understanding the Ṭhākura's mind, the Lord did not call him to eat with the other Vaiṣṇavas again. Govinda always set aside the Lord's remnants and delivered them to Haridāsa Ṭhākura very carefully.

Rathayātrā Saṅkīrtana

When participating in the Rathayātrā festival, Haridāsa Ṭhākura was appointed by Śrī Caitanya Mahāprabhu to dance in one of the *saṅkīrtana* parties, composed of Vāsudeva, Gopīnātha, Murāri, Śrīkānta and Vallabha Sena. In that party Mukunda was the chief singer. Altogether there were seven *saṅkīrtana* parties, each one composed of exalted devotees, expert in dancing, singing and playing *mṛdaṅgas*, *karatālas* and other instruments. When the Lord wanted to dance, all seven groups combined together. At that time, under the supervision of Svarūpa Dāmodara, the associates of the Lord: Śrīvāsa, Rāmāi, Raghu, Govinda, Mukunda, Haridāsa, Govindānanda, Mādhava, and a second Govinda all combined together to augment the Lord's pleasure.

When the Lord wanted to jump and leap while dancing, He placed these nine devotees in the charge of Svarūpa Dāmodara. These devotees sang along with the Lord, and they also ran beside Him. All the other groups of men also sang. It is described that: "When Śrī Caitanya Mahāprabhu danced and jumped high, roaring like thunder and moving in a circle like a wheel, He appeared like a circling firebrand."[16]

In this way Haridāsa Ṭhākura was a primary participant in all of the Lord's Rathayātrā pastimes, and all of his *saṅkīrtana līlās*. When it came to performing service and dancing and singing loudly in public, Haridāsa was not shy. It would appear from this example that shyness is not equivalent to humility. The fact that Haridasa often took part with so much enthusiasm would also indicate that he was bold for the sake of Śrī Caitanya Mahāprabhu's happiness and a talented singer and dancer as well. Despite his advanced years, he never hesitated to take part in the Lord's Rathayātrā pastimes.

Rūpa Gosvāmī

Prior to Śrīla Rūpa Gosvāmī's coming to Jagannātha Purī to see the Lord, he had a dream in which a celestially beautiful woman ordered him: "Write a separate drama about me. By my mercy, it will be extraordinarily beautiful."[15] Rūpa Gosvāmī had composed a drama of all the pastimes of Kṛṣṇa in Vṛndāvana and Dvārakā. After this dream he understood that Satyabhāmā intended for him to compose two dramas, one delineating the Dvārakā-līlā and the other the Vṛndāvana-līlā. This was later confirmed by Śrī Caitanya Mahāprabhu by direct instruction at Purī. When Śrīla Rūpa Gosvāmī came to see the Lord at Jagannātha Purī, he first came to the hut of Haridāsa Ṭhākura. Rūpa and Sanātana Gosvāmīs also exhibited their heartfelt sentiment of being fallen souls, due to their years of government service to the Muslim king of Bengal, the Nawab Hussain Shah.

Haridāsa Ṭhākura informed Śrīla Rūpa Gosvāmī that Lord Caitanya had already intimated that Rūpa Gosvāmī would come to Haridāsa's *bhajana-kuṭira*. After the *upala-bhoga* (morning refreshments) ceremony of Lord Jagannātha, the Lord came regularly to see Haridāsa Ṭhākura, and suddenly He arrived. Śrīla Rūpa Gosvāmī fell at the Lord's feet, and Haridāsa Ṭhākura informed Śrī Caitanya Mahāprabhu, "This is Rūpa Gosvāmī offering You obeisances."[18] The Lord immediately embraced Rūpa Gosvāmī, and the three sat and talked for some time. It is described in *Śrī Caitanya-caritāmṛta* that Śrī Caitanya Mahāprabhu would go every day to see Haridāsa Ṭhākura and Śrīla Rūpa Gosvāmī, and He would deliver whatever *prasādam* He had received from the temple to them.[19] It is further described that when those two fortunate Vaiṣṇavas received the remnants of Śrī Caitanya Mahāprabhu through Govinda, they respected it, and then danced in ecstasy. It appears that according to the social etiquette of the time, Śrīla Rūpa Gosvāmī, although born in a *brāhmaṇa* family, was considered proper association for Haridāsa. This was due to his having served a Muslim ruler and, by association, was considered to have become a Mus lim. Devotees are generally well aware that Haridāsa Ṭhākura was considered an outcaste, and they view Rūpa Gosvāmī as the exalted head of the *sampradāya* after Mahāprabhu

Himself. However, both Haridāsa Ṭhākura and Rūpa Gosvāmī had to deal with very critical attitudes from society regarding their social status. Both of them took very humble positions in the face of such materialistic attitudes and preached as well as they could under the circumstances. The Vaiṣṇavas understood their exalted status as devotees, but others did not. Śrīla Rupa and Sanātana Gosvāmīs, after arriving in Vrndavana, wrote advanced literatures in Sanskrit which targeted the educated *brāhmaṇa* class. They also used their experience in government in dealing with the Moghul government in Agra. However, at heart, they considered themselves to be like Haridāsa, or friends of Haridāsa. This is certainly so, since their deep humility is on a par with Haridāsa Ṭhākura's.

After the four months of the rainy season had passed, all of the Vaiṣṇavas from Bengal returned to their homes, but Śrīla Rūpa Gosvāmī remained under the shelter of Śrī Caitanya Mahāprabhu's lotus feet. On one occasion, as Śrīla Rūpa Gosvāmī was composing his transcendental drama, the Lord came to see Haridāsa Ṭhākura and Rūpa Gosvāmī. Both of them offered their obeisances, and Śrī Caitanya Mahāprabhu embraced them both and then sat down. He began to examine the manuscript of Rūpa Gosvāmī, noting that the handwriting was "...just like rows of pearls."[20] While reading, Śrī Caitanya Mahāprabhu came to a wonderful verse:

"I do not know how much nectar the two syllables '*Kṛṣ ṇa*' have produced. When the holy name of Kṛṣṇa is chanted, it appears to dance within the mouth. We then desire many, many mouths. When that name enters the holes of the ears, we desire many millions of ears. And when the holy name dances in the courtyard of the heart, it conquers the activities of the mind, and therefore all the senses become inert."[21]

When Śrī Caitanya Mahāprabhu chanted this wonderful verse, Haridāsa Ṭhākura began jubilantly dancing and praising its meaning. Haridāsa Ṭhākura had a very deep realization of Śrīla Rūpa Gosvāmī's ecstatic verse which expressed the full, joyful taste he experienced daily. Haridāsa Ṭhākura perfectly understood Mahāprabhu's message and mood. The Namācārya lived this verse at every moment, and here he wonderfully and spontaneously interacted with the Lord and augmented His ecstatic mood which He experienced while reading the verse.

On another occasion Śrīla Rūpa Gosvāmī composed a verse in response to one chanted by Śrī Caitanya Mahāprabhu during the Rathayātrā celebration. No one knew why Śrī Caitanya Mahāprabhu chanted that particular verse, except for Svarūpa Dāmodara Gosvāmī, and yet the poetic composition by Rūpa Gosvāmī perfectly illustrated the mood and sentiment of Śrī Caitanya Mahāprabhu. Later Lord Caitanya discovered the companion verse composed by Rūpa Gosvāmī stuck in the straw roof of Rūpa Gosvāmī's hut and experienced great happiness and surprise that Śrīla Rūpa Gosvāmī understood His heart so well. On the next day the Lord, accompanied by Śrī Rāmānanda Rāya, Sārvabhauma Bhaṭṭācārya, and Svarūpa Dāmodara Gosvāmī, went to see Śrīla Rūpa Gosvāmī, and, on the way, Śrī Caitanya Mahāprabhu glorified the qualities of Śrīla Rūpa Gosvāmī.

After Haridāsa Ṭhākura and Rūpa Gosvāmī greeted the Lord and His intimate associates, the visiting party was seated on a raised platform. They repeatedly asked Rūpa Gosvāmī and Haridāsa Ṭhākura to sit with them, but they would not do it. Śrī Caitanya Mahāprabhu wanted Śrīla Rūpa Gosvāmī to recite the verse expressing His internal mood, but Rūpa

Gosvāmī was shy and became silent, so Svarūpa Dāmodara Gosvāmī recited it with great happiness:

"My dear friend, now I have met My very old and dear friend Kṛṣṇa on this field of Kurukṣetra. I am the same Rādhārāṇī, and now We are meeting together. It is very pleasant, but I would still like to go to the bank of the Yamunā beneath the trees of the forest there. I wish to hear the vibration of His sweet flute playing the fifth note within that forest of Vṛndāvana."[22]

All of Śrī Caitanya Mahāprabhu's associates were amazed at this poetic and deep verse which perfectly purported the mysterious verse sung by Śrī Caitanya Mahāprabhu during the Rathayātrā festival. They all confirmed that Śrīla Rūpa Gosvāmī had received the special mercy of the Lord. The Lord insisted that Rūpa Gosvāmī recite other verses from his writing, and Rāmānanda Rāya and the others exulted in the perfection of Rūpa Gosvāmī's compositions which were like showers of nectar. All of them bestowed their mercy on Rūpa Gosvāmī at the request of the Lord, and then took their leave. Haridāsa Ṭhākura embraced Rūpa Gosvāmī and told him: "There is no limit to your good fortune. No one can understand the glories of what you have described."[23] Haridāsa was a senior member of Mahāprabhu's entourage, and, as such, he took Śrīla Rūpa Gosvāmī under his wing. Rūpa Gosvāmī was certainly recognized by the Lord and by Svarūpa Dāmodara Gosvāmī, Mahāprabhu's personal secretary. However, it appears that Haridāsa Ṭhākura was also Rūpa Gosvāmī's intimate friend and associate, and they lived as roommates and friends in Purī. As Rūpānugas, or followers of Śrī Rūpa, all Gaudiya Vaiṣṇavas should feel a special debt to the Nāmācārya for his personal care of the beautiful personality who would become the most prominent preceptor of the Brahmā-Madhva-Gauḍīya *sampradāya.*

Sanātana Gosvāmī

When Śrīla Rūpa Gosvāmī returned to Vṛndāvana, after residing for many months in Jagannātha Purī, Sanātana Gosvāmī simultaneously left Mathurā and proceeded to Jagannātha Purī. He traveled through the Jhārikhaṇḍa Forest; sometimes he fasted and sometimes he was able to eat. Due to drinking some contaminated water in the forest, Sanātana Gosvāmī contracted a disease which covered his body with itching, oozing sores. Thinking of himself in excruciatingly humble terms, he considered his body useless, and without qualification to go to Śrī Caitanya Mahāprabhu in Purī, worrying for the fate of those who might come in contact with him in that holy place. He thus concluded that he would give up his life under the wheel of Lord Jagannātha's cart in the presence of Śrī Caitanya Mahāprabhu, and that such a death would be the highest benediction. Sanātana Gosvāmī, having come to this resolution, then inquired, upon reaching Purī, as to the whereabouts of the residence of Haridāsa Ṭhākura. After receiving directions, he found the Ṭhākura, and they embraced each other in intense happiness. Haridāsa Ṭhākura happily informed him: "The Lord is coming here very soon."[24]

At that very moment Śrī Caitanya Mahāprabhu, after attending the *upala-bhoga* ceremony of Jagannātha, came with other devotees to see Haridāsa Ṭhākura. Sanātana Gosvāmī and Haridāsa Ṭhākura immediately fell flat like rods to offer obeisances. Śrī Caitanya Mahāprabhu embraced Haridāsa Ṭhākura, and, as he had when Rūpa Gosvāmī had first arrived, Haridāsa Ṭhākura announced, "Here is Sanātana Gosvāmī offering his obeisances."[25] The Lord was greatly surprised and stepped forward to embrace him, but Sanātana

Gosvāmī backed away on the plea of his fallen condition and bodily sores. However, Śrī Caitanya Mahāprabhu forcefully embraced Sanātana Gosvāmī and introduced him to all of the Vaiṣṇavas accompanying Him. Sanātana Gosvāmī was informed by the Lord of the disappearance (death) of his brother Anupama, a great devotee of Lord Rāmacandra. Then the Lord ordered, "It is very good that you have arrived here. Now stay in this room with Haridāsa Ṭhākura.[26] Both of you are expert in understanding the mellows of Lord Kṛṣṇa's devotional service. Therefore you should both continue relishing the taste for such activities and chanting the Hare Kṛṣṇa *mahā-mantra*."[27]

Then Śrī Caitanya Mahāprabhu got up and left and arranged for Govinda to bring them *prasādam*. Every day Śrī Caitanya Mahāprabhu would visit the two stalwarts, Haridāsa Ṭhākura and Sanātana Gosvāmī, and bring them *prasādam* and discuss topics about Kṛṣṇa.

On one such occasion the Lord suddenly began speaking to Sanātana Gosvāmī:

"My dear Sanātana, if I could attain Kṛṣṇa by committing suicide I would certainly give up millions of bodies without a moment's hesitation. You should know that one cannot attain Kṛṣṇa simply by giving up the body. Kṛṣṇa is attainable by devotional service. There is no other means to attain Him."[28]

Śrī Caitanya Mahāprabhu then proceeded to establish His points by logic and scripture and concluded by stating:

"Give up all your nonsensical desires, for they are unfavorable for getting shelter at the lotus feet of Kṛṣṇa. Engage yourself in chanting and hearing. Then you will soon achieve the shelter of Kṛṣṇa without a doubt."[29]

Sanātana Gosvāmī made some humble replies, understanding the Lord's displeasure with his plan, and then Śrī Caitanya Mahāprabhu strongly reinforced His argument by pointing out that Sanātana Gosvāmī's body was His property:

"...you no longer have any claim to your body. Why should you want to destroy another's property? Can't you consider what is right and wrong?"[30]

Lord Caitanya then described all of the services He later expected to execute with his servant's body in Vraja: "Your body is My principal instrument for executing many necessary functions. By your body I shall carry out many important tasks. You shall have to ascertain the basic principles of a devotee, devotional service, love of Godhead, Vaiṣṇava duties, and Vaiṣṇava characteristics. You will also have to explain Kṛṣṇa's devotional service, establish centers for cultivation of love of Kṛṣṇa, excavate lost places of pilgrimage and teach people how to adopt the renounced order. Mathurā-Vṛndāvana is My own very dear abode. I want to do many things there to preach Kṛṣṇa consciousness."[31] Sanātana Gosvāmī was overwhelmed and expressed his willingness to do whatever the Lord desired. Just as Lord Caitanya described to Sanātana Gosvāmī that He had much to accomplish through the body of Śrīla Sanātana Gosvāmī in the future, Śrīla Prabhupāda expressed his sense of ownership of his disciples' bodies in his last days in Vṛndāvana and his confidence that they would accomplish wonderful things in his worldwide mission:

Rāmeśvara: Yayāti. King Yayāti traded his old age.
Kīrtanānanda: With his son. You can do that.
Prabhupāda: (laughs) Who did?
Rāmeśvara: King Yayāti.
Prabhupāda: Ah. Yayāti. **No, why? *You are my body. So you live on. There is no difference. Just like I am working, so my Guru Mahārāja is there, Bhaktisiddhānta Sarasvatī. Physically he may not be, but in every action he is there* [italics and underlining added]. I think actually I have written that.**
Tamāla Kṛṣṇa: Yeah, it's in the *Bhāgavatam*, that "He who lives with him, he lives eternally. He who remembers his words lives eternally."
Prabhupāda: So I am not going to die. *Kīrtir yasya sa jīvati*: "One who has done something substantial, he lives forever." He doesn't die.[32]

Śrīla Prabhupāda humbly explains how his body was simply a vehicle for the preaching of his spiritual master: "By his [Śrīla Bhaktivinoda Ṭhākura's] prayers to the Lord he had as his child *Bhaktisiddhānta Sarasvatī Gosvami Maharaja, who, at the present moment, is preaching the philosophy of Lord Caitanya throughout the entire world through his bona fide disciples*." [italics added][33] The bodies of genuine disciples are really only meant for this purpose: to preach Kṛṣṇa consciousness according to the desires of the bona fide spiritual master. Such a disciple is not to consider the body, which belongs to the spiritual master, as his own, as Śrī Caitanya Mahāprabhu explains.

The Lord then turned to Haridāsa Ṭhākura and said, "My dear Haridāsa, please hear Me. This gentleman wants to destroy another's property. One who is entrusted with another's property does not distribute it or use it for his own purposes. Therefore, tell him not to do such an unlawful thing."[34]

Haridāsa Ṭhākura replied, "We are falsely proud of our capabilities. Actually we cannot understand Your deep intentions. Unless You inform us, we cannot understand what

Your purpose is nor what You want to do through whom. My dear sir, since You, a great personality, have accepted Sanātana Gosvāmī, he is greatly fortunate; no one can be as fortunate as he."[35]

The Lord then left to perform His noon duties, and Haridāsa Ṭhākura embraced Sanātana Gosvāmī[36], telling him:

"My dear Sanātana, no one can find the limits of your good fortune. Śrī Caitanya Mahāprabhu has accepted your body as His own property. Therefore no one can equal you in good fortune. What Śrī Caitanya Mahāprabhu cannot do with His personal body He wants to do through you, and He wants to do it in Mathurā. Whatever the Supreme Personality of Godhead wants us to do will successfully be accomplished. This is your great fortune. That is my considered opinion. I can understand from the words of Śrī Caitanya Mahāprabhu that He wants you to write books about the conclusive decision of devotional service and about the regulative principles ascertained from the revealed scriptures. My body could not be used in the service of Śrī Caitanya Mahāprabhu. Therefore although it took birth in the land of India, this body has been useless."[37]

Upon hearing the heartfelt and humble words of Haridāsa Ṭhākura, Sanātana Gosvāmī spoke the following perfectly realized assessment of the glories of the *mahā-bhāgavata* Nāmācārya Haridāsa Ṭhākura:

"O Haridāsa Ṭhākura, who is equal to you? You are one of the associates of Śrī Caitanya Mahāprabhu. Therefore you are the most fortunate. The mission of Śrī Caitanya Mahāprabhu, for which He has descended as an incarnation, is to spread the importance of chanting the holy name of the Lord.

Now instead of personally doing so, He is spreading it through you. My dear sir, you are chanting the holy name 300,000 times daily and informing everyone of the importance of such chanting. Some behave very well but do not preach the cult of Kṛṣṇa consciousness, whereas others preach but do not behave properly. You simultaneously perform both duties in relation to the holy name by your personal behavior and by your preaching. Therefore you are the spiritual master of the entire world, for you are the most advanced devotee in the world."[38]

Śrīla Prabhupāda comments:

> "Sanātana Gosvāmī clearly defines herein the bona fide spiritual master of the world. The qualifications expressed in this connection are that one must act according to the scriptural injunctions and at the same time preach. One who does so is a bona fide spiritual master. Haridāsa Ṭhākura was the ideal spiritual master because he regularly chanted on his beads a prescribed number of times. Indeed, he was chanting the holy name of the Lord 300,000 times a day. Similarly, the members of the Kṛṣṇa consciousness movement chant a minimum of sixteen rounds a day, which can be done without difficulty, and at the same time they must preach the cult of Caitanya Mahāprabhu according to the gospel of *Bhagavad-gītā As It Is*. One who does so is quite fit to become a spiritual master for the entire world."[39]

While Sanātana Gosvāmī stayed in Purī, his itching sores continued to cause him grief. Every time the Lord came to see him, He would embrace him, and thus the oozing discharge from the sores would touch the body of Śrī Caitanya Mahāprabhu. On one occasion when the Lord invited Sanātana Gosvāmī for lunch, he avoided the shaded path to the garden of Yameśvara (Lord Śiva) and went along the beach, being fearful that he might come in contact with the servants of Lord Jagannātha. The sand was as hot as fire, and his feet became blistered as he proceeded, but out of transcendental joy, thinking of how he would soon see the Lord, he did not notice it. When the Lord ascertained what Sanātana Gosvāmī had done, He embraced him, noting his strict and humble observance of consideration for others. When He embraced his servant, despite the protestations and actual forbidding by Sanātana Gosvāmī, His body was smeared with moisture from Sanātana's body. Sanātana was greatly distressed by this. Sanātana later consulted Jagadānanda Paṇḍita who suggested that he go to Vṛndāvana after the observance of the Rathayātrā festival. In Sanātana's next meeting with Śrī Caitanya Mahāprabhu, the Lord again forcefully embraced him, and Sanātana Gosvāmī lamented that he simply committed offenses by remaining in Purī and told the Lord that Jagadānanda Paṇḍita had advised him to go to Vṛndāvana. The Lord then began to chastise Jagadānanda Paṇḍita and glorify Sanātana Gosvāmī. However, Sanātana Gosvāmī then submitted that to be an object of chastisement means that one is an intimate associate of the Lord, and to be formally glorified is a sign of being an outsider. Śrī Caitanya Mahāprabhu was somewhat embarrassed to hear Sanātana Gosvāmī talk like this, and began to give many scriptural and logical explanations about the detachment and equal vision of a transcendentalist in relation to the body, and concludes by saying: "Since I am in the renounced order, My duty is to make no distinction but instead to be equipoised. My knowledge must be equally disposed toward sandalwood pulp and dirty mud. For this reason, I cannot reject you. If I hated you, I would deviate from My occupational duty." Thus, Lord Caitanya replied philosophically to counter the thrust of Sanātana Gosvāmī's lamentation at being treated as an outsider.

Haridāsa Ṭhākura then boldly countered the Lord's scriptural logic with *bhakti*, and stated: "My dear Lord, what You have spoken deals with external formalities. I do not accept it. My Lord, we are all fallen, but You have accepted us due to Your attribute of being merciful to the fallen. This is well known all over the world."[40]

Haridāsa went to the heart of the matter—that Śrī Caitanya Mahāprabhu accepted them both out of love and mercy, and that was the actual platform of His exchanges with His followers.

Śrī Caitanya Mahāprabhu smiled at being defeated with *bhakti* and then admitted that he saw Haridāsa Ṭhākura and Sanātana Gosvāmī as one sees children. If a child even passes stool or urine, the mother doesn't take it seriously, seeing it as sandalwood. He explained, "Now I am speaking the truth about how My mind is attached to you...I always think of Myself as deserving no respect, but because of affection I always consider you to be like My little children. When a child passes stool and urine that touch the body of the mother, the mother never hates the child. On the contrary, she takes much pleasure in cleansing him...when the foul moisture oozing from the itches of Sanātana touches My body, I have no hatred for him...The body of a devotee is never material. It is considered to be transcendental, full of spiritual bliss. At the time of initiation, when a devotee fully surrenders unto the service of the Lord, Kṛṣṇa accepts him to be as good as Himself. When the devotee's body is thus transformed into spiritual existence, the devotee, in that transcendental body, renders service to the lotus feet of the Lord...Kṛṣṇa somehow or other manifested these itching sores on the body of Sanātana Gosvāmī and sent him here to test Me. If I had hated Sanātana Gosvāmī and had not embraced him, I would certainly have been chastised for offenses to Kṛṣṇa. Sanātana Gosvāmī is one of the associates of Kṛṣṇa. There could not be any bad odor from his body. On the first day I embraced him, I smelled the aroma of *catuḥsama* [a mixture of sandalwood pulp, camphor, *aguru* and musk]."[41]

Haridasa Ṭhākura then replied: "My dear sir, You are the Supreme Personality of Godhead and are most merciful toward us. No one can understand what is within Your deeply affectionate heart. You embraced the leper Vāsudeva, whose body was fully infected by worms. You are so kind that in spite of his condition You embraced him. By embracing him You made his body as beautiful as that of Cupid. We cannot understand the waves of Your mercy."[42]

When the Lord embraced Sanātana Gosvāmī, an odor of sandalwood emanated from his body, and he ordered Sanātana Gosvāmī to remain in Jagannātha Purī for one year and then he could go to Vṛndāvana. Firmly embracing Sanātana Gosvāmī again, the itches immediately disappeared, and his entire body became golden.

Haridāsa Ṭhākura was astonished and exclaimed: "This is Your pastime...You made Sanātana Gosvāmī drink the water of Jhārikhaṇḍa, and You actually generated the consequent itching sores on his body. After thus causing these itching sores, You examined Sanātana Gosvāmī. No one can understand Your transcendental pastimes."[43]

Śrī Caitanya Mahāprabhu embraced Sanātana Gosvāmī and Haridāsa Ṭhākura, and the two fortunate devotees, experiencing the ecstasy of Lord Caitanya's association, began to describe His transcendental attributes. Sanātana Gosvāmī remained under the care of Śrī Caitanya Mahāprabhu and always discussed the transcendental qualities of Śrī Caitanya Mahāprabhu with Haridāsa Ṭhākura.

Kṛṣṇadāsa Kavirāja Gosvāmī explains something about the wonderful behavior of Śrī Caitanya Mahāprabhu in relation to devotees who have been born in non-*brāhmaṇa* families:

"The Supreme Personality of Godhead, Śrī Caitanya Mahāprabhu, knows very well how to demonstrate the qualities of His devotees. Therefore, acting like an artistic painter, He does so in various ways and considers this His personal profit. There is another characteristic of Lord Śrī Caitanya Mahāprabhu, O devotees, listen carefully to how He manifests His opulence and characteristics, although they are exceptionally deep.

"To vanquish the false pride of so-called renunciates and learned scholars, He spreads real religious principles, even through a *śūdra*, or lowborn fourth-class man. Śrī Caitanya Mahāprabhu preached about devotional service, ecstatic love and the Absolute Truth by making Rāmānanda Rāya, a *gṛhastha* born in a low family, the speaker. Then Śrī Caitanya Mahāprabhu Himself, the exalted *brāhmaṇa-sannyāsī*, and Pradyumna Miśra, the purified *brāhmaṇa*, both became the hearers of Rāmānanda Rāya.

"Śrī Caitanya Mahāprabhu exhibited the glories of the holy name of the Lord through Haridāsa Ṭhākura, who was born in a Mohammedan family. Similarly, He exhibited the essence of devotional service through Sanātana Gosvāmī, who had almost been converted into a Mohammedan. The Lord also fully exhibited the ecstatic love and transcendental pastimes of Vṛndāvana through Rūpa Gosvāmī. Considering all this, who can understand the deep plans of Lord Śrī Caitanya Mahāprabhu. The activities of Śrī Caitanya Mahāprabhu are just like an ocean of nectar. Even a drop of this ocean can inundate all the three worlds.

"O devotees, relish daily the nectar of *Śrī Caitanya-caritāmṛta* and the pastimes of Śrī Caitanya Mahāprabhu, for by doing so one can merge in the transcendental bliss and full knowledge of devotional service."[44]

Glorified by the Lord

There is a description in the seventh chapter of the *Antya-līlā* of *Caitanya-caritāmṛta* of a meeting between Vallabha Bhaṭṭa and Śrī Caitanya Mahāprabhu. They had previously met in Vṛndāvana and had some very sweet exchanges. Later when they met in Purī, Vallabha Bhaṭṭa glorified Śrī Caitanya

Mahāprabhu extensively, but Śrī Caitanya Mahāprabhu indicated to him that He was a Māyāvādī *sannyāsī* and knew nothing of *bhakti*. However, His saving grace was that He had been purified by association of many great Vaiṣṇavas. He then began to list and glorify all of his exalted associates like Advaita Ācārya, Nityānanda Prabhu, Sārvabhauma Bhaṭṭācārya, Rāmānanda Rāya, and then He came to Haridāsa Ṭhākura. About him, the Lord spoke as follows:

"Haridāsa Ṭhākura, the teacher of the holy name, is among the most exalted of all devotees. Every day he chants 300,000 holy names of the Lord. I have learned about the glories of the Lord's holy name from Haridāsa Ṭhākura, and by his mercy I have understood these glories."[45]

Endnotes

[1] *CC Madhya* 1.246.
[2] *CC Madhya* 11.86.
[3] *CC Madhya* 11.161.
[4] *CC Madhya* 11.165–167.
[5] *CC Madhya* 11.188, 189.
[6] *CC Madhya* 11.189 purport.
[7] The flower garden where Haridāsa Ṭhākura stayed was formerly known as Mudra Math. According to legend, a *bakula* twig that was offered to Lord Jagannātha as a tooth brush was planted in the ground by Śrī Caitanya Mahāprabhu near Haridāsa's place of *bhajana*, and that twig grew into a great tree to give shade to the saint. A great yearly festi val is still held there called *Danta-kāṣṭha-ropaṇa mahotsava* to celebrate that occasion.
[8] *CC Madhya* 11.194, 195.
[9] Śrīla Prabhupāda has paraphrased the first two verses of *Duṣṭa Mana* by Śrīla Bhaktisiddhānta Sarasvatī Ṭhākura. The complete form of the two verses from the 19-verse address to the mind, which desires the prestige of a solitary renunciant and which desires to imitate exalted souls like Haridāsa Ṭhākura, are as follows:

duṣṭa mana! tumi kiser vaiṣṇava?
pratiṣṭhār tare, nirjaner ghare,
tava 'hari nāma' kevala 'kaitava'

"O wicked mind! What kind of Vaiṣṇava do you think you are? Your pretentious show of chanting Lord Hari's holy name in a solitary place is only for the sake of attaining the false prestige of a worldly reputation—it is nothing but pure hypocrisy.

jaḍer pratiṣṭhā, śukarer viṣṭhā,
jāno nā ki tāhā 'māyār vaibhava'
kanaka kāminī, divasa-yāminī,
bhāviyā ki kāja, anitya se saba

"Such materialistic prestige is as disgusting as the stool of a hog. Do you not know that it is only a mere illusion cast by the potency of Māyā? What is the value of contemplating day and night your plans for enjoying wealth and women? All these things are only temporary."

[10] *CC Madhya* 11.195 purport.

[11] *CC Madhya* 12.161, 162.

[12] *Śrī Śrī Śikṣāṣṭaka*, verse 3.

[13] SP Lecture, August 12, 1973, London, England (730822.VP.LON)

[14] SP Morning Walk, October 28, 1975, Nairobi, Kenya (751028.mw.nai)

[15] *CC Madhya* 7.130 purport.

[16] *CC Madhya* 13.82.

[17] *CC Antya* 1.42.

[18] *CC Antya* 1.48.

[19] *CC Antya* 1.59.

[20] *CC Antya* 1.97.

[21] *CC Antya* 1.99, quoted from *Vidagdha-mādhava* 1.15 from a seven-act play by Śrīla Rūpa Gosvāmī describing Kṛṣṇa's pastimes in Vṛndāvana.

[22] *CC Antya* 1.114.

[23] *CC Antya* 1.210.

[24] *CC Antya* 4.15.

[25] *CC Antya* 4.18.

[26] This statement is proof of the care Mahāprabhu took of His disciples, regardless of caste. He did not artificially try to elevate them to a higher social position, but, at the same time, he did not refuse to meet with them and even embrace them. Many *brāhmaṇas* of that time, and even

today, would not pay any attention to the "lower" classes. *Brāhmaṇas* were so disdainful that they would purify themselves if they crossed paths with, or even saw a low-class person.

According to the example of Mahāprabhu, followers of the *varṇāśrama* class system need not worry about contamination when associating with devotees of a different social class. Śrīla Prabhupāda explains: "The cooperation between the head, arms, stomach and legs is the perfect situation of human society. [...]Not that 'Because I am head, *brāhmaṇa*, oh, here is a *śūdra*. Oh, don't see his face.' Why? *Śūdra* is also required. Leg is also required. [...]But the *śūdras* were hated like anything, and they became Mohammedans. And there was no reacceptance. [...]Kṛṣṇa and the *śāstra*, it does not say that if one has fallen, you cannot reclaim him. No, why not reclaim him?" (SP Room Conversation, Vrindavan, India, April 20, 1975, VD 19, conversation with governor)

[27] *CC Antya* 4.48, 49.

[28] *CC Antya* 4.55, 56.

[29] *CC Antya* 4.65.

[30] *CC Antya* 4.76, 77.

[31] *CC Antya* 4.78—4.81.

[32] SP Room Conversations, May 27, 1977, Vṛndāvana, India (770527r2.vrn)

[33] *SB* 3.22.19 purport.

[34] *CC Antya* 4.87, 88.

[35] *CC Antya* 4.89—91.

[36] Again, it appears that Haridāsa Ṭhākura took intimate, loving care of Sanātana Gosvāmī, who was later to perform incalculably important service in Vṛndāvana that was essential to the expansion of Mahāprabhu's movement. Although Haridāsa had joined Mahāprabhu's party in Navadvīpa, he befriended the new member, Sanātana. This is a great example for all devotees. It is not enough to give a lecture or sell a book to be considered a preacher. Good preachers care for their wards, befriending and encouraging them. Who knows who they may turn out to be or what wonderful things they may accomplish in the future? All devotees will take part and remain in the Kṛṣṇa consciousness movement due to receiving the loving care of Vaiṣṇavas. Loving dealings are the basis of a healthy society. Śrīla Prabhupāda once wrote to me, "We are persons, and Krishna is a Person, and our relationship with Krishna He leaves open as a voluntary agreement always, and that voluntary attitude—Yes, Krishna, I shall gladly co-operate whatever You say—that ready willingness to obey is only possible if there is love. Forcing will not

make me agree. But if there is love, oh, I shall gladly do it. That is bhakti, that is Krishna consciousness." (SP Letter, November 18, 1972)

[37] *CC Antya* 4.93—98.

[38] *CC Antya* 4.99—103.

[39] *CC Antya* 4.103 purport.

[40] *CC Antya* 4.181, 182.

[41] *CC Antya* 4.183, 185—187, 191—193, 195—197.

[42] *CC Antya* 4.188—190.

[43] *CC Antya* 4.202—204.

[44] *CC Antya* 5.82—89.

[45] *CC Antya* 7.48, 49.

kṛṣṇa-nāma-mahā-mantrera ei ta' svabhāva
yei jape, tāra kṛṣṇe upajaye bhāva

IT IS THE NATURE OF THE HARE KṚṢṆA *MAHĀ-mantra* that anyone who chants it immediately develops his loving ecstasy for Kṛṣṇa."

Śrī Caitanya-caritāmṛta Ādi-līlā 7.83
[Īśvara Purī to Lord Caitanya]

By descending as an incarnation in Navadvīpa, You, just like Kṛṣṇa, have already delivered all the living entities of the universe. One may say that he understands the glories of Śrī Caitanya Mahāprabhu. He may know whatever he may know, but as far as I am concerned, this is my conclusion. My dear Lord, Your pastimes are just like an ocean of nectar. It is not possible for me to conceive how great that ocean is or even to understand a drop of it."

Śrī Caitanya-caritāmṛta Antya-līlā 3.86—88
[Haridāsa Ṭhākura to Lord Caitanya]

CHAPTER EIGHT

Glorious Revelations & Departure

Relieving Lord Caitanya's Anxiety

ONE DAY ŚRĪ CAITANYA MAHĀPRABHU CAME to see Haridāsa Ṭhākura at Siddha-bakula and expressed His anxiety for the fallen souls of Kali-yuga:

"My dear Ṭhākura Haridāsa, in this age of Kali most people are bereft of Vedic culture, and therefore they are called *yavanas*. They are concerned only with killing cows and brahminical culture. In this way they all engage in sinful acts. How will these *yavanas* be delivered?[1] To my great unhappiness, I do not see any way."[2]

Śrīla Prabhupāda explains in the above verses of *Śrī Caitanya-caritāmṛta* that the term "*yavana*" does not refer to a particular group, but rather to those persons who are "violent killers of cows and brahminical culture."[3] Sometimes the term "*yavana*" is used to refer to the 15th century Turkish invaders whose conquering of India was foretold in the Vedic literature—the predicted conquest actually took place.[4] However, Lord Caitanya was universally concerned for all such persons who were cow-killers and destroyers of brahminical culture, since by such activities they were creating a very inauspicious future for themselves. It is also significant that such persons are the majority of the populace in Kali-yuga.

Śrī Caitanya Mahāprabhu was referring, in this instance, to cultural habits, not people or places. In general, India, Pakistan, Afghanistan, and Iran were all vegetarian cultures in ancient times. Broadly, these people followed Zorastrianism, Buddhism, Janism, Vedic religion, Vaiṣṇavism, and other religions that prohibited or discouraged meat-eating. In contrast, part of *yavana* culture was and is meat-eating. Since the time of Alexander and even before, the meat-eating cultures of the *yavanas* gradually influenced and overtook the vegetarian cultures. In response to these influences, Vaiṣṇavas, in general, and followers of Mahāprabhu, in particular, strongly oppose meat-eating, finding it abominable. Other cultural practices of the *yavanas* may be more or less acceptable, but meat-eating is not a worthy act for a human being.

When Haridāsa Ṭhākura heard this question, he immediately felt inspired to pacify the Lord.[5] This is the nature of a confidential devotee of the Lord—he wants to relieve Him of His anxiety for the suffering of the conditioned souls. This is the true nature of confidentiality—understanding the Lord's compassionate desire to help those souls who are caught in the meshes of the illusory energy and acting to relieve the anxiety of the Lord. Sometimes persons with a superficial theistic understanding imagine that confidential devotees are those who have so-called "high" realizations and spend their time delivering lengthy expositions on arcane and esoteric scriptural topics. Such persons and their followers often mistake *jñāna* (book or theoretical knowledge) for *vijñāna* (spiritual realization) and neglect making serious efforts to bring Kṛṣṇa consciousness to those souls lost in the material world. In their hierarchy of concern, understanding "high" topics, personal spiritual enjoyment and advancement come first, and relieving the Lord's anxiety to deliver conditioned souls follows as a distant second, not understanding that their greed for realization can be best accomplished by putting the relief of the Lord's anxiety in the first position. The Lord is extremely anxious to bring bewildered souls back to the spiritual world where they may achieve the happiness which they have sought for many lifetimes in the material world, where there are so many anxieties and miseries. Those devotees who dedicate themselves to relieving the anxiety of the Lord by practical service to the *saṅkīrtana* movement of Śrī Caitanya Mahāprabhu are truly confidential associates of the Lord.

Haridāsa Ṭhākura began to explain how such *yavanas* can be delivered by *nāmābhāsa*. *Nāmābhāsa* is an amazingly merciful arrangement of the Lord allowing a person to benefit from chanting the holy name inadvertently, even though intending something else. Such chanting still receives the credit derived from offenseless chanting. Haridasa Thakura gave the example of Muslims who use the expression *hārām* to indicate something abominable. Nevertheless, by such chanting they receive the benefit of *nāmābhāsa*, which can deliver a conditioned soul. When a Vaiṣṇava chants the same expression [*hārām*] he is vibrating the name of Lord Rāma. However, despite the intention, the vibration's effect and transcendental power is not destroyed.

There are so many words in various languages containing the holy name. For example, in English we have many words which are commonly vibrated which contain the embedded syllable *oṁ*—like home, comb, dome, gnome, tome, etc. There are cities which contain names of God like Rome, Nome, Tallahassee (Allah), motels like Ramada Inn (Rāma), etc. Haridāsa Ṭhākura points out that the Lord is so merciful that He even credits such unconscious chanting of the holy name as *nāmābhāsa*. Even if the syllables of the holy name are pronounced incorrectly, they will still act. However, the inconceivable power or mystery of the Holy Name does not permit us to abuse that power. When we have come in contact with a devotee, he or she instructs us to have respect for the Name, and to pronounce it in the proper attitude. Similarly, other religious traditions also prescribe devotional attitudes when chanting the Lord's name.

Haridāsa Ṭhākura also gives the examples of giving the Lord's names to children, so that throughout the day we are vibrating the holy name, citing the incidence of Ajāmila, who was delivered by sincerely chanting the name of his son, Nārāyaṇa, despite Ajāmila's many previous sinful acts.

Haridāsa Ṭhākura states: "Even a faint light from the holy name of the Lord can eradicate all the reactions of sinful life...Because of even the faintest rays of the effulgence of the Lord's holy name, one can attain liberation."[6]

When Śrī Caitanya Mahāprabhu heard this, He was very pleased, but inquired further about the moving and nonmoving living beings like trees, plants, insects, and other living entities—how would they be delivered? Haridāsa Ṭhākura immediately replied that by the Lord's own chanting, such deliverance had already been accomplished by His chanting in the Jhārikhaṇḍa forest, and by the benediction given to Vāsudeva Datta by the Lord to deliver all the living beings in the universe. The delivery of all living beings had been achieved simply by the desire of Vāsudeva Datta, a great devotee whose compassion and affection for all living beings had reached a level inconceivable to most human beings.[7]

Although secretly amazed and very pleased by Haridāsa Ṭhākura's analysis, the Lord raised a doubt:

"If all living entities were liberated, the entire universe would be devoid of living beings."[8]

Haridāsa Ṭhākura immediately explained that when the Lord delivered all moving and nonmoving beings in different species, He then awakened the living beings who were not yet embodied and thus repopulated the universe. In the purport, Śrīla Prabhupāda explains that a prison never remains empty. There are always criminals to refill it.[9]

The Ṭhākura explained how in Lord Rāma's and Lord Kṛṣṇa's appearances, They similarly freed all the living entities. He then spoke with great awe and appreciation of the Lord's kindness, quoting the *Viṣṇu Purāṇa* 4.15.17:

"Although the Supreme Personality of Godhead may be seen, glorified or remembered with an attitude of envy, He nevertheless awards the most confidential liberation, which is rarely achieved by the demigods and demons. What can be said of those who are already fully engaged in devotional service to the Lord?"

Haridāsa Ṭhākura continued: "By descending as an incarnation in Navadvīpa, You, just like Kṛṣṇa, have already delivered all the living entities of the universe. One may say that he understands the glories of Śrī Caitanya Mahāprabhu. He may know whatever he may know, but as far as I am concerned, this is my conclusion. My dear Lord, Your pastimes are just like an ocean of nectar. It is not possible for me to conceive how great that ocean is or even to understand a drop of it."[10]

When Śrī Caitanya Mahāprabhu heard all of these conclusive and profound remarks, He was astonished. He began to silently consider: "These are actually My confidential pastimes. How could Haridāsa have understood them?"[11]

To summarize, if one were to look at the conversation between Haridāsa Ṭhākura and Mahāprabhu as a discussion about how to deliver people from the *yavana* influence, a few items are prominent. First Mahāprabhu presented the problem of the *yavana* culture. Then, Haridāsa elevated the conversation to the spiritual level by citing the power of chanting the Lord's name. Mahāprabhu countered by asking about other entities aside from humans. Such a question follows perfectly, because Haridāsa had put the discussion on the spiritual level where there are no bodily distinctions. Again, Haridāsa Ṭhākura gives a wonderful answer, explaining that deliverance is ultimately the pleasure of the Lord.

In reverse order, the pleasure of the Lord is the highest goal of the living being. The chanting of His Name is the most important way to make connection with the Lord, and offer Him some service, some pleasure. Finally, in a cultural setting, individuals and societies that avoid meat-eating and elevate the devotees of the Lord provide the basis for spiritual advancement, or the path toward giving pleasure to the Lord. In this way, the Lord and His devotee, Haridāsa Ṭhākura, have stressed the Lord's pleasure, or His service, and His name as the greatest strategies for deliverance and for counteracting the *yavana* influence.

Śrī Caitanya Mahāprabhu then embraced Haridāsa Ṭhākura and avoided further discussion on this topic. Kṛṣṇadāsa Kavirāja Gosvāmī explains that although Śrī Caitanya Mahāprabhu attempts to cover His opulences, He cannot do so before His devotees.[12]

"Then Śrī Caitanya Mahāprabhu went to His personal devotees and began speaking about Haridāsa Ṭhākura's transcendental qualities as if He had hundreds of mouths. Śrī Caitanya Mahāprabhu derives great pleasure from glorifying His devotees, and among the devotees, Haridāsa Ṭhākura is the foremost. The transcendental qualities of Haridāsa Ṭhākura are innumerable and unfathomable. One may describe a portion of them, but to count them all is impossible.

"In *Caitanya-maṅgala* [*Caitanya-bhāgavata*], Śrīla Vṛndāvana dāsa Ṭhākura has described the attributes of Haridāsa Ṭhākura to some extent. No one can describe all the qualities of Haridāsa Ṭhākura. One may say something about them just to purify himself."[13]

In this way Haridāsa Ṭhākura passed his time in Jagannātha Purī in the secluded garden of Siddha-bakula: associating on a daily basis with Śrī Caitanya Mahāprabhu; chanting three *lakhs* of rounds every day without fail; being personally brought *prasādam* by Śrī Caitanya Mahāprabhu or by Śrī Caitanya Mahāprabhu's exalted God-brother, Govinda, the personal servant of both Īśvara Purī and Śrī Caitanya Mahāprabhu; giving encouragement and inspiration to all devotees who came to him; and personifying the principle of Vaiṣṇava humility and determination to always be absorbed in chanting of the holy name, day and night. Whenever, Śrī Caitanya Mahāprabhu performed His pastimes of *nāma-saṅkīrtana* at Jagannātha Purī, Haridāsa was one of the principal dancers and singers. He was a very beautiful personality and an incomparable topmost devotee of the Lord. All of his desires to associate with the Lord and to assist the Lord in expressing the paramount importance of chanting the holy name were fulfilled.

He grew old. He had appeared some 35 years prior to Śrī Caitanya Mahāprabhu, and it became increasingly difficult for him to continue his rigid vows.

The Passing of Haridāsa Ṭhākura

Kṛṣṇadāsa Kavirāja Gosvāmī summarizes the *līlā* of Śrī Caitanya Mahāprabhu in Purī:

"Śrī Caitanya Mahāprabhu thus resided at Jagannātha Purī with His personal devotees and enjoyed the congregational chanting of the Hare Kṛṣṇa *mahā-mantra*. In the daytime Śrī Caitanya Mahāprabhu engaged in dancing and chanting and in seeing the temple of Lord Jagannātha. At night, in the company of His most confidential devotees, such as Rāmānanda Rāya and Svarūpa Dāmodara Gosvāmī, He tasted the nectar of the transcendental mellows of Lord Śrī Kṛṣṇa's pastimes.

"Śrī Caitanya Mahāprabhu very happily passed His days in this way at Nilācala, Jagannātha Purī. Feeling separation from Kṛṣṇa, He exhibited many transcendental symptoms all over His body. Day after day the symptoms increased, and at night they increased even more. All these symptoms, such as transcendental anxiety, agitation, and talking like a madman, were present, just as they are described in the *śāstras* [scriptures]."[14]

One day Govinda went to deliver the remnants of Lord Jagannātha to Haridāsa Ṭhākura in great jubilation, but when he arrived he saw that exalted devotee lying on his back and chanting his rounds very slowly. He requested Haridāsa to rise and take the *mahā-prasāda*, but Haridāsa insisted that he would fast as he had not finished his rounds.

However, since it was *mahā-prasāda*, he offered prayers and honored a tiny portion. The situation was immediately reported to the Lord by Govinda, and the next day Lord Caitanya came to see Haridāsa and asked him if he was well.

Haridāsa Ṭhākura replied, "My body is all right, but my mind and intelligence are not well."[15]

Śrī Caitanya Mahāprabhu asked him if he could ascertain the disease, and the Ṭhākura replied: "My disease is that I cannot complete my rounds."[16]

Śrīla Prabhupāda points out that although the activities of Haridāsa Ṭhākura cannot be imitated, sixteen rounds (minimum) must be chanted by initiated disciples, loudly enough so that both the chanter and others hearing the chanting can hear. He further comments: "If one cannot complete the fixed number of rounds he is assigned, he should be considered to be in a diseased condition of spiritual life."[17]

Lord Caitanya then reassured Haridāsa Ṭhākura that it was no longer necessary for him to keep such a rigid chanting vow. "Your role in this incarnation is to deliver the people in general. You have sufficiently preached the glories of the holy name in this world."[18]

Lord Caitanya uses the words *tomāra avatāra* (your incarnation) to describe Haridāsa. Whenever the Lord descends, so many great devotees also descend to assist Him in His pastimes. The Lord repeatedly reassured Haridāsa that he could reduce the fixed number of rounds he had been chanting.

Regarding Śrīla Prabhupāda's comments about being in a "diseased condition of spiritual life...:" the only medicine which is powerful enough to effect a complete and perfect cure is *nāma-auṣadhi—enechi auṣadhi māyā nāśibāro lāgi'/ hari-nāma-mantra lao tumi magi.'* According to our *ācārya*, Śrīla Bhaktivinoda Ṭhākura (the Seventh Gosvāmī), Lord Gaurāṅga Himself preaches to all living beings: "I have brought the medicine for destroying the illusion of Māyā. Now pray for this *hari-nāma mahā-mantra* and take it."[19] Śrīla Bhaktivinoda Ṭhākura also sings: "Whether you are a householder or a *sannyāsī*, constantly chant 'Hari! Hari!' Do not forget this chanting, whether you are in a happy condition or a distressful one. Just fill your lips with the *hari-nāma*."[20] And he conclusively states: "There is nothing except the holy name [the Lord Himself] within all the fourteen worlds."[21]

Haridāsa Ṭhākura then replied:

"Kindly hear my real plea..." He proceeded to make many excruciatingly humble remarks about himself and then stated, "...You have made me dance in many ways.

For example, I was offered the *śrāddha-pātra*[22] that should have been offered to first-class *brāhmaṇas*. I ate from it even though I was born in a family of meat-eaters."[23]

"I have had one desire for a very long time. I think that quite soon, my Lord, You will bring to a close Your pastimes within this material world. I wish that You not show me this closing chapter of Your pastimes. Before that time comes, kindly let my body fall down in Your presence. I wish to catch Your lotus-like feet upon my heart and see Your moon-like face. With my tongue I shall chant Your holy name, 'Śrī Kṛṣṇa Caitanya!' That is my desire. Kindly let me give up my body in this way. O most merciful Lord, if by Your mercy it is possible, kindly grant my desire. Let this lowborn body fall down before You. You can make possible this perfection of all my desires."[24]

Śrī Caitanya Mahāprabhu immediately expressed His dismay that Haridāsa Ṭhākura wanted to depart from the world and simultaneously affirmed his capacity and right to do whatever he wished. Lord Caitanya indicated that Kṛṣṇa [Lord Caitanya] was obligated out of love to do as Haridāsa Ṭhākura desired, and yet He simultaneously appealed to him to stay on.

"My dear Haridāsa, Kṛṣṇa is so merciful that He must execute whatever you want. But whatever happiness is Mine is all due to your association. It is not fitting for you to go away and leave Me aside."[25]

Haridāsa Ṭhākura did not want Lord Caitanya to avoid his request by reference to His loving attachment to His servant. The Ṭhākura immediately caught hold of the feet of the Lord and pleaded with Him:

"My Lord, do not create an illusion! Although I am so fallen, You must certainly show me this mercy! My Lord there are so many respectable personalities, millions of devotees, who are fit to sit on my head. They are all helpful in Your pastimes. My Lord, if an insignificant insect like me dies, what is the loss? If an ant dies, where is the loss to the material world? My Lord, You are always affectionate to Your devotees. I am just an imitation devotee, but nevertheless I wish that You fulfill my desire. That is my expectation."[26]

This insistence of Haridāsa Ṭhākura that Śrī Caitanya Mahāprabhu fulfill his desire appears to be confusing. A pure devotee has no desire other than to please the Lord. Yet, Lord Caitanya is requesting Haridāsa Ṭhākura to stay, and Haridāsa Ṭhākura is insisting that he be allowed to go. Several questions arise: First, why would Haridāsa wish to separate himself from the company of the Lord? Second, why would a great Vaiṣṇava insist on the fulfillment of his own desire in preference to the desire of the Lord? There are several ways to view this apparent contradiction. On one hand, there was no question of Haridāsa Ṭhākura being separated from the Lord under any circumstance, as he was an eternal servant of the Lord, and could never be without the company of the Lord at any time. Haridāsa Ṭhākura understood the desires of the Lord perfectly. Śrī Caitanya Mahāprabhu wanted Haridāsa Ṭhākura, the perfect *ācārya*, to show the world how to die gloriously chanting. At the same time, Śrī Caitanya Mahāprabhu also exhibits the affection that the Lord feels for His pure devotee by asking him not to leave. Haridāsa Ṭhākura had never exhibited any separate desire in all of his dealings with Śrī Caitanya Mahāprabhu. This incident was no exception. The glorious passing of Haridāsa Ṭhākura exhibits perfection in the art of dying. Just as Haridāsa Ṭhākura had understood the most confidential aspects of Lord Caitanya's mission in their discussions about the deliverance of all *jīvas* by the holy name, he now exhibits his perfect understanding of the Lord's desire for the final chapter of his appearance in the material world. [27] From another angle of vision, to be a pure devotee of the Lord does not mean to become a sycophantic automaton, who simply channels Kṛṣṇa and completely suppresses his own personality and desire. When there is love between the Lord and His devotee, the Lord also loves the devotee's unique qualities and personality and even their contrary nature. Where there is love, there can even be disagreement, a difference of opinion. For Haridāsa Ṭhākura it was too painful for him to even contemplate the Lord's disappearance. He is expressing his individuality, knowing full well that such an exhibition of his unique personality would ultimately be pleasing to Lord Caitanya.

Śrī Caitanya Mahāprabhu did not give an immediate answer to His servant's request. He agreed to meet Haridāsa on the following day and give him His decision. He embraced Haridāsa and left to perform His noon duties and took His bath in the ocean.

On the next morning, after seeing Lord Jagannātha, Śrī Caitanya Mahāprabhu, accompanied by all of His devotees, came to visit Haridāsa Ṭhākura. Haridāsa offered obeisances to the Lord and all the assembled Vaiṣṇavas.

The Lord asked, "My dear Haridasa, what is the news?"[28]

The Lord's question could have been taken in the conventional sense. For example, we commonly say, "What's going on? What's happening? What's the latest?" Such questions generally refer to the everyday events in a person's life or various material developments. However, Haridāsa Ṭhākura's answer brushed aside such possible interpretations. Firmly fixed in his position as the Lord's eternal servant, he replied with a complete understanding of his position:

"My Lord, whatever mercy You can bestow upon me."[29]

This reply by Ṭhākura Haridāsa exhibited his perfect understanding of the existential position of a pure living being. As a servant of the Lord the only news is whatever mercy the Lord bestows in His dealings with his sold-out servant. A servant has no independence; he depends only on the Lord in all circumstances. "News" is the revelation of the Lord's mercy.

Śrī Caitanya Mahāprabhu began congregational chanting with all of His followers; great devotees like Sārvabhauma Bhaṭṭācārya and Rāmānanda Rāya were present, chanting ecstatically. Lord Caitanya began to glorify Haridāsa Ṭhākura, enumerating his divine attributes as though He possessed five mouths. As He described Haridāsa Ṭhākura's qualities and glories, He became increasingly happy. Upon hearing the glories of the exalted Haridāsa, all of the Vaiṣṇavas were stunned and wonderstruck. They all immediately fell down and offered obeisances to the Ṭhākura.

Haridāsa Ṭhākura forced the Lord to sit down in front of him and took the Lord's feet and placed them on his heart. He took the dust of the feet of all the assembled Vaiṣṇavas on his head, and then fixed his eyes like two bumblebees on the Lord's beautiful face. He began to chant the Lord's name, "Śrī Kṛṣṇa Caitanya," again and again, as tears glided down from his eyes.

While chanting in this way, he gave up his body and left for the spiritual world. All who witnessed his passing were reminded of the passage of Bhīṣmadeva. When Grandfather Bhīṣma was ready to depart this world, Kṛṣṇa appeared before him because Bhīṣmadeva was the unflinching servant of Kṛṣṇa. Haridāsa Ṭhākura was also an unflinching servitor, the *nāmācārya*, and therefore Lord Caitanya was obligated out of love to come before His servitor at the last moments of his earthly existence.

Bhīṣmadeva had declared:

"Yet, despite His being equally kind to everyone, He has graciously come before me while I am ending my life, for I am His unflinching servitor."[30]

Śrīla Prabhupāda comments on this verse from the *Śrīmad-Bhāgavatam*:

> "The Supreme Lord, the Absolute Personality of Godhead, Śrī Kṛṣṇa, although equal to everyone, is still more inclined to His unflinching devotee who is completely surrendered and knows no one else as his protector and master. Having unflinching faith in the Supreme Lord as one's protector, friend and master is the natural condition of eternal life. A living entity is so made by the will of the Almighty that he is most happy when placing himself in a condition of absolute dependence. The opposite tendency is the cause of falldown. The living entity has this tendency of falling down by dint of misidentifying himself as fully independent to lord it over the material world. The root cause of all troubles is there in false egotism. One must draw towards the Lord in all circumstances.
>
> "The appearance of Lord Kṛṣṇa at the deathbed of Bhīṣmajī is due to his being an unflinching devotee of the Lord. Arjuna had some bodily relation with Kṛṣṇa because the Lord happened to be his maternal cousin. But Bhīṣma had no such bodily relation. Therefore

the cause of attraction was due to the intimate relation of the soul. Yet because the relation of the body is very pleasing and natural, the Lord is more pleased when He is addressed as the son of Mahārāja Nanda, the son of Yaśodā, the lover of Rādhārāṇī. This affinity by bodily relation with the Lord is another feature of reciprocating loving service with the Lord. Bhīṣmadeva is conscious of this sweetness of transcendental humor, and therefore he likes to address the Lord as Vijaya-Sakhe, Pārtha-Sakhe, etc., exactly like Nanda-nandana or Yaśodā-nandana. The best way to establish our relation in transcendental sweetness is to approach Him through His recognized devotees. One should not try to establish the relation directly; there must be a via medium which is transparent and competent to lead us to the right path."[31]

"Thereupon that man who spoke on different subjects with thousands of meanings and who fought on thousands of battlefields and protected thousands of men, stopped speaking and, being completely freed from all bondage, withdrew his mind from everything else and fixed his wide-open eyes upon the original Personality of Godhead, Śrī Kṛṣṇa, who stood before him, four-handed, dressed in yellow garments that glittered and shined."[32]

After glorifying Kṛṣṇa and instructing Yudhiṣṭhira and the other Pāṇḍavas on all the duties of kingship, Bhīṣmadeva entered into *samādhi* (trance) by meditation on the divine form of Kṛṣṇa. Śrīla Prabhupāda comments on Bhīṣma's having attained the highest perfectional stage of life:

"The stage attained by Bhīṣmadeva while quitting his material body is called *nirvikalpa-samādhi* because he merged his self into thinking of the Lord and his mind into remembering His different activities. He chanted the glories of the Lord, and by his sight he began to see the Lord personally present before him, and thus all his activities became concentrated upon the Lord without deviation. This is the highest stage of perfection, and it is possible for everyone to attain this stage by practice of devotional service. The devotional service of the Lord consists of nine principles of service

> activities, and they are (1) hearing, (2) chanting, (3) remembering, (4) serving the lotus feet, (5) worshiping, (6) praying, (7) executing the orders, (8) fraternizing, and (9) fully surrendering. Any one of them or all of them are equally competent to award the desired result, but they require to be practiced persistently under the guidance of an expert devotee of the Lord."[33]

Therefore, the passing of Haridāsa Ṭhākura can be compared to Bhīṣma's as both of them left this world by their own will, both were compared to mystic *yogīs*, and both were such great devotees that the Lord felt personally compelled to appear before them at the point of death. Such occurrences are extraordinary and amazing. The Lord personally certified the greatness of His servitors by agreeing to appear directly before them in this way.

After the departure of Haridāsa Ṭhākura, tumultuous *kīrtana* continued, and Lord Caitanya was overwhelmed with ecstatic love. He raised the body of Haridāsa Ṭhākura and began to dance in the courtyard. All of the devotees were helpless with spiritual emotion and continued chanting and dancing. After some time Svarūpa Dāmodara Gosvāmī informed the Lord of the rituals that needed to be performed. The Ṭhākura's body was placed on a carrier that resembled an airship[34] and taken to the ocean, accompanied by constant congregational chanting. Lord Caitanya led the procession, and when reaching the sea, He bathed the body of Haridāsa Ṭhākura with the ocean's water and declared, "From this day on, this sea has become a great pilgrimage site."[35]

Everyone drank the water that had touched the feet of Haridāsa Ṭhākura, and they then smeared the remnants of Lord Jagannatha's sandalwood over his body. After a hole was dug in the sand, Haridāsa Ṭhākura was placed in *samādhi*[36], along with sandalwood pulp, silken ropes, food and cloth from Lord Jagannātha. The devotees chanted as Vakreśvara Paṇḍita danced. Śrī Caitanya Mahāprabhu personally covered the Ṭhākura's transcendental form with sand, chanting "Haribol! Haribol!" All the Vaiṣṇavas present took part in covering the body of Haridāsa Ṭhākura with sand, and a platform was constructed on the site. Tremendous *saṅkīrtana* was performed, described as both roaring and tumultuous. Afterwards all the devotees bathed and sported in the sea.[37] After bathing, all of the devotees, led by Śrī Caitanya Mahāprabhu circumambulated the tomb and then proceeded to the Siṁha-dvāra gate of the Jagannātha temple. The whole city of Jagannātha Purī vibrated with the chanting of the holy names.

Lord Caitanya then personally began to beg for *prasādam* so that a wonderful festival for Haridāsa Ṭhākura could be observed. All of the shopkeepers were eager to serve, but Svarūpa Dāmodara Gosvāmī, in a mood of service, began to organize everything for the pleasure of Lord Caitanya. After the *prasādam* was collected, Śrī Caitanya Mahāprabhu began to distribute the *prasādam*, but He began serving portions that five men would have trouble eating. Again, Svarūpa Dāmodara, desiring to be of service, insisted that the Lord be seated and that he, along with Jagadānanda, Kāśīśvara, and Śaṅkara would handle the distribution of Jagannātha's *prasāda*. Kāśī Miśra personally served the Lord, and as the Lord took, all the other Vaisnavas also honored the *prasādam*. Everyone took to their full satisfaction, and Lord Caitanya repeatedly enjoined the servers, "Give them more! Give them more!"[38] When no one could eat any more, they washed their hands and mouths and were personally decorated with sandalwood pulp and garlands by Śrī Caitanya Mahāprabhu.

Out of ecstatic feeling, Śrī Caitanya Mahāprabhu gave the following benediction: "Anyone who has seen the festival of Śrī Haridāsa Ṭhākura's passing away, anyone who has chanted and danced here, anyone who has offered sand on the body of Haridāsa Ṭhākura and anyone who has joined this festival to partake of the *prasāda* will achieve the favor of Kṛṣṇa very soon. There is such wonderful power in seeing Haridāsa Ṭhākura.

"Being merciful upon Me, Kṛṣṇa gave Me the association of Haridāsa Ṭhākura. Being independent in His desires, He has now broken that association. When Haridāsa Ṭhākura wanted to leave this material world, it was not within My power to detain him. Simply by his will, Haridāsa Ṭhākura could give up his life and go away exactly like Bhīṣma, who previously died simply by his own desire, as we have heard from *śāstra*. Haridāsa Ṭhākura was the crown jewel on the head of this world; without him, this world is now bereft of its valuable jewel."[39]

The Lord then commanded all of the Vaiṣṇavas: "Say 'All glories to Haridāsa Ṭhākura!' and chant the holy name of Hari." The Lord then began to dance. Everyone began to chant and exclaim: "All glories to Haridāsa Ṭhākura, who revealed the importance of chanting the holy name of the Lord!"[40]

Kṛṣṇadāsa Kavirāja Gosvāmī then offers this wonderful benediction to the readers of *Śrī Caitanya-caritāmṛta*: "Anyone who hears this narration will certainly fix his mind firmly in devotional service to Kṛṣṇa."[41]

Kavirāja Gosvāmī then concludes: "Haridāsa Ṭhākura was not only the topmost devotee of the Lord, but also a great and learned scholar. It was his great fortune that he passed away before Śrī Caitanya Mahāprabhu."[42]

A question may be raised as to why and how, when Haridāsa Ṭhākura was outwardly not well educated or even literate, could he possibly be described as a great and learned scholar. Śrīla Prabhupāda addresses the point as follows: "Actually, the most important science to know is the science of getting out of the clutches of material existence. Anyone who knows this science must be considered the greatest learned person. Anyone who knows the temporary situation of this material world and is expert in achieving a permanent situation in the spiritual world, who knows that the Supreme Personality of Godhead is beyond the jurisdiction of our experimental knowledge, is understood to be the most learned scholar. Haridāsa Ṭhākura knew this science perfectly. Therefore, he is described in this connection as *parama-vidvān*. He personally preached the importance of chanting the Hare Kṛṣṇa *mahā-mantra*, which is approved by the revealed scriptures...Haridāsa Ṭhākura knew this science very well, and he can therefore be called, technically, *sarva-śāstrādhītī*. Anyone who has learned the essence of Vedic scripture is to be known as a first-class educated person, with full knowledge of all *śāstra*."[43]

Haridāsa Ṭhākura is the emblem of the perfect preacher of Kṛṣṇa consciousness, since he was a perfect example of both practice *and* precept. Whenever he spoke, he spoke perfectly according to time, place, and circumstance and according to *guru, sādhu,* and *śāstra*. He also behaved perfectly, being always absorbed in chanting the holy name, day and night and thinking how others might be delivered, even at the risk of his own life. Therefore, he is unsurpassed as a preacher of Kṛṣṇa consciousness, and the greatest inspiration for all succeeding generations of preachers in the Kṛṣṇa consciousness movement who come from *yavana* backgrounds. He was born into a meat-eater's family and was uneducated in the ordinary sense of the term, and yet he was the most refined and learned person. He was extremely humble in all his dealings but also bold as a lion in distributing Kṛṣṇa consciousness. He was timid but completely fearless. He was deferential in his behavior with other Vaiṣṇavas, yet he possessed unshakeable and immovable conviction. His only aspiration was to be the servant of the Vaiṣṇavas. He is the Nāmācārya! Hare Kṛṣṇa Hare Kṛṣṇa Kṛṣṇa Kṛṣṇa Hare Hare Hare Rāma Hare Rāma Rāma Rāma Hare Hare!

sanātana kahe,—"tomā-sama kebā āche āna
mahāprabhura gaṇe tumi—mahā-bhāgyavān!

Sanātana Gosvāmī[44] replied, "O Haridāsa Ṭhākura, who is equal to you? You are one of the associates of Śrī Caitanya Mahāprabhu. Therefore you are the most fortunate.

avatāra-kārya prabhura—nāma-pracāre
sei nija-kārya prabhu karena tomāra dvāre

"The mission of Śrī Caitanya Mahāprabhu, for which He has descended as an incarnation, is to spread the importance of chanting the holy name of the Lord. Now instead of personally doing so, He is spreading it through you.

pratyaha kara tina-lakṣa nāma-saṅkīrtana
sabāra āge kara nāmera mahimā kathana

"My dear sir, you are chanting the holy name 300,000 times daily and informing everyone of the importance of such chanting.

Nāmācārya Śrīla Haridāsa Ṭhākura

āpane ācare keha, nā kare pracāra
pracāra karena keha, nā karena ācāra

"Some behave very well but do not preach the cult of Kṛṣṇa consciousness, whereas others preach but do not behave properly.

'ācāra', 'pracāra',—nāmera karaha 'dui' kārya
tumi—sarva-guru, tumi jagatera ārya

"You simultaneously perform both duties in relation to the holy name by your personal behavior and by your preaching. Therefore you are the spiritual master of the entire world, for you are the most advanced devotee in the world."[45]

NĀMĀCĀRYA ŚRĪLA HARIDĀSA ṬHĀKURA KI JĀYA!

ENDNOTES

[1] Here again we find evidence of Śrī Caitanya Mahāprabhu's interest in developing preaching strategies. He and Haridāsa Ṭhākura were most certainly absorbed in the names and pastimes of Śrī Kṛṣṇa; however, they were also discussing how others might be influenced and inspired. Since Haridāsa Ṭhākura with his Muslim background had practical knowledge of that culture, it is significant that Mahaprabhu is approaching him as an experienced person, who simultaneously had deep attachment to the holy name.

[2] *CC Antya* 3.50, 51.

[3] Scholars often identify the word "yavana" with Ionia, or Greece (see Monier-Williams dictionary). The term has also shifted in meaning over time. In this following quote from Śrīla Prabhupāda, he refers to a prediction that Yavanas would conquer India, and it was true that Alexander conquered India (or part of it—the Punjab) in the third century BCE. Later, of course, the Turks, or actually Turco-Mongols who were steeped in the Persian language and culture, conquered India in the 15th century. In ancient and medieval times the boundaries of countries shifted as empires rose and fell. Suffice it to say that the term "yavana" has generally meant Western(er), and more specifically, further west than

Iran (Persia). Thus, one could argue that "yavana" refers to a Western race or place.

[4] *SB 2.4.18* purport: Śrīla Prabhupāda writes: "**Yavanas**: Yavana was the name of one of the sons of Mahārāja Yayāti who was given the part of the world known as Turkey to rule. Therefore the Turks are Yavanas due to being descendants of Mahārāja Yavana. The Yavanas were therefore *kṣatriyas*, and later on, by giving up the brahminical culture, they became *mleccha-yavanas*. Descriptions of the Yavanas are in the *Mahābhārata (Ādi-parva* 85.34). Another prince called Turvasu was also known as Yavana, and his country was conquered by Sahadeva, one of the Pāṇḍavas. The western Yavana joined with Duryodhana in the Battle of Kurukṣetra under the pressure of Karṇa. It is also foretold that these Yavanas also would conquer India, and it proved to be true."

[5]An entire book has been composed by Śrīla Bhaktivinoda Ṭhākura on the exchanges of Haridāsa Ṭhākura and Śrī Caitanya Mahāprabhu called *Śrī Harināma-cintāmaṇi*. This book details the science of chanting the holy names in wonderful detail. Śrīla Bhaktivinoda Ṭhākura writes in the introduction to the book: "Inspired by certain Vaiṣṇavas, we compiled the teachings of Haridāsa Ṭhākura into the present book form. We received several other books about Śrīla Haridāsa. Unfortunately, many of them contained unauthorized and scripturally fallacious statements, and had to be rejected. One of them, however, appeared to have been written by an elevated Vaiṣṇava. It explained the esoteric mellow of chanting the holy name. Reading it gave us considerable joy. We could surmise that Śrīla Haridāsa must have instructed a saintly Vaiṣṇava on the philosophy of the holy name. That Vaiṣṇava in turn penned these valuable teachings in a book dedicated to his initiating spiritual master. We extended our heartfelt gratitude to the sender of the book from Śrīhaṭṭa. The *Harināma-cintāmaṇi* has recorded these precious edicts glorifying the holy name. This book, therefore, is being published for the pleasure of the devotees surrendered to the Lord and His transcendental name. We firmly believe that only those who have taken shelter of the holy name will read the book; others will not. Therefore we do not expect any arguments or challenges about the holy name from them." Readers who are serious about chanting the holy name are recommended to study this book carefully.

[6] *CC Antya* 3.63, 65.

[7] *CC Antya* 3.67—76.

[8] *CCAntya* 3.77.

[9] *CC Antya* 3.80 purport.

[10] *CC Antya* 3.86—88.

[11] *CC Antya* 3.89

[12] *CC Antya* 3.91, 3.92. "This is a characteristic of the Supreme Personality of Godhead. Although He wants to cover His opulence, He cannot do so before His devotees. This is well-known everywhere.

"'O my Lord, everything within material nature is limited by time, space and thought. Your characteristics, however, being unequaled and unsurpassed, are always transcendental to such limitations. You sometimes cover such characteristics by Your own energy, but nevertheless Your unalloyed devotees are always able to see You under all circumstances.'" (*Stotra-ratna* of Yamunācārya)

[13] *CC Antya* 3.96, 97.

[14] *CC Antya* 11.11—14.

[15] *CC Antya* 11.22.

[16] *CC Antya* 11.23.

[17] *CC Antya* 11.23 purport.

[18] *CC Antya* 11.25.

[19] *Songs of the Vaiṣṇava Ācāryas*, Songs of Śrīla Bhaktivinoda Ṭhākura, from *Gitāvalī, Aruṇodaya-kīrtana* (part 2) (to be sung at dawn), pg. 37, Bhaktivedanta Book Trust, 1979.

[20] *Songs of the Vaiṣṇava Ācāryas*, Songs of Śrīla Bhaktivinoda Ṭhākura, from *Gitāvalī, Śrī Nāma*, pg. 37, Bhaktivedanta Book Trust, 1979.

[21] *Songs of the Vaiṣṇava Ācāryas*, Songs of Śrīla Bhaktivinoda Ṭhākura, from *Gitāvalī, Aruṇodaya-kīrtana* (part 1) (to be sung at dawn) pg. 35, Bhaktivedanta Book Trust, 1979.

[22] *CC Adi* 10.48: "There was no end to the transcendental qualities of Haridāsa Ṭhākura. Here I mention but a fraction of His qualities. He was so exalted that Advaita Gosvāmī, when performing the *śrāddha* ceremony of his father, offered him the first plate." *CC Antya* 3.222: "Feeding you is equal to feeding ten million *brāhmaṇas*. Therefore, accept this *śrāddha-pātra*." Thus Advaita Ācārya made him eat. Śrīla Prabhupāda comments: "The *śrāddha-pātra*, or plate offered to the forefathers, is then offered to the best of the *brāhmaṇas* in society. Instead of offering the *śrāddha-pātra* to any other *brāhmaṇa*, Advaita Ācārya offered it to Haridāsa Ṭhākura, considering him greater than any of the foremost *brāhmaṇas*."

[23] *CC Antya* 11.26, 30.

[24] *CC Antya* 11.31—36.

[25] *CC Antya* 11.37, 38.

[26] *CC Antya* 11.39—42.

[27] The loving exchanges between Śrī Caitanya Mahāprabhu and Śrīla Haridāsa Ṭhākura are on a very intimate level. A very elevated devotee

may sometimes argue with or disagree with the Lord. The *gopīs* even used to chastise and challenge the Lord. It was possible for Haridāsa to see deeply into the intention of the Lord and to know when to disagree in a manner which augmented the Lord's pleasure. As *sādhakas* (neophyte devotees), we are obligated to attempt to become expert in serving the Lord's desires as explicitly expressed by the spiritual master and Kṛṣṇa and not to think we can leapfrog into the internal *līlā* of the Lord. First, there must be complete purity, and then there can be intimate dealings.

[28] *CC Antya* 11.47.

[29] *CC Antya* 11.47.

[30] *SB* 1.9.22.

[31] *SB* 1.9.22 purport.

[32] *SB* 1.9.30.

[33] *SB* 1.9.43 purport.

[34] The Bengali and Sanskrit word for airship is *vimāna*. For thousands of years the Indian traditions have understood that some beings could fly. Thus, the recent aeronautical accomplishments of the last one hundred years are not really so extraordinary.

[35] *CC Antya* 11.64.

[36] Ordinary people, and even many devotees, are cremated; however, Śrīla Haridāsa Ṭhākura was placed in *samādhi*, which is reserved for those great souls who have given up attachment to the world, and whose bodies have become pure by complete absorption in the service of the Lord.

[37] In this case there was not much cause for lamentation, at least not for Haridāsa Ṭhākura. He had lived a long life, he had served the Lord wonderfully, and he had left his body gloriously, in the way in which he desired. Those left behind would be bereft of his association; however, as Vaiṣṇavas, they were happy that Haridāsa had finished his service in Kali-yuga, where he had been subjected to so much abuse, and he could now return to serve the Lord in the pure environment of the spiritual world.

[38] *CC Antya* 11.88.

[39] *CC Antya* 11.91—97.

[40] *CC Antya* 11.98, 99.

[41] *CC Antya* 11.101.

[42] *CC Antya* 11.105.

[43] *CC Antya* 11.105 purport.

[44] The transcendental roommate of Śrīla Haridāsa Ṭhākura.

[45] *CC Antya* 4.99—103.

kṛṣṇa-mantra haite habe saṁsāra-mocana
kṛṣṇa-nāma haite pābe kṛṣṇera caraṇa

IN THIS AGE OF KALI there is no religious principle other than the chanting of the holy name, which is the essence of all Vedic hymns. This is the purport of all scriptures.'

Śrī Caitanya-caritāmṛta Ādi-līlā 7.73-74
[Lord Caitanya to Prakāśānanda Sarasvatī]

Appendix I
— Quotes from —
Śrīla Prabhupāda's Books

A DEVOTEE OF KṚṢṆA IS FRIENDLY TO EVERYONE. Therefore it is said here that he has no enemy (*nirvairaḥ*). How is this? A devotee situated in Kṛṣṇa consciousness knows that only devotional service to Kṛṣṇa can relieve a person from all the problems of life. He has personal experience of this, and therefore he wants to introduce this system, Kṛṣṇa consciousness, into human society. There are many examples in history of devotees of the Lord who risked their lives for the spreading of God consciousness. The favorite example is Lord Jesus Christ. He was crucified by the nondevotees, but he sacrificed his life for spreading God consciousness. Of course, it would be superficial to understand that he was killed. Similarly, in India also there are many examples, such as Ṭhākura Haridāsa and Prahlāda Mahārāja. Why such risk? Because they wanted to spread Kṛṣṇa consciousness, and it is difficult. A Kṛṣṇa conscious person knows that if a man is suffering it is due to his forgetfulness of his eternal relationship with Kṛṣṇa. Therefore, the highest benefit one can render to human society is relieving one's neighbor from all material problems. In such a way, a pure devotee is engaged in the service of the Lord. Now, we can imagine how merciful Kṛṣṇa is to those engaged in His service, risking everything for Him. Therefore it is certain that such persons must reach the supreme planet after leaving the body.

(*BG* 2.62)

ŚRĪ RĀMĀNANDA RĀYA WAS A SELF-REALIZED SOUL, although outwardly he belonged to a caste lower than the *brāhmaṇa* in social status. He was not in the renounced order of life, and besides that he was a high government servant in the state. Still, Śrī Caitanya Mahāprabhu accepted him as a liberated soul on the strength of the high order of his realization of transcendental knowledge. Similarly, the Lord accepted Śrīla Haridāsa Ṭhākura, a veteran devotee of the Lord coming from a Mohammedan family. And there are many other great devotees of the Lord who came from different communities, sects and castes. The Lord's only criterion was the standard of devotional service of the particular person. He was not concerned with the outward dress of a man; He was concerned only with the inner soul and its activities. Therefore all the missionary activities of the Lord are to be understood to be on the spiritual plane, and as such the cult of Śrī Caitanya Mahāprabhu, or the cult of *Bhāgavata-dharma*, has nothing to do with mundane affairs, sociology, politics, economic development or any such sphere of life. *Śrīmad-Bhāgavatam* is the purely transcendental urge of the soul.

(*SB* Canto I, Introduction)

THE LORD IS SO MERCIFUL that even if there is some impediment for the devotee, He Himself manages matters in such a way that the devotee is not bereft of having audience at His lotus feet. There is a very good example in the life of Haridāsa Ṭhākura. When Caitanya Mahāprabhu was residing at Jagannātha Purī, Haridāsa Ṭhākura, who happened to be Muhammadan by birth, was with Him. In Hindu temples, especially in those days, no one but a Hindu was allowed to enter. Although Haridāsa Ṭhākura was the greatest of all Hindus in his behavior, he considered himself a Muhammadan and did not enter the temple. Lord Caitanya could understand his humility, and since he did not go to see the temple, Lord Caitanya Himself, who is nondifferent from Jagannātha, used to come and sit with Haridāsa Ṭhākura daily. Here in *Śrīmad-Bhāgavatam* we also find this same behavior of the Lord. His devotees were prevented from seeing His lotus feet, but the Lord Himself came to see them on the same lotus feet for which they aspired. It is also significant that He was accompanied by the goddess of fortune. The goddess of fortune is not to be seen by ordinary persons, but the Lord was so kind that although the devotees did not aspire for such an honor, He appeared before them with the goddess of fortune.

(*SB* 3.16.2)

THE LORD ACCEPTS SACRIFICIAL OFFERINGS from the *brāhmaṇas* and devotees, and elsewhere it is stated that whatever is given for the *brāhmaṇas* and Vaiṣṇavas to eat is also accepted by the Lord. But here it is said that He accepts offerings to the mouths of *brāhmaṇas* and Vaiṣṇavas with even greater relish. The best example of this is found in the life of Advaita Prabhu in his dealings with Haridāsa Ṭhākura. Even though Haridāsa was born of a Muhammadan family, Advaita Prabhu offered him the first dish of *prasāda* after the performance of a sacred fire ceremony. Haridāsa Ṭhākura informed him that he was born of a Muhammadan family and asked why Advaita Prabhu was offering the first dish to a Muhammadan instead of an elevated *brāhmaṇa*. Out of his humbleness, Haridāsa condemned himself Muhammadan, but Advaita Prabhu, being an experienced devotee, accepted him as a real *brāhmaṇa*. Advaita Prabhu asserted that by offering the first dish to Haridāsa Ṭhākura, he was getting the result of feeding one hundred thousand *brāhmaṇas*. The conclusion is that if one can feed a *brāhmaṇa* or Vaiṣṇava, it is better than performing hundreds of thousands of sacrifices. In this age, therefore, it is recommended that *harer nāma* [Cc. Ādi 17.21]—chanting the holy name of God—and pleasing the Vaiṣṇava are the only means to elevate oneself to spiritual life.

(*SB* 3.16.8)

WHEN SOMETHING IS ARRANGED BY THE SUPREME Personality of Godhead, one should not be disturbed by it, even if it appears to be a reverse according to one's calculations. For example, sometimes we see that a powerful preacher is killed, or sometimes he is put into difficulty, just as Haridāsa Ṭhākura was. He was a great devotee who came into this material world to execute the will of the Lord by preaching the Lord's glories. But Haridāsa was punished at the hands of the Kazi by being beaten in twenty-two marketplaces. Similarly, Lord Jesus Christ was crucified, and Prahlāda Mahārāja was put through so many tribulations. The Pāṇḍavas, who were direct friends of Kṛṣṇa, lost their kingdom, their wife was insulted, and they had to undergo many severe tribulations. Seeing all these reverses affect devotees, one should not be disturbed; one should simply understand that in these matters there must be some plan of the Supreme Personality of Godhead. The *Bhāgavatam's* conclusion is that a devotee is never disturbed by such reverses. He accepts even reverse conditions as the grace of the

Lord. One who continues to serve the Lord even in reverse conditions is assured that he will go back to Godhead, back to the Vaikuṇṭha planets. Lord Brahmā assured the demigods that there was no use in talking about how the disturbing situation of darkness was taking place, since the actual fact was that it was ordered by the Supreme Lord. Brahmā knew this because he was a great devotee; it was possible for him to understand the plan of the Lord.

(*SB* 3.16.37)

A *SĀDHU*, AS DESCRIBED ABOVE, IS A DEVOTEE of the Lord. His concern, therefore, is to enlighten people in devotional service to the Lord. That is his mercy. He knows that without devotional service to the Lord, human life is spoiled. A devotee travels all over the country, from door to door, preaching, "Be Kṛṣṇa conscious. Be a devotee of Lord Kṛṣṇa. Don't spoil your life in simply fulfilling your animal propensities. Human life is meant for self-realization, or Kṛṣṇa consciousness." These are the preachings of a *sādhu*. He is not satisfied with his own liberation. He always thinks about others. He is the most compassionate personality towards all the fallen souls. One of his qualifications, therefore, is *kāruṇika*, great mercy to the fallen souls. While engaged in preaching work, he has to meet with so many opposing elements, and therefore the *sādhu*, or devotee of the Lord, has to be very tolerant. Someone may ill-treat him because the conditioned souls are not prepared to receive the transcendental knowledge of devotional service. They do not like it; that is their disease. The *sādhu* has the thankless task of impressing upon them the importance of devotional service. Sometimes devotees are personally attacked with violence. Lord Jesus Christ was crucified, Haridāsa Ṭhākura was caned in twenty-two marketplaces, and Lord Caitanya's principal assistant, Nityānanda, was violently attacked by Jagāi and Mādhāi. But still they were tolerant because their mission was to deliver the fallen souls. One of the qualifications of a *sādhu* is that he is very tolerant and is merciful to all fallen souls. He is merciful because he is the well-wisher of all living entities. He is not only a well-wisher of human society, but a well-wisher of animal society as well. It is said here, *sarva-dehinām*, which indicates all living entities who have accepted material bodies. Not only does the human being have a material body, but other living entities, such as cats and dogs, also have material bodies. The devotee of the Lord is merciful to everyone-the cats, dogs, trees, etc. He treats all living entities in such a way that they can ultimately get salvation from this material entanglement. Śivānanda Sena, one of the disciples of Lord Caitanya, gave liberation to a dog by treating the dog transcendentally. There are many instances where a dog got salvation by association with a *sādhu*, because a *sādhu* engages in the highest philanthropic activities for the benediction of all living entities. Yet although a *sādhu* is not inimical towards anyone, the world is so ungrateful that even a *sādhu* has many enemies.

What is the difference between an enemy and a friend? It is a difference in behavior. A *sādhu* behaves with all conditioned souls for their ultimate relief from material entanglement. Therefore, no one can be more friendly than a *sādhu* in relieving a conditioned soul. A *sādhu* is calm, and he quietly and peacefully follows the principles of scripture. A *sādhu* means one who follows the principles of scripture and at the same time is a devotee of the Lord. One who actually follows the principles of scripture must be a devotee of God because all the *śāstras* instruct us to obey the orders of the Personality of Godhead. *Sādhu*, therefore, means a follower of the scriptural injunctions and a devotee of the Lord. All these characteristics are prominent in a devotee. A devotee develops all the good qualities of the demigods, whereas a nondevotee, even though academically qualified, has no actual good qualifications or good characteristics according to the standard of transcendental realization.

(*SB* 3.25.22)

THE HOLY NAME HAS TO BE CHANTED to please the Supreme Lord, and not for any sense gratification or professional purpose. If this pure mentality is there, then even though a person is born of a low family, such as a dog-eater's, he is so glorious that not only has he purified himself, but he is quite competent to deliver others. He is competent to speak on the importance of the transcendental name, just as Ṭhākura Haridāsa did. He was apparently born in a family of Muhammadans, but because he was chanting the holy name of the Supreme Lord offenselessly, Lord Caitanya empowered him to become the authority, or *ācārya*, of spreading the name. It did not matter that he was born in a family which was not following the Vedic rules and regulations. Caitanya Mahāprabhu and Advaita Prabhu accepted him as an authority because he was offenselessly chanting the name of the Lord. Authorities like Advaita Prabhu and Lord Caitanya immediately accepted that he had already performed all kinds of austerities, studied the Vedas and performed all sacrifices. That is automatically understood. There is a hereditary class of brāhmaṇas called the *smārta-brāhmaṇas*, however, who are of the opinion that even if such persons who are chanting the holy name of the Lord are accepted as purified, they still have to perform the Vedic rites or await their next birth in a family of *brāhmaṇas* so that they can perform the Vedic rituals. But actually that is not the case. Such a man does not need to wait for the next birth to become purified. He is at once purified. It is understood that he has already performed all sorts of rites. It is the so-called *brāhmaṇas* who actually have to undergo different kinds of austerities before reaching that point of purification. There are many other Vedic performances which are not described here. All such Vedic rituals have been already performed by the chanters of the holy name.

(*SB* 3.33.7)

FIRE IS CERTAINLY DEVOID OF LIFE, but devotees and *brāhmaṇas* are the living representatives of the Supreme Lord. Therefore to feed *brāhmaṇas* and Vaiṣṇavas is to feed the Supreme Personality of Godhead directly. It may be concluded that instead of offering fire sacrifices, one should offer foodstuffs to *brāhmaṇas* and Vaiṣṇavas, for that process is more effective than fire *yajña.* The vivid example of this principle in action was given by Advaita Prabhu. When He performed the *śrāddha* ceremony for His father, He first of all called Haridāsa Ṭhākura and offered him food. It is the practice that after finishing the *śrāddha* ceremony, one should offer food to an elevated *brāhmaṇa*. But Advaita Prabhu offered food first to Haridāsa Ṭhākura, who had taken his birth in a Muhammadan family. Therefore Haridāsa Ṭhākura asked Advaita Prabhu why He was doing something which might jeopardize His position in *brāhmaṇa* society.

Advaita Prabhu replied that He was feeding millions of first-class *brāhmaṇas* by offering the food to Haridāsa Ṭhākura. He was prepared to talk with any learned *brāhmaṇa* on this point and prove definitely that by offering food to a pure devotee like Haridāsa Ṭhākura, He was equally as blessed as He would have been by offering food to thousands of learned *brāhmaṇas*. When performing sacrifices, one offers oblations to the sacrificial fire, but when such oblations are offered to Vaiṣṇavas, they are certainly more effective.

(*SB* 4.21.41)

THE WORD *ASAKṚT* IS SIGNIFICANT, for it means not just for a few minutes but continuously. That is the instruction given by Lord Caitanya Mahāprabhu in His *Śikṣāṣṭaka* 3. *Kīrtanīyaḥ sadā hariḥ*: [*Cc. Ādi* 17.31] "The holy name of the Lord should be chanted twenty-four hours daily." Therefore in this Kṛṣṇa consciousness movement we request the devotees to chant at least sixteen rounds on their beads daily. Actually one has to chant twenty-four hours daily, just like Ṭhākura Haridāsa, who was chanting the Hare Kṛṣṇa mantra three hundred thousand times daily. Indeed, he had no other business. Some of the Gosvāmīs, like Raghunātha dāsa Gosvāmī, were also chanting very rigidly and also offering obeisances very rigidly. As stated in Śrīnivāsācārya's prayer to the six Gosvāmīs (*Ṣaḍ-gosvāmy-aṣṭaka*): *saṅkhyā-pūrvaka-nāma-gāna-natibhiḥ kālāvasānī-kṛtau*. The word *saṅkhyā-pūrvaka* means "maintaining a numerical strength." Not only was Raghunātha dāsa Gosvāmī chanting the holy name of the Lord, but he was also offering obeisances in the same prolific numbers.

(*SB* 4.24.70)

IN THIS VERSE THE WORDS *DAYĀ JĪVEṢU*, meaning "mercy to other living entities," indicate that a living entity must be merciful to other living entities if he wishes to make progress in self-realization. This means he must preach this knowledge after perfecting himself and understanding his own position as an eternal servant of Kṛṣṇa. Preaching this is showing real mercy to living entities. Other types of humanitarian work may be temporarily beneficial for the body, but because a living entity is spirit soul, ultimately one can show him real mercy only by revealing knowledge of his spiritual existence. As Caitanya Mahāprabhu says, *jīvera 'svarūpa' haya-kṛṣṇera 'nitya-dāsa'*: [*Cc. Madhya* 20.108] "Every living entity is constitutionally a servant of Kṛṣṇa." One should know this fact perfectly and should preach it to the mass of people. If one realizes that he is an eternal servant of Kṛṣṇa but does not preach it, his realization is imperfect. Śrīla Bhaktisiddhānta Sarasvatī Ṭhākura therefore sings, *duṣṭa mana, tumi kisera vaiṣṇava? pratiṣṭhāra tare, nirjanera ghare, tava hari-nāma kevala kaitava*: "My dear mind, what kind of Vaiṣṇava are you? Simply for false prestige and a material reputation you are chanting the Hare Kṛṣṇa mantra in a solitary place." In this way people who do not preach are criticized. There are many Vaiṣṇavas in Vṛndāvana who do not like preaching; they chiefly try to imitate Haridāsa Ṭhākura. The actual result of their so-called chanting in a secluded place, however, is that they sleep and think of women and money. Similarly, one who simply engages in temple worship but does not see to the interests of the mass of people or cannot recognize devotees is called a *kaniṣṭha-adhikāri*:

arcāyām eva haraye
pūjāṁ yaḥ śraddhayehate

na tad-bhakteṣu cānyeṣu
sa bhaktaḥ prākṛtaḥ smṛtaḥ

(*SB* 11.2.47)

IN THIS REGARD, *CAITANYA-CARITĀMṚTA* (*Antya* 3.177-188) describes Haridāsa Ṭhākura's confirmation of the effect of chanting the holy name of the Lord.

keha bale–'nāma haite haya pāpa-kṣaya'
keha bale–'nāma haite jīvera mokṣa haya'

Some say that by chanting the holy name of the Lord one is freed from all the reactions of sinful life, and others say that by chanting the holy name of the Lord one attains liberation from material bondage.

haridāsa kahena,–"nāmera ei dui phala naya
nāmera phale kṛṣṇa-pade prema upajaya

Haridāsa Ṭhākura, however, said that the desired result of chanting the holy name of the Lord is not that one is liberated from material bondage or freed from the reactions of sinful life. The actual result of chanting the holy name of the Lord is that one awakens his dormant Kṛṣṇa consciousness, his loving service to the Lord.

ānuṣaṅgika phala nāmera–'mukti', 'pāpa-nāśa'
tāhāra dṛṣṭānta yaiche sūryera prakāśa

Haridāsa Ṭhākura said that liberation and freedom from the reactions of sinful activities are only by-products of chanting the holy name of the Lord. If one chants the holy name of the Lord purely, he attains the platform of loving service to the Supreme Personality of Godhead. In this regard Haridāsa Ṭhākura gave an example comparing the power of the holy name to sunshine.

ei ślokera artha kara paṇḍitera gaṇa"
sabe kahe,—'tumi kaha artha-vivaraṇa'

He placed a verse before all the learned scholars present, but the learned scholars asked him to state the purport of the verse.

haridāsa kahena,—"yaiche sūryera udaya
udaya nā haite ārambhe tamera haya kṣaya

Haridāsa Ṭhākura said that as the sun begins to rise, it dissipates the darkness of night, even before the sunshine is visible.

caura-preta-rākṣasādira bhaya haya nāśa
udaya haile dharma-karma-ādi parakāśa

Before the sunrise even takes place, the light of dawn destroys the fear of the dangers of the night, such as disturbances by thieves, ghosts and Rākṣasas, and when the sunshine actually appears, one engages in his duties.

aiche nāmodayārambhe pāpa-ādira kṣaya
udaya kaile kṛṣṇa-pade haya premodaya

Similarly, even before one's chanting of the holy name is pure, one is freed from all sinful reactions, and when he chants purely he becomes a lover of Kṛṣṇa.

'mukti' tuccha-phala haya nāmābhāsa haite
ye mukti bhakta nā laya, se kṛṣṇa cāhe dite"

A devotee never accepts *mukti*, even if Kṛṣṇa offers it. Mukti, freedom from all sinful reactions, is obtained even by *nāmābhāsa*, or a glimpse of the light of the holy name before its full light is perfectly visible.

The *nāmābhāsa* stage is between that of *nāma-aparādha*, or chanting of the holy name with offenses, and pure chanting. There are three stages in chanting the holy name of the Lord. In the first stage, one commits ten kinds of offenses while chanting. In the next stage, *nāmābhāsa*, the offenses have almost stopped, and one is coming to the platform of pure chanting. In the third stage, when one chants the Hare Kṛṣṇa mantra without offenses, his dormant love for Kṛṣṇa immediately awakens. This is the perfection.

(*SB* 5.24.20)

THOSE WHO ARE NOT *NĀRĀYAṆA-PARA*, pure devotees, must be disturbed by this duality of the material world, whereas devotees who are simply attached to the service of the Lord are not at all disturbed by it. For example, Haridāsa Ṭhākura was beaten with cane in twenty-two bazaars, but he was never disturbed; instead, he smilingly tolerated the beating. Despite the disturbing dualities of the material world, devotees are not disturbed at all. Because they fix their minds on the lotus feet of the Lord and concentrate on the holy name of the Lord, they do not feel the so-called pains and pleasures caused by the dualities of this material world.

(*SB* 6.17.29)

NĀRADA MUNI IS A GREAT SAINT and is transcendentally situated. Therefore, although he was a young man, he could give shelter to a young woman and accept her service. Haridāsa Ṭhākura also spoke with a young woman, a prostitute, in the dead of night, but the woman could not deviate his mind. Instead, she became a Vaiṣṇavī, a pure devotee, by the benediction of Haridāsa Ṭhākura. Ordinary persons, however, should not imitate such highly elevated devotees. Ordinary persons must strictly observe the rules and regulations by staying aloof from the association of women. No one should imitate Nārada Muni or Haridāsa Ṭhākura. It is said, *vaiṣṇavera kriyā-mudrā vijñe nā bujhaya*. Even if a man is very advanced in learning, he cannot understand the behavior of a Vaiṣṇava. Anyone can take shelter of a pure Vaiṣṇava, without fear. Therefore in the previous verse it has been distinctly said, *devarṣer antike sākuto-bhayā*: Kayādhu, the mother of Prahlāda Mahārāja, stayed under the protection of Nārada Muni without fear from any direction. Similarly, Nārada Muni, in his transcendental position, stayed with the young woman without fear of deviation. Nārada Muni, Haridāsa Ṭhākura and similar *ācāryas* especially empowered to broadcast the glories of the Lord cannot be brought down to the material platform. Therefore one is strictly forbidden to think that the *ācārya* is an ordinary human being (*guruṣu nara-matiḥ*).

(*SB* 7.7.14)

ONE WHO RESTRAINS THE SENSES and organs of action, but whose mind dwells on sense objects, certainly deludes himself and is called a pretender." (Bg. 3.6) One should act for Kṛṣṇa very seriously in order to become fully Kṛṣṇa conscious and should not sit down to imitate such great personalities as Haridāsa Ṭhākura. Śrīla Bhaktisiddhānta Sarasvatī Ṭhākura condemned such imitation. He said:

duṣṭa mana! tumi kisera vaiṣṇava?
pratiṣṭhāra tare, nirjanera ghare,
tava hari-nāma kevala kaitava

"My dear mind, what kind of devotee are you? Simply for cheap adoration, you sit in a solitary place and pretend to chant the Hare Kṛṣṇa *mahā-mantra*, but this is all cheating." Recently at Māyāpur an African devotee wanted to imitate Haridāsa Ṭhākura, but after fifteen days he became restless and went away. Do not suddenly try to imitate Haridāsa Ṭhākura. Engage yourself in Kṛṣṇa conscious activities, and gradually you will come to the stage of liberation (*muktir hitvānyathā rūpaṁ svarūpeṇa vyavasthitiḥ* [*SB* 2.10.6]).

(*SB* 7.7.14)

THE *ĀCĀRYA'S* DUTY, THEREFORE, is to find the means by which devotees may render service according to references from śāstra. Rūpa Gosvāmī, for example, in order to help subsequent devotees, published such devotional books as *Bhakti-rasāmṛta-sindhu*. Thus it is the duty of the *ācārya* to publish books that will help future candidates take up the method of service and become eligible to return home, back to Godhead, by the mercy of the Lord. In our Kṛṣṇa consciousness movement, this same path is being prescribed and followed. Thus the devotees have been advised to refrain from four sinful activities—illicit sex, intoxication, meat-eating and gambling—and to chant sixteen rounds a day. These are bona fide instructions. Because in the Western countries constant chanting is not possible, one should not artificially imitate Haridāsa Ṭhākura, but should follow the regulative principles and the method prescribed in the various books and literatures published by the authorities. The *ācārya* gives the suitable method for crossing the ocean of nescience by accepting the boat of the Lord's lotus feet, and if this method is strictly followed, the followers will ultimately reach the destination, by the grace of the Lord. This method is called *ācārya-sampradāya*. It is therefore said, *sampradāya-vihīnā ye mantrās te niṣphalā matāḥ* (*Padma Purāṇa*). The *ācārya-sampradāya* is strictly bona fide. Therefore one must accept the *ācārya-sampradāya*; otherwise one's endeavor will be futile. Śrīla Narottama dāsa Ṭhākura therefore sings:

tāṅdera caraṇa sevi bhakta sane vāsa
janame janame haya, ei abhilāṣa

One must worship the lotus feet of the *ācārya* and live within the society of devotees. Then one's endeavor to cross over nescience will surely be successful.

(*SB* 10.2.31)

THE TWENTIETH BRANCH of the Caitanya tree was Haridāsa Ṭhākura. His character was wonderful. He used to chant the holy name of Kṛṣṇa 300,000 times a day without fail.

PURPORT

Certainly the chanting of 300,000 holy names of the Lord is wonderful. No ordinary person can chant so many names, nor should one artificially imitate Haridāsa Ṭhākura's behavior. It is essential, however, that everyone fulfill a specific vow to chant the Hare Kṛṣṇa mantra. Therefore we have prescribed in our Society that all our students must chant at least sixteen rounds daily. Such chanting must be offenseless in order to be of high quality. Mechanical chanting is not as powerful as chanting of the holy name without offenses. It is stated in the *Caitanya-bhāgavata, Ādi-khaṇḍa*, Chapter Two, that Haridāsa Ṭhākura was born in a village known as Buḍhana but after some time came to live on the bank of the Ganges at Phuliyā, near Śāntipura. From the description of his chastisement by a Muslim magistrate, which is found in the Sixteenth Chapter of the *Ādi-khaṇḍa* of *Caitanya-bhāgavata*, we can understand how humble and meek Haridāsa Ṭhākura was and how he achieved the causeless mercy of the Lord. In the dramas performed by Lord Caitanya Mahāprabhu, Haridāsa Ṭhākura played the part of a police chief. While chanting the Hare Kṛṣṇa *mahā-mantra* in Benāpola, he was personally tested by Māyādevī herself. Haridāsa Ṭhākura's passing away is described in the *Antya-līlā* of *Caitanya-caritāmṛta*, Eleventh Chapter. It is not definitely certain whether Śrī Haridāsa Ṭhākura appeared in the village named Buḍhana that is in the district of Khulnā. Formerly this village was within a district of twenty-four *pargaṇas* within the Sātakṣīrā division.

(*Cc Adi* 10.43)

ONE SUBBRANCH OF HARIDĀSA ṬHĀKURA consisted of the residents of Kulīna-grāma. The most important among them was Satyarāja Khān, or Satyarāja Vasu, who was a recipient of all the mercy of Haridāsa Ṭhākura.

PURPORT

Satyarāja Khān was the son of Guṇarāja Khān and father of Rāmānanda Vasu. Haridāsa Ṭhākura lived for some time during the Cāturmāsya period in the village named Kulīna-grāma, where he chanted the holy name, the Hare Kṛṣṇa *mahā-mantra*, and distributed his mercy to the descendants of the Vasu family. Satyarāja Khān was allotted the service of supplying silk ropes for the Jagannātha Deity during the Ratha-yātrā festival. Śrī Caitanya Mahāprabhu's answers to his inquiries about the duty of householder devotees are vividly described in the *Madhya-līlā*, Chapters Fifteen and Sixteen.

The village of Kulīna-grāma is situated two miles from the railway station named Jaugrāma on the Newcord line from Howrah to Burdwan. Lord Caitanya Mahāprabhu very highly praised the people of Kulīna-grāma, and He stated that even a dog of Kulīna-grāma was very dear to Him.

(Cc Adi 10.48)

TO AVOID TURMOIL, three great personalities—Haridāsa Ṭhākura, Śrīla Rūpa Gosvāmī and Śrīla Sanātana Gosvāmī—did not enter the temple of Jagannātha.

PURPORT

It is still the practice at the Jagannātha temple not to allow those to enter who do not strictly follow the Vedic culture known as Hinduism. Śrīla Haridāsa Ṭhākura, Śrīla Rūpa Gosvāmī and Śrīla Sanātana Gosvāmī had had previous intimate connections with Muslims. Haridāsa Ṭhākura had been born in a Muslim family, and Śrīla Rūpa Gosvāmī and Śrīla Sanātana Gosvāmī, having given up their social status in Hindu society, had been appointed ministers in the Muslim government. They had even changed their names to Dabira Khāsa and Sākara Mallika. Thus they had supposedly been expelled from *brāhmaṇa* society. Consequently, out of humility they did not enter the temple of Jagannātha, although the Personality of Godhead, Jagannātha, in His form of Caitanya Mahāprabhu, personally came to see them every day. Similarly, the members of this Kṛṣṇa consciousness society are sometimes refused entrance into some of the temples in India. We should not feel sorry about this as long as we engage in chanting the Hare Kṛṣṇa *mantra*. Kṛṣṇa Himself associates with devotees who are chanting His holy name, and there is no need to be unhappy over not being able to enter a certain temple. Such dogmatic prohibitions were not approved by Lord Caitanya Mahāprabhu. Those who were thought unfit to enter the Jagannātha temple were daily visited by Caitanya Mahāprabhu, and this indicates that Caitanya Mahāprabhu did not approve of the prohibitions. To avoid unnecessary turmoil, however, these great personalities would not enter the Jagannātha temple.

(*Cc Madhya* 1.63)

HARIDĀSA ṬHĀKURA SAID, "I am the most sinful and lowest among men. Later I shall eat one palmful of *prasādam* while waiting outside."

PURPORT

Although the Hindus and Muslims lived together in a very friendly manner, still there were distinctions between them. The Muslims were considered *yavanas*, or low-born, and whenever a Muslim was invited, he would be fed outside of the house. Although personally called by Śrī Caitanya Mahāprabhu and Nityānanda Prabhu to take *prasādam* with Them, still, out of great humility, Haridāsa Ṭhākura submitted, "I shall take the *prasādam* outside of the house." Although Haridāsa Ṭhākura was an exalted Vaiṣṇava accepted by Advaita Ācārya, Nityānanda Prabhu and Śrī Caitanya Mahāprabhu, nonetheless, in order not to disturb social tranquillity, he humbly kept himself in the position of a Muslim, outside the jurisdiction of the Hindu community. Therefore he proposed to take *prasādam* outside the house. Although he was in an exalted position and equal to other great Vaiṣṇavas, he considered himself a *pāpiṣṭha*, a most sinful man, and *adhama*, the lowest among men. Although a Vaiṣṇava may be very advanced spiritually, he keeps himself externally humble and submissive.

(*Cc Madhya* 3.63)

ALTHOUGH ŚRĪLA HARIDĀSA ṬHĀKURA was born in a Muslim family, he was accepted as a properly initiated *brāhmaṇa*. As such, he had every right to enter the temple of Jagannātha Purī, but because there were some rules and regulations stipulating that only *brāhmaṇas, kṣatriyas, vaiśyas* and *śūdras* (members of the *varṇāśrama-dharma* system) could enter, Haridāsa Ṭhākura, out of his great humility, did not want to violate these existing rules. He therefore said that he did not have the strength to enter into the temple, and he pointed out that if Lord Śrī Caitanya Mahāprabhu lived within the temple, there would be no way for Haridāsa Ṭhākura to see Him. Later, when Haridāsa Ṭhākura went to Jagannātha Purī, he lived outside the temple, at a place called

Siddhabakula. A monastery has now been erected there, known as Siddhabakula Maṭha. People who visit Jagannātha Purī often go to see Siddhabakula and the tomb of Haridāsa Ṭhākura, on the beach by the sea.

(*Cc Madhya* 3.194)

ALTHOUGH HARIDĀSA ṬHĀKURA was such a highly exalted Vaiṣṇava that he was addressed as Haridāsa Gosvāmī, he still did not like to disturb the common sense of the general populace. Haridāsa Ṭhākura was so exalted that he was addressed as *ṭhākura* and *gosāñi*, and these titles are offered to the most advanced Vaiṣṇavas. The spiritual master is generally called *gosāñi*, and *ṭhākura* is used to address the *paramahaṁsas*, those in the topmost rank of spirituality. Nonetheless, Haridāsa Ṭhākura did not want to go near the temple, although he was called there by Śrī Caitanya Mahāprabhu Himself. The Jagannātha temple still accepts only those Hindus who are in the *varṇāśrama* order. Other castes, especially those who are not Hindu, are not allowed to enter the temple. This is a long-standing regulation, and thus Haridāsa Ṭhākura, although certainly competent and qualified to enter the temple, did not want even to go near it. This is called Vaiṣṇava humility.

(*Cc Madhya* 11.165)

THIS STATEMENT OF ŚRĪ CAITANYA MAHĀPRABHU is significant. *Nibhṛte vasiyā tāhāṅ kariba smaraṇa*: "I shall sit down there in that solitary place and remember the lotus feet of the Lord." Neophyte students are not to imitate sitting in a solitary place and remembering the lotus feet of the Lord by chanting the Hare Kṛṣṇa *mahā-mantra*. We should always remember that it was Śrī Caitanya Mahāprabhu Himself who wanted such a place, either for Himself or Haridāsa Ṭhākura. No one can suddenly attain the level of Haridāsa Ṭhākura and sit down in a solitary place to chant the Hare Kṛṣṇa *mahā-mantra* and remember the lotus feet of the Lord. Only an exalted person like Haridāsa Ṭhākura or Śrī Caitanya Mahāprabhu, who is personally exhibiting the proper behavior for an *ācārya*, can engage in such a practice.

At the present moment we see that some of the members of the International Society for Krishna Consciousness are tending to leave their preaching activities in order to sit in a solitary place. This is not a very good sign. It is a fact that Śrīla Bhaktisiddhānta Sarasvatī Ṭhākura has condemned this process for neophytes. He has even stated in a song, *pratiṣṭhāra tare, nirjanera ghare, tava hari-nāma kevala kaitava*: "Sitting in a solitary place intending to chant the Hare Kṛṣṇa *mahā-mantra* is considered a cheating process." This practice is not possible for neophytes at all. The neophyte devotee must act and work very laboriously under the direction of the spiritual master, and he must thus preach the cult of Śrī Caitanya Mahāprabhu. Only after maturing in devotion can he sit down in a solitary place to chant the Hare Kṛṣṇa *mahā-mantra* as Śrī Caitanya Mahāprabhu Himself did. Although Śrī Caitanya Mahāprabhu is the Supreme Personality of Godhead, to teach us a lesson He traveled all over India continuously for six years and only then retired at Jagannātha Purī. Even at Jagannātha Purī the Lord chanted the Hare Kṛṣṇa *mahā-mantra* in great meetings at the Jagannātha temple. The point is that one should not try to imitate Haridāsa Ṭhākura at the beginning of one's transcendental life. One must first become very mature in devotion and thus receive the approval of Śrī Caitanya Mahāprabhu. Only at such a time may one actually sit down peacefully in a solitary place to chant the Hare Kṛṣṇa *mahā-mantra* and remember the lotus feet of the Lord. The senses are very strong, and if a neophyte devotee imitates Haridāsa Ṭhākura, his enemies (*kāma, krodha, lobha, moha, mada* and *mātsarya*) will disturb and fatigue him. Instead of chanting the Hare Kṛṣṇa *mahā-mantra*, the neophyte will simply sleep soundly. Preaching work is meant for advanced devotees, and when an advanced devotee is further elevated on the devotional scale, he may retire to chant the Hare Kṛṣṇa *mantra* in a solitary place. However, if one simply imitates advanced spiritual life, he will fall down, just like the *sahajiyās* in Vṛndāvana.

(*Cc Madhya* 11.176)

BY HIS PRACTICAL EXAMPLE, Śrī Caitanya Mahāprabhu has shown us that all the grains of sand must be picked up thoroughly and thrown outside. Śrī Caitanya Mahāprabhu also cleansed the outside of the temple, fearing that the grains of sand would again come within. In this connection, Śrīla Bhaktisiddhānta Sarasvatī Ṭhākura explains that even though one may become free from the desire for fruitive activity, sometimes the subtle desire for fruitive activity again comes into being within the heart. One often thinks of conducting business to improve devotional activity. But the contamination is so strong that it may later develop into misunderstanding, described as *kuṭi-nāṭi* (faultfinding) and *pratiṣṭhāśā* (the desire for name and fame and for high position), *jīva-hiṁsā* (envy of other living entities), *niṣiddhācāra* (accept ing things forbidden in the *śāstra*), *kāma* (desire for material gain) and *pūjā* (hankering for popularity). The word *kuṭi-nāṭi* means "duplicity." As an example of *pratiṣṭhāśā*, one may attempt to imitate Śrīla Haridāsa Ṭhākura by living in a solitary place. One's real desire may be for name and fame—in other words, one thinks that fools will accept one to be as good as Haridāsa Ṭhākura just because one lives in a solitary place. These are all material desires. A neophyte devotee is certain to be attacked by other material desires as well, namely desires for women and money. In this way the heart is again filled with dirty things and becomes harder and harder, like that of a materialist. Gradually one desires to become a reputed devotee or an *avatāra* (incarnation).

(*Cc Madhya* 12.135)

AT NOON, WHEN THERE WAS an *upala-bhoga* offering in a place called *bhoga-vardhana-khaṇḍa*, Śrī Caitanya Mahāprabhu would go outside the temple. Before going outside, He used to stand near the Garuḍa-stambha column and offer His obeisances and prayers. Afterwards, the Lord would visit Siddha-bakula, where Haridāsa Ṭhākura lived. After visiting with Haridāsa Ṭhākura, the Lord would return to His own place at the abode of Kāśī Miśra.

(*Cc Madhya* 15.6)

THE LOUD CHANTING OF THE HARE KṚṢṆA MANTRA is so powerful that it can even penetrate the ears of trees and creepers, what to speak of those of animals and human beings. Śrī Caitanya Mahāprabhu once asked Haridāsa Ṭhākura how trees and plants could be delivered, and Haridāsa

Ṭhākura replied that the loud chanting of the Hare Kṛṣṇa *mahā-mantra* would benefit not only trees and plants but insects and all other living beings. One should therefore not be disturbed by the loud chanting of Hare Kṛṣṇa, for it is beneficial not only to the chanter but to everyone who gets an opportunity to hear.

(*Cc Madhya* 17.45)

SOMETIMES PEOPLE ACCEPT AS *mahājanas* those who have been designated by Śrīla Vṛndāvana dāsa Ṭhākura as *ḍhaṅga-vipras* (imposter *brāhmaṇas*). Such imposters imitate the characteristics of Śrīla Haridāsa Ṭhākura, and they envy Haridāsa Ṭhākura, who was certainly a *mahājana*. They make great artificial endeavors, advertising themselves as great devotees of the Lord or as mystic hypnotists knowledgeable in witchcraft, hypnotism and miracles. Sometimes people accept as *mahājanas* demons like Pūtanā, Tṛṇāvarta, Vatsa, Baka, Aghāsura, Dhenuka, Kālīya and Pralamba. Some people accept imitators and adversaries of the Supreme Personality of Godhead, such as Pauṇḍraka, Śṛgāla Vāsudeva, the spiritual master of the demons (Śukrācārya), or atheists like Cārvāka, King Vena, Sugata and Arhat. People who accept such imitators as *mahājanas* have no faith in Śrī Caitanya Mahāprabhu as the Supreme Personality of Godhead. Rather, they accept godless cheaters who present themselves as incarnations of God and cheat foolish people within the material world by word jugglery. Thus many rascals are accepted as *mahājanas*.

(*Cc Madhya* 17.185)

ALTHOUGH KṚṢṆA WANTS everyone to surrender to His lotus feet, because of people's sinful activities they cannot do this. *Na māṁ duṣkṛtino mūḍhāḥ prapadyante narādhamāḥ*: [Bg. 7.15] rascals and fools, the lowest of men, who engage in sinful activities, cannot suddenly surrender to the lotus feet of Kṛṣṇa. Nevertheless, if they begin chanting the Hare Kṛṣṇa mantra and rendering service unto the *tulasī* plant, they will very soon be able to surrender. One's real duty is to surrender to the lotus feet of Kṛṣṇa, but if one is unable to do so, he should adopt this process, as introduced by Śrī Caitanya Mahāprabhu and His most confidential servant, Nāmācārya Śrīla Haridāsa Ṭhākura. This is the way to achieve success in Kṛṣṇa consciousness.

(*Cc Antya* 3.137)

THUS HARIDĀSA ṬHĀKURA WAS AFRAID that Advaita Ācārya would be put into some difficulty because of His familiarity with Haridāsa Ṭhākura. Śrī Advaita Ācārya treated Haridāsa Ṭhākura as a most elevated Vaiṣṇava, but others, like Rāmacandra Khān, were envious of Haridāsa Ṭhākura. Of course, we have to follow in the footsteps of Advaita Ācārya, not caring for people like Rāmacandra Khān. At present, many Vaiṣṇavas are coming to our Kṛṣṇa consciousness movement from among the Europeans and Americans, and although men like Rāmacandra Khān are always envious of such Vaiṣṇavas, one should follow in the footsteps of Śrī Advaita Ācārya by treating all of them as Vaiṣṇavas. Although they are not as exalted as Haridāsa Ṭhākura, such Americans and Europeans, having accepted the principles of Vaiṣṇava philosophy and behavior, should never be excluded from Vaiṣṇava society.
(*Cc Antya* 3.220)

ŚRĀDDHA IS *PRASĀDAM* OFFERED to the forefathers at a certain date of the year or month. The *śrāddha-pātra*, or plate offered to the forefathers, is then offered to the best of the *brāhmaṇas* in society. Instead of offering the *śrāddha-pātra* to any other *brāhmaṇa*, Advaita Ācārya offered it to Haridāsa Ṭhākura, considering him greater than any of the foremost *brāhmaṇas*. This act by Śrī Advaita Ācārya proves that Haridāsa Ṭhākura was always situated in a transcendental position and was therefore always greater than even the most exalted *brāhmaṇa*, for he was situated above the mode of goodness of the material world.

(*Cc Antya* 3.222)

ŚRĪ CAITANYA MAHĀPRABHU further inquired from Haridāsa, "Can you ascertain what your disease is?" Haridāsa Ṭhākura replied, "My disease is that I cannot complete my rounds."

PURPORT

If one cannot complete the fixed number of rounds he is assigned, he should be considered to be in a diseased condition of spiritual life. Śrīla Haridāsa Ṭhākura is called *nāmācārya*. Of course, we cannot imitate Haridāsa Ṭhākura, but everyone must chant a prescribed number of rounds. In our Kṛṣṇa consciousness movement we have fixed sixteen rounds as the minimum so that the Westerners will not feel burdened. These sixteen rounds must be chanted, and chanted loudly, so that one can hear himself and others.

(*Cc Antya* 11.23)

UNLESS ONE HAS COME to the platform of spontaneous love of God, he must follow the regulative principles. Ṭhākura Haridāsa was the living example of how to follow the regulative principles.

(*Cc Antya* 11.24)

YOUR ROLE IN THIS INCARNATION is to deliver the people in general. You have sufficiently preached the glories of the holy name in this world."

PURPORT

Haridāsa Ṭhākura is known as *nāmācārya* because it is he who preached the glories of chanting *hari-nāma*, the holy name of God. By using the words *tomāra avatāra* ("your incarnation"), Śrī Caitanya Mahāprabhu confirms that Haridāsa Ṭhākura is the incarnation of Lord Brahmā. Śrīla Bhaktisiddhānta Sarasvatī Ṭhākura says that advanced devotees help the Supreme Personality of Godhead in His mission and that such devotees or personal associates incarnate by the will of the Supreme Lord. The Supreme Lord incarnates by His own will, and, by His will, competent devotees also incarnate to help Him in His mission. Haridāsa Ṭhākura is thus the incarnation of Lord Brahmā, and other devotees are likewise incarnations who help in the prosecution of the Lord's mission.

(*Cc Antya* 11.25)

ŚRĪ CAITANYA MAHĀPRABHU gave this benediction: "Anyone who has seen the festival of Śrī Haridāsa Ṭhākura's passing away, anyone who has chanted and danced here, anyone who has offered sand on the body of Haridāsa Ṭhākura, and anyone who has joined this festival to partake of the *prasādam* will achieve the favor of Kṛṣṇa very soon. There is such wonderful power in seeing Haridāsa Ṭhākura.

TRANSLATION

"Being merciful upon Me, Kṛṣṇa gave Me the association of Haridāsa Ṭhākura. Being independent in His desires, He has now broken that association.

"When Haridāsa Ṭhākura wanted to leave this material world, it was not within My power to detain him.

"Simply by his will, Haridāsa Ṭhākura could give up his life and go away, exactly like Bhīṣma, who previously died simply by his own desire, as we have heard from *śāstra*.

"Haridāsa Ṭhākura was the crown jewel on the head of this world; without him, this world is now bereft of its valuable jewel."

Śrī Caitanya Mahāprabhu then told everyone, "Say 'All glories to Haridāsa Ṭhākura!' and chant the holy name of Hari." Saying this, He personally began to dance.

Everyone began to chant, "All glories to Haridāsa Ṭhākura, who revealed the importance of chanting the holy name of the Lord!"

(*Cc Antya* 11.91-99)

HARIDĀSA ṬHĀKURA WAS NOT ONLY the topmost devotee of the Lord but also a great and learned scholar. It was his great fortune that he passed away before Śrī Caitanya Mahāprabhu.

PURPORT

Haridāsa Ṭhākura is mentioned here as the most learned scholar, *parama-vidvān*. Actually, the most important science to know is the science of getting out of the clutches of material existence. Anyone who knows this science must be considered the greatest learned person. Anyone who knows the temporary situation of this material world and is expert in achieving a permanent situation in the spiritual world, who knows that the Supreme Personality of Godhead is beyond the jurisdiction of our experimental knowledge, is understood to be the most learned scholar. Haridāsa Ṭhākura knew this science perfectly. Therefore, he is described in this connection as *parama-vidvān*. He personally preached the importance of chanting the Hare Kṛṣṇa *mahā-mantra*, which is approved by the revealed scriptures. As stated in the *Śrīmad-Bhāgavatam* (7.5.24):

iti puṁsārpitā viṣṇau bhaktiś cen nava-lakṣaṇā
kriyeta bhagavaty addhā tan manye 'dhītam uttamam

There are nine different processes of devotional service to Kṛṣṇa, the most important being *śravaṇaṁ kīrtanam* [SB 7.5.23]—hearing and chanting. Haridāsa Ṭhākura knew this science very well, and he can therefore be called, technically, *sarva-śāstrādhītī*. Anyone who has learned the essence of all the Vedic scriptures is to be known as a first-class educated person, with full knowledge of all *śāstra*.

(*Cc Antya* 11.105)

HARIDĀSA ṬHĀKURA, A MUHAMMADAN BY BIRTH, was a very great devotee and was always chanting Hare Kṛṣṇa.

That was his only fault. However, the Muslim Kazi called him forth and said, "You are a Muhammadan, born in a great Muhammadan family, yet you are chanting this Hindu Hare Kṛṣṇa mantra. What is this?" Haridāsa Ṭhākura mildly replied, "My dear sir, there are many Hindus who have become Muhammadans. Suppose I have become a Hindu? What is wrong with this?" The Kazi became very angry and ordered Haridāsa Ṭhākura to be whipped in twenty-two bazaars. This essentially meant that he was to be beaten to death, but because he was such a great devotee he did not actually feel the pain. Although a devotee may sometimes have to suffer, he tolerates the suffering. At the same time, he is very kind to conditioned souls and tries to elevate them to Kṛṣṇa consciousness. This is one of the primary features of a devotee's life. People are always putting a *sādhu* into difficulties, but he does not give up his job, which is to spread Kṛṣṇa consciousness so that others may become happy.

(*TLK* verse 23, purport)

WHERE THERE IS KṚṢṆA, there is no question of hell; every place is Vaikuṇṭha. Haridāsa Ṭhākura, for instance, did not enter the Jagannātha temple at Purī, for he was born in a Muhammadan family, and the Hindus opposed the Muhammadans' entering the temple. Haridāsa Ṭhākura did not let this disturb him, however. He thought, "Oh, why should I go and disturb them? I shall chant here." Consequently Lord Caitanya, who is Lord Jagannātha Himself, came daily to see Haridāsa. This is the power of a pure devotee: he doesn't have to go to Jagannātha; Jagannātha comes to him. Lord Caitanya Mahāprabhu used to go see Haridāsa Ṭhākura daily when the Lord was going to bathe in the sea. The Lord would enter Haridāsa's cottage and ask, "Haridāsa, what are you doing?" and Haridāsa would reply, "Please come in, my Lord." This then is the actual position of a devotee. Therefore Kṛṣṇa says that worship of His devotee is even more valuable than worship of Himself.

(*SSR* chapter 8)

ŚRĪLA GAURAKIŚORA DĀSA BĀBĀJĪ always tried to dissuade his disciple, Śrīla Bhaktisiddhānta Sarasvatī Ṭhākura, from going to Calcutta, which he considered a bastion of Kali-yuga. Yet though some might think Śrīla Bhaktisiddhānta Sarasvatī Ṭhākura disobeyed his guru's order, he preached not only in Calcutta but in other capitals of Kali-yuga, such as London, Berlin, Bombay, Madras, and Delhi. He vehemently opposed the idea of constructing a temple in some quiet spot and leading a passive and uneventful life in the monastery. He represented perfectly the ideal of utilizing 100 percent of one's energy in God's service for the spiritual upliftment of humanity. A certain Gujarati friend offered to build him a temple in Ville Parle, a quiet and remote section of Bombay. He immediately refused. We had the greatest good fortune of seeing him act and preach in this way. And now it is our ill fate that after the passing away of Śrīla Bhaktisiddhānta Sarasvatī Ṭhākura, the exemplar of *patita-pāvana*, we have returned to our lowly, fallen ways. Is there a glimmer of hope for our deliverance?

(*RTW* 2.3 about Gaurikisora and BSST)

ŚRĪLA RAGHUNĀTHA DĀSA GOSVĀMĪ'S father and uncle—Hiraṇya Majumdara and Govardhana Majumdara, respectively—were big landowners of the ancient village of

Cāndapura at Saptagrāma. One of their employees, a *brāhmaṇa* by birth named Gopāla Cakravartī, locked the great Vaiṣṇava saint Śrīla Haridāsa Ṭhākura in a debate on the scriptures. The *brāhmaṇa* was a sheer empiricist, and the Vaiṣṇava saint was an absolute authority on the chanting of the holy names of God, Kṛṣṇa. The *brāhmaṇa* asked Śrīla Haridāsa at what stage of realization liberation is attained. Citing many appropriate verses from the scriptures, Śrīla Haridāsa explained that just as fear of nocturnal creatures like thieves, ghosts, and hobgoblins evaporates at dawn's first light, so all sins and offences are erased and liberation is attained in the clearing stage of chanting the holy name, called *nāmābhāsa*, which comes long before pure chanting. Only a liberated, highly evolved soul can utter the Lord's name purely and thus achieve the highest realization, untainted love of Godhead. The speculative philosopher *brāhmaṇa*, who was very much addicted to sophism, could not fathom the saint's instructions and so ended up offending him. The foolish *brāhmaṇa* tried to impose his own interpretations on the excellences of the holy name and concluded that Śrīla Haridāsa Ṭhākura was a mere sentimentalist. He insolently rebuked the saint in public and tried to ridicule his explanations and character.

Argumentative impersonalists fail to grasp that without first properly understanding the science of the Absolute Truth, one cannot possibly develop firm devotion to the Supreme Lord. Hence when a person is seen to be situated on the platform of pure devotional service, it is to be understood that his ignorance has been destroyed. We have discussed this point in some detail in the previous essay, "The Science of Devotion." The empirical philosophers generally put forward the idea that human life is meant for achieving perfect knowledge. To them, knowledge means the ability to discern reality from illusion. By eradicating illusion and establishing that truth and reality are nondifferent from Brahman, they want to merge into the existence of Brahman. This, then, is their definition of perfect knowledge, which they aspire to attain birth after birth. They declare that the highest stage of knowledge is reached when the knower, the knowledge, and the object of knowledge become one entity, which then finally merges into Brahman, attaining liberation. Lord Caitanya has described this state of liberation as *bhava-mahādāvāgni-nirvāpanam*, "extinguishing the flames of material existence." He cited many verses from the revealed scriptures proving that a pure devotee easily attains this state of liberation by chanting the holy names of God.

The *brāhmaṇa* Gopāla Cakravartī believed that *jñāna*, perfect knowledge, is far superior to devotional service of the Lord. But as recorded in the *Caitanya-caritāmṛta* (*Antya* 3.201):

balāi-purohita tāre karilā bhartsana
"ghaṭa-paṭiyā mūrkha tumi bhakti kāṅhā jāna?"

The priest named Balarāma Ācārya chastised Gopāla Cakravartī. "You are a foolish logician," he said. "What do you know about the devotional service of the Lord?"

If one pretends to be a devotee of the Lord but does not understand the difference between dry speculative knowledge and knowledge of the Supreme Absolute Truth, then such a person's devotion borders on impersonalism and is rank with cheap sentimentalism, which is totally against the spiritual teachings of Śrīla Rūpa Gosvāmī. Therefore *jñāna-yoga* is not speculation or empirical research; nor is it the sudden emotional outbursts of upstarts pretending to be devotees. By practicing genuine *jñāna-yoga*, even an empirical philosopher will develop a taste for hearing purely spiritual topics from the scriptures. Eventually he will come to understand the Supreme Lord's transcendental position and potency, and ultimately he will relish the Lord's form, which is eternal and full of knowledge and bliss. He will perceive the Lord as the embodiment of all transcendental mellows. And if the pretentious nondevotee sentimentalists, who like to imitate the empiricists, practice genuine *jñāna-yoga*, then they too will gain an accurate perspective on the Absolute Truth. They will become firmly established in the understanding that the Supreme Lord's form is spiritual and transcendental, and then they will begin to render unflinching devotional service.

(*RTW* 3.1)

SIMILARLY, SOMEONE SENT a young prostitute to disturb Haridāsa Ṭhākura, and upon hearing her appeals for intercourse, Haridāsa Ṭhākura said, "Yes, your proposal is very nice. Please sit down and let me finish my chanting, and then we shall enjoy." Morning came and the prostitute became impatient, but Haridāsa Ṭhākura replied, "I'm very sorry. I could not finish my chanting. Come tonight again." The prostitute came for three nights, and on the third night she fell down at his feet, confessed her intentions, and pleaded with him, "I was induced to perform this act by a man who is your enemy. Kindly excuse me." Haridāsa Ṭhākura then replied, "I know all about that, but I allowed you to come here for three days so that you could be converted and become a devotee. Now take these chanting beads, and go on chanting. I am leaving this place." Here is an other example of a *dhīra* who has control of his body (*deha*), words (*vāc*), and intelligence (*buddhi*). One's body, words and intelligence (*buddhi*). One's body, words and intelligence should be controlled by one who is *dhīra* and who actually knows the principles of religion.

(*Kṛṣṇa Consciousness the Matchless Gift* MG5)

END OF APPENDIX I

Appendix II
— The Holy Name —

nāma vinu kali-kāle nāhi āra dharma
sarva-mantra-sāra nāma, ei śāstra-marma

"'In this Age of Kali there is no religious principle other than the chanting of the holy name, which is the essence of all Vedic hymns. This is the purport of all scriptures.'

The principles of the *paramparā* system were strictly honored in previous ages—Satya-yuga, Tretā-yuga and Dvāpara-yuga—but in the present age, Kali-yuga, people neglect the importance of this system of *śrauta-paramparā*, or receiving knowledge by disciplic succession. In this age, people are prepared to argue that they can understand that which is beyond their limited knowledge and perception through so-called scientific observations and experiments, not knowing that actual truth comes down to man from authorities. This argumentative attitude is against the Vedic principles, and it is very difficult for one who adopts it to understand that the holy name of Kṛṣṇa is as good as Kṛṣṇa Himself. Since Kṛṣṇa and His holy name are identical, the holy name is eternally pure and beyond material contamination. It is the Supreme Personality of Godhead as a transcendental vibration. The holy name is completely different from material sound, as confirmed by Narottama dāsa Ṭhākura: *golokera prema-dhana, hari-nāma-saṅkīrtana.* The transcendental vibration of *hari-nāma-saṅkīrtana* is imported from the spiritual world. Thus although materialists who are addicted to experimental knowledge and the so-called "scientific method" cannot place their faith in the chanting of the Hare Kṛṣṇa *mahā-mantra*, it is a fact that simply by chanting the Hare Kṛṣṇa *mantra* offenselessly one can be freed from all subtle and gross material conditions. The spiritual world is called Vaikuṇṭha, which means "without anxiety." In the material world everything is full of anxiety (*kuṇṭha*), whereas in the spiritual world (Vaikuṇṭha) everything is free from anxiety. Therefore those who are afflicted by a combination of anxieties cannot understand the Hare Kṛṣṇa *mantra*, which is free from all anxiety. In the present age the vibration of the Hare Kṛṣṇa *mahā-mantra* is the only process that is in a transcendental position, beyond material contamination. Since the holy name can deliver a conditioned soul, it is explained here to be *sarva-mantra-sāra*, the essence of all Vedic hymns.

A name that represents an object of this material world may be subjected to arguments and experimental knowledge, but in the absolute world a name and its owner, the fame and the famous, are identical, and similarly the qualities, pastimes and everything else pertaining to the Absolute are also absolute. Although Māyāvādīs profess monism, they differentiate between the holy name of the Supreme Lord and the Lord Himself. For this offense of nāmāparādha they gradually glide down from their exalted position of *brahma-jñāna*, as confirmed in *Śrīmad-Bhāgavatam* (10.2.32):

āruhya kṛcchreṇa paraṁ padaṁ tataḥ
patanty adho 'nādṛta-yuṣmad-aṅghrayaḥ

Although by severe austerities they rise to the exalted position of *brahma-jñāna*, they nevertheless fall down due to imperfect knowledge of the Absolute Truth. Although they profess to understand the Vedic *mantra sarvaṁ khalv idaṁ brahma* (Chāndogya Up. 3.14.1), which means "Everything is Brahman," they are unable to understand that the holy name is also Brahman. If they regularly chant the *mahā-mantra*, however, they can be relieved from this misconception. Unless one properly takes shelter of the holy name, he cannot be relieved from the offensive stage in chanting the holy name.

Śrī Caitanya-caritāmṛta Ādi-līlā 7.74 and purport
[Lord Caitanya to Prakāśānanda Sarasvatī]

---

harer nāma harer nāma
harer nāmaiva kevalam
kalau nāsty eva nāsty eva
nāsty eva gatir anyathā

"In this age of Kali there is no alternative, there is no alternative, there is no alternative for spiritual progress than the holy name, the holy name, the holy name of the Lord."

Bṛhan-nāradīya Purāṇa
[cited: *Śrī Caitanya-caritāmṛta Ādi-līlā* 7.76]

---

kṛṣṇa-varṇaṁ tviṣākṛṣṇaṁ
sāṅgopāṅgāstra-pārṣadam
yajñaiḥ saṅkīrtana-prāyair
yajanti hi su-medhasaḥ

"In the age of Kali, intelligent persons perform congregational chanting to worship the incarnation of Godhead who constantly sings the name of Kṛṣṇa. Although His complexion is not blackish, He is Kṛṣṇa Himself. He is

accompanied by His associates, servants, weapons and confidential companions."

Śrīmad-Bhāgavatam 11.5.32
[cited: *Śrī Caitanya-caritāmṛta Antya-līlā* 20.10]
[Karabhājana Ṛṣi to Mahārāja Nimi]

---

hare kṛṣṇa hare kṛṣṇa kṛṣṇa kṛṣṇa hare hare
hare rāma hare rāma rāma rāma hare hare
iti ṣoḍaśakaṁ nāmnāṁ kali-kalmaṣa-nāśanam
nātaḥ paratаropāyaḥ sarva-vedeṣu dṛśyate

"Hare Kṛṣṇa, Hare Kṛṣṇa, Kṛṣṇa Kṛṣṇa, Hare Hare/ Hare Rāma, Hare Rāma, Rāma Rāma, Hare Hare—these sixteen names composed of thirty-two syllables are the only means to counteract the evil effects of Kali-yuga. In all the *Vedas* it is seen that to cross the ocean of nescience there is no alternative to the chanting of the holy name."

Kalisantaraṇa Upaniṣad
[cited: *Śrī Caitanya-caritāmṛta Ādi-līlā* 7.76
transliteration given: *Śrī Caitanya-caritāmṛta Ādi-līlā* 3.40]

---

kaler doṣa-nidhe rājann
asti hy eko mahān guṇaḥ
kīrtanād eva kṛṣṇasya
mukta-saṅgaḥ paraṁ vrajet

"My dear King, although Kali-yuga is full of faults, there is still one good quality about this age. It is that simply by chanting the Hare Kṛṣṇa *mahā-mantra*, one can become free from material bondage and be promoted to the transcendental kingdom."

Śrīmad-Bhāgavatam 12.3.51
[cited: *Śrī Caitanya-caritāmṛta Madhya-līlā* 20.344]
[Śukadeva Gosvāmī to Mahārāja Parīkṣit]

---

kṛte yad dhyāyato viṣṇuṁ
tretāyāṁ yajato makhaiḥ
dvāpare paricaryāyāṁ
kalau tad dhari-kīrtanāt

"Whatever result was obtained in Satya-yuga by meditating on Viṣṇu, in Tretā-yuga by performing sacrifices and in Dvāpara-yuga by serving the Lord's lotus feet can also be obtained in Kali-yuga simply by chanting the Hare Kṛṣṇa *mahā-mantra.*"

Śrīmad-Bhāgavatam 12.3.52
[cited: *Śrī Caitanya-caritāmṛta Madhya-līlā* 20.345]
[Śukadeva Gosvāmī to Mahāraja Parīkṣit]

---

dhyāyan kṛte yajan yajñais
tretāyāṁ dvāpare 'rcayan
yad āpnoti tad āpnoti
kalau saṅkīrtya keśavam

"Whatever is achieved by meditation in Satya-yuga, by performance of yajña in Tretā-yuga or by the worship of Kṛṣṇa's lotus feet in Dvāpara-yuga is also obtained in the age of Kali simply by chanting and glorifying Lord Keśava."

Viṣnu Purāṇa (6.2.17),

dvāparīyair janair viṣṇuḥ
pañcarātrais tu kevalaiḥ
kalau tu nāma-mātreṇa
pūjyate bhagavān hariḥ

"In the Dvāpara-yuga one could satisfy Kṛṣṇa or Viṣṇu only by worshiping opulently according to the *pāñcarātrikī* system; but in the age of Kali, one can satisfy and worship the Supreme Personality of Godhead Hari simply by chanting His holy name."

Nārāyaṇa-saṁhitā
(quoted by Śrīla Madhvācārya in his commentary on *Muṇḍaka Upaniṣad*)
[cited: *Śrī Caitanya-caritāmṛta Antya-līlā* 7.12]

---

kaliṁ sabhājayanty āryā
guṇa jñāḥ sāra-bhāginaḥ
yatra saṅkīrtanenaiva
sarva-svārtho 'bhilabhyate

"Those who are advanced and highly qualified and are interested in the essence of life know the good qualities of Kali-yuga. Such people worship the age of Kali because in this age, simply by chanting the Hare Kṛṣṇa *mahā-mantra* one can advance in spiritual knowledge and attain life's goal."

Śrīmad-Bhāgavatam 11.5.36
[cited: *Śrī Caitanya-caritāmṛta Madhya-līlā* 20.347]
[Karabhājana Ṛṣi to Mahārāja Nimi]

nāma vinu kali-kāle nāhi āra dharma
sarva-mantra-sāra nāma, ei śāstra-marma

"In this age of Kali there is no other religious principle than the chanting of the holy name, which is the essence of all Vedic hymns. This is the purport of all scriptures."

Śrī Caitanya-caritāmṛta Ādi-līlā 7.74
[Īśvara Purī to Lord Caitanya]

---

etāvān eva loke 'smin
puṁsāṁ dharmaḥ paraḥ smṛtaḥ
bhakti-yogo bhagavati
tan-nāma-grahaṇādibhiḥ

"Devotional service, beginning with the chanting of the holy name of the Lord, is the ultimate religious principle for the living entity in human society."

Śrīmad-Bhāgavatam 6.3.22
[Yamarāja to the Yamadutas]

---

etan nirvidyamānānām
icchatām akuto-bhayam
yoginām nṛpa nirṇītaṁ
harer nāmānukīrtanam

"O King, constant chanting of the holy name of the Lord after the ways of the great authorities is the doubtless and fearless way of success for all, including those who are free from all material desires, those who are desirous of

all material enjoyment, and also those who are self-satisfied by dint of transcendental knowledge."

Śrīmad-Bhāgavatam 2.1.11
[Śukadeva Gosvāmī to Mahārāja Parīkṣit]

---

tattva-vastu-kṛṣṇa, kṛṣṇa-bhakti, prema-rūpa
nāma-saṅkīrtana-saba ānanda-svarūpa

"The Absolute Truth is Śrī Kṛṣṇa, and loving devotion to Śrī Kṛṣṇa exhibited in pure love is achieved through congregational chanting of the holy name, which is the essence of all bliss."

Śrī Caitanya-caritāmṛta Ādi-līlā 1.96

---

iti mūrty-abhidhānena
mantra-mūrtim amūrtikam
yajate yajña-puruṣaṁ
sa samyag darśanaḥ pumān

"Thus he is the actual seer who worships, in the form of transcendental sound representation, the Supreme Personality of Godhead, Viṣṇu, who has no material form."

Śrīmad-Bhāgavatam 1.5.38
[Nārada Muni to Vyāsadeva]

---

ceto-darpaṇa-mārjanaṁ bhava-mahā-dāvāgni-nirvāpaṇaṁ
śreyaḥ-kairava-candrikā-vitaraṇaṁ vidyā-vadhū-jīvanam
ānandāmbudhi-vardhanaṁ prati-padaṁ pūrṇāmṛtāsvādanaṁ
sarvātma-snapanaṁ paraṁ vijayate śrī-kṛṣṇa-saṅkīrtanam

"Let there be all victory for the chanting of the holy name of Lord Kṛṣṇa, which can cleanse the mirror of the heart and stop the miseries of the blazing fire of material existence. That chanting is the waxing moon that spreads the white lotus of good fortune for all living entities. It is the life and soul of all education. The chanting of the holy name of Kṛṣṇa expands the blissful ocean of transcendental life. It gives a cooling effect to everyone and enables one to taste full nectar at every step."

Śrī Śrī Śikṣāṣṭaka (verse 1), by Lord Caitanya
[cited: *Śrī Caitanya-caritāmṛta Antya-līlā* 20.12]

---

nāmnām akāri bahudhā nija-sarva-śaktis
tatrārpitā niyamitaḥ smaraṇe na kālaḥ
etādṛśī tava kṛpā bhagavan mamāpi
durdaivam īdṛśam ihājani nānurāgaḥ

"My Lord, O Supreme Personality of Godhead, in Your holy name there is all good fortune for the living entity, and therefore You have many names, such as Kṛṣṇa and Govinda, by which You expand Yourself. You have invested all Your potencies in those names, and there are no hard and fast rules for remembering them. My dear Lord, although You bestow such mercy upon the fallen, conditioned souls by liberally teaching Your holy names, I am so unfortunate that I commit offenses while chanting the holy name, and therefore I do not achieve attachment for chanting."

Śrī Śrī Śikṣāṣṭaka (verse 2), by Lord Caitanya
[cited: *Śrī Caitanya-caritāmṛta Antya-līlā* 20.16]

ākṛṣṭiḥ kṛta-cetasāṁ sumanasām uccāṭanaṁ cāṁhasām
ācaṇḍālam amūka-loka-sulabho vaśyaś ca mukti-śriyaḥ
no dīkṣāṁ na ca sat-kriyāṁ na ca puraścaryāṁ manāg īkṣate
mantro 'yaṁ rasanā-spṛg eva phalati śrī-kṛṣṇa-nāmātmakaḥ

"The holy name of Lord Kṛṣṇa is an attractive feature for many saintly, liberal people. It is the annihilator of all sinful reactions and is so powerful that save for the dumb who cannot chant it, it is readily available to everyone, including the lowest type of man, the *caṇḍāla*. The holy name of Kṛṣṇa is the controller of the opulence of liberation, and it is identical with Kṛṣṇa. Simply by touching the holy name with one's tongue, immediate effects are produced. Chanting the holy name does not depend on initiation, pious activities or the *puraścaryā* regulative principles generally observed before initiation. The holy name does not wait for all these activities. It is self-sufficient."

Padyāvalī (29), by Rūpa Gosvāmī
[cited: *Śrī Caitanya-caritāmṛta Madhya-līlā* 15.110]

---

nāma cintāmaṇiḥ kṛṣṇaś
caitanya-rasa-vigrahaḥ
pūrṇaḥ śuddho nitya-mukto
'bhinnatvān nāma-nāminoḥ

"The holy name of Kṛṣna is transcendentally blissful. It bestows all spiritual benedictions, for it is Kṛṣna Himself, the reservoir of all pleasure. Kṛṣṇa's name is complete, and it is the form of all transcendental mellows. It is not a material name under any condition, and it is no less powerful than Kṛṣṇa Himself. Since Kṛṣṇa's name is not contaminated by the material qualities, there is no question of its being involved with *māyā*. Kṛṣṇa's name is always liberated and spiritual; it is never conditioned by the laws of material nature. This is because the name of Kṛṣṇa and Kṛṣṇa Himself are identical."

Padma Purāṇa
[cited: *Śrī Caitanya-caritāmṛta Madhya-līlā* 17.133]

---

jayati jayati nāmānanda-rūpaṁ murārer
viramita-nija-dharma-dhyāna-pūjādi-yatnam
kathamapi sakṛd-āttaṁ muktidaṁ prāṇīnāṁ yat
paramam amṛtam ekaṁ jīvanaṁ bhūṣaṇaṁ me

"All glories, all glories to the all-blissful holy name of Śrī Kṛṣṇa, which causes the devotee to give up all conventional religious duties, meditation and worship. When somehow or other uttered even once by a living entity, the holy name awards him liberation. The holy name of Kṛṣṇa is the highest nectar. It is my very life and my only treasure."

Bṛhad-bhāgavatāmṛta (1.9), by Sanātana Gosvāmī
[cited: *Śrī Caitanya-caritāmṛta Antya-līlā* 4.71]

---

nikhila-śruti-mauli-ratna-mālā-
dyuti-nīrājita-pāda-paṅkajānta
ayi mukta-kulair upāsyamānaṁ
paritas tvāṁ hari-nāma saṁśrayāmi

"O Hari-nāma! The tips of the toes of Your lotus feet are constantly being worshiped by the glowing radiance emanating from the string of gems known as the *Upaniṣads*, the

by liberated souls such as Nārada and Śukadeva. O Hari-nāma! I take complete shelter of You."

Nāmāṣṭaka (verse 1), by Rūpa Gosvāmī
[cited: *Śrī Caitanya-caritāmṛta Antya-līlā* 4.71]

---

trayo vedāḥ ṣaḍ-aṅgāni
chandāṁsi vividhāḥ surāḥ
sarvam aṣṭākṣarāntaḥstham
yac cānyad api vāṅ-mayam
sarva-vedānta-sārārthaḥ
saṁsārārṇava-tāraṇaḥ

"The essence of all Vedic knowledge—comprehending the three kinds of Vedic activity [*karma-kāṇḍa, jñāna-kāṇḍa* and *upāsanā-kāṇḍa*], the *chandaḥ* or Vedic hymns, and the processes for satisfying the demigods—is included in the eight syllables Hare Kṛṣṇa, Hare Kṛṣṇa. This is the reality of all *Vedānta*. The chanting of the holy name is the only means to cross the ocean of nescience."

Nārada-pañcarātra
[cited: *Śrī Caitanya-caritāmṛta Ādi-līlā* 7.76]

---

taṁ nirvyājaṁ bhaja guṇa-nidhe pāvanaṁ pāvanānāṁ
śraddhā-rajyan-matir atitarām uttamaḥ-śloka-maulim
prodyann antaḥ-karaṇa-kuhare hanta yan-nāma-bhānor
ābhāso 'pi kṣapayati mahā-pātaka-dhvānta-rāśim

"O reservoir of all good qualities, just worship Śrī Kṛṣṇa, the purifier of all purifiers, the most exalted of the personalities worshiped by choice poetry. Worship Him with a faithful, unflinching mind, without duplicity and in a highly elevated manner. Thus worship the Lord, whose name is like the sun, for just as a slight appearance of the sun dissipates the darkness of night, so a slight appearance of the holy name of Kṛṣṇa can drive away all the darkness of ignorance that arises in the heart due to greatly sinful activities performed in previous lives."

Bhakti-rasāmṛta-sindhu (2.1.103), by Rūpa Gosvāmī
[cited: *Śrī Caitanya-caritāmṛta Antya-līlā* 3.62]

---

nāmno hi yāvatī śaktiḥ
pāpa-nirharaṇe hareḥ
tāvat kartuṁ na śaknoti
pātakaṁ pātakī naraḥ

"Simply by chanting one holy name of Hari, a sinful man can counteract the reactions to more sins than he is able to commit."

Bṛhad-Viṣṇu Purāṇa
[cited: *Śrīmad-Bhāgavatam* 6.2.7]

---

avaśenāpi yan-nāmni
kīrtite sarva-pātakaiḥ
pumān vimucyate sadyaḥ
siṁha-trastair mṛgair iva

"If one chants the holy name of the Lord, even in a helpless condition or without desiring to do so, all the reactions of his sinful life depart, just as when a lion roars, all the small animals flee in fear."

"My dear King, this word 'Kṛṣṇa' is so auspicious that anyone who chants this holy name immediately gets rid of the resultant actions of sinful activities from many, many births."

Viṣṇu-dharma
[cited: *The Nectar of Devotion*]

'eka' kṛṣṇa-nāme kare sarva-pāpa nāśa
premera kāraṇa bhakti karena prakāśa

"Simply chanting the Hare Kṛṣṇa *mahā-mantra* without offenses vanquishes all sinful activities. Thus pure devotional service, which is the cause of love of Godhead, becomes manifest."

Śrī Caitanya-caritāmṛta Ādi-līlā 8.26

āpannaḥ saṁsṛtiṁ ghorāṁ
yan-nāma vivaśo gṛṇan
tataḥ sadyo vimucyeta
yad bibheti svayaṁ bhayam

"Living beings who are entangled in the complicated meshes of birth and death can be freed immediately by even unconsciously chanting the holy name of Kṛṣṇa, which is feared by fear personified."

Śrīmad-Bhāgavatam 1.1.14
[The sages at Naimiṣāraṇya to Sūta Gosvāmī]

sakṛd uccāritaṁ yena
harir ity akṣara-dvayam
baddha-parikaras tena
mokṣāya gamanaṁ prati

"By once chanting the holy name of the Lord, which consists of the two syllables ha-ri, one guarantees his path to liberation."

Skanda Purāṇa
[cited: *Śrīmad-Bhāgavatam* 6.2.7]

"For any person who is chanting the holy name either softly or loudly, the paths to liberation and even heavenly happiness are at once open."

Padma Purāṇa
[cited: *The Nectar of Devotion*]

kṛṣṇa-mantra haite habe saṁsāra-mocana
kṛṣṇa-nāma haite pābe kṛṣṇera caraṇa

"Simply by chanting the holy name of Kṛṣṇa, one can obtain freedom from material existence. Indeed, simply by chanting the Hare Kṛṣṇa *mantra* one will be able to see the lotus feet of the Lord."

Śrī Caitanya-caritāmṛta Ādi-līlā 7.73
[Īśvara Purī to Lord Caitanya]

tāra madhye sarva-śreṣṭha nāma-saṅkīrtana
niraparādhe nāma laile pāya prema-dhana

"Of the nine processes of devotional service, the most important is to always chant the holy name of the Lord. If one does so, avoiding the ten kinds of offenses, one very easily obtains the most valuable love of Godhead."

Śrī Caitanya-caritāmṛta Antya-līlā 4.71
[Lord Caitanya to Sanātana Gosvāmī]

---

kṛṣṇa-ādi, āra yata sthāvara-jaṅgame
kṛṣṇa-preme matta kare kṛṣṇa-saṅkīrtane

"The holy name of Kṛṣṇa is so attractive that anyone who chants it—including all living entities, moving and non-moving, and even Lord Kṛṣṇa Himself—becomes imbued with love of Kṛṣṇa. This is the effect of chanting the Hare Kṛṣṇa *mahā-mantra*."

Śrī Caitanya-caritāmṛta Antya-līlā 3.268

---

anāyāse bhava-kṣaya, kṛṣṇera sevana
eka kṛṣṇa-nāmera phale pāi eta dhana

"As a result of chanting the Hare Kṛṣṇa *mahā-mantra*, one makes such great advancement in spiritual life that simultaneously his material existence terminates and he receives love of Godhead. The holy name of Kṛṣṇa is so powerful that by chanting even one name, one very easily achieves these transcendental riches."

Śrī Caitanya-caritāmṛta Ādi-līlā 8.28

saṅkīrtana haite pāpa-saṁsāra-nāśana
citta-śuddhi, sarva-bhakti-sādhana-udgama
kṛṣṇa-premodgama, premāmṛta-āsvādana
kṛṣṇa-prāpti, sevāmṛta-samudre majjana

"By performing congregational chanting of the Hare Kṛṣṇa *mantra*, one can destroy the sinful condition of material existence, purify the unclean heart and awaken all varieties of devotional service. The result of chanting is that one awakens his love for Kṛṣṇa and tastes transcendental bliss. Ultimately, one attains the association of Kṛṣṇa and engages in His devotional service, as if immersing himself in a great ocean of love."

Śrī Caitanya-caritāmṛta Antya-līlā 20.13-14
[Lord Caitanya to Svarūpa Dāmodara and Rāmānanda Rāya]

---

kṛṣṇa-nāma-mahā-mantrera ei ta' svabhāva
yei jape, tāra kṛṣṇe upajaye bhāva

"It is the nature of the Hare Kṛṣṇa *mahā-mantra* that anyone who chants it immediately develops his loving ecstasy for Kṛṣṇa."

Śrī Caitanya-caritāmṛta Ādi-līlā 7.83
[Īśvara Purī to Lord Caitanya]

---

evaṁ-vrataḥ sva-priya-nāma-kīrtyā
jātānurāgo druta-citta uccaiḥ
hasaty atho roditi rauti gāyaty
unmāda-van nṛtyati loka-bāhyaḥ

"When a person is actually advanced and takes pleasure in chanting the holy name of the Lord, who is very dear to him, he is agitated and loudly chants the holy name. He also laughs, cries, becomes agitated and chants just like a madman, not caring for outsiders."

Śrīmad-Bhāgavatam 11.2.40
[cited: *Śrī Caitanya-caritāmṛta Madhya-līlā* 9.262]
[Kavi to Mahārāja Nimi]

---

nayanaṁ galad-aśru-dhārayā
vadanaṁ gadgada-ruddhayā girā
pulakair nicitaṁ vapuḥ kadā,
tava nāma-grahaṇe bhaviṣyati

"My dear Lord, when will My eyes be beautified by filling with tears that constantly glide down as I chant Your holy name? When will My voice falter and all the hairs on My body stand erect in transcendental happiness as I chant Your holy name?"

Śrī Śrī Śikṣāṣṭaka (verse 6), by Lord Caitanya
[cited: *Śrī Caitanya-caritāmṛta Antya-līlā* 20.36]

---

tuṇḍe tāṇḍavinī ratiṁ vitanute tuṇḍāvalī-labdhaye
karṇa-kroḍa-kaḍambinī ghaṭayate karṇārbudebhyaḥ spṛhām
cetaḥ-prāṅgaṇa-saṅginī vijayate sarvendriyāṇāṁ kṛtiṁ
no jāne janitā kiyadbhir amṛtaiḥ kṛṣṇeti varṇa-dvayī

"I do not know how much nectar the two syllables 'Kṛṣ-ṇa' have produced. When the holy name of Kṛṣṇa is chanted, it appears to dance within the mouth. We then desire many,

many mouths. When that name enters the holes of the ears, we desire many millions of ears. And when the holy name dances in the courtyard of the heart, it conquers the activities of the mind, and therefore all the senses become inert."

Vidagdha-mādhava (1.15), by Rūpa Gosvāmī
[cited: *Śrī Caitanya-caritāmṛta Antya-līlā* 1.99]

---

mriyamāṇo harer nāma
gṛṇan putropacāritam
ajāmilo 'py agād dhāma
kim uta śraddhayā gṛṇan

"While suffering at the time of death, Ajāmila chanted the holy name of the Lord, and although the chanting was directed toward his son, he nevertheless returned home, back to Godhead. Therefore if one faithfully and inoffensively chants the holy name of the Lord, where is the doubt that he will return to Godhead?"

Śrīmad-Bhāgavatam 6.2.49
[Śukadeva Gosvāmī to Mahārāja Parīkṣit]

---

ataḥ śrī-kṛṣṇa-nāmādi
na bhaved grāhyam indriyaiḥ
sevonmukhe hi jihvādau
svayam eva sphuraty adaḥ

"Therefore material senses cannot appreciate Kṛṣṇa's holy name, form, qualities and pastimes. When a conditioned soul is awakened to Kṛṣṇa consciousness and renders

taste the remnants of the Lord's food, the tongue is purified, and one gradually comes to understand who Kṛṣṇa really is."

Bhakti-rasāmṛta-sindhu (1.2.234), by Rūpa Gosvāmī [cited: *Śrī Caitanya-caritāmṛta Madhya-līlā* 17.136]

---

syāt kṛṣṇa-nāma-caritādi-sitāpy avidyā-
pittopatapta-rasanasya na rocikā nu
kintv ādarād anudinaṁ khalu saiva juṣṭā
svādvī kramād bhavati tad-gada-mūla-hantrī

"The holy name, character, pastimes and activities of Kṛṣṇa are all transcendentally sweet like sugar candy. Although the tongue of one afflicted by the jaundice of *avidyā*, ignorance, cannot taste anything sweet, it is wonderful that simply by carefully chanting these sweet names every day, a natural relish awakens within his tongue, and his disease is gradually destroyed at the root."

Śrī Upadeśāmṛta (The Nectar of Instruction), Text 7

'kāṅhāra smaraṇa jīva karibe anukṣaṇa?'
'kṛṣṇa-nāma-guṇa-līlā-pradhāna smaraṇa'

Śrī Caitanya Mahāprabhu asked, "What should all living entities constantly remember?" Rāmānanda Rāya replied, "The chief object of remembrance is always the holy name of the Lord, His qualities and pastimes."

Śrī Caitanya-caritāmṛta Madhya-līlā 8.252

yasya smṛtyā ca nāmoktyā
tapo-yajña-kriyādiṣu
nūnaṁ sampūrṇatām eti
sadyo vande tam acyutam

"I offer my obeisances unto Him, the infallible, because simply by either remembering Him or vibrating His holy name one can attain the perfection of all penances, sacrifices or fruitive activities, and this process can be universally followed."

Skanda Purāna [cited: *Śrīmad-Bhāgavatam* 2.9.36]

---

yan-nāmadheya-śravaṇānukīrtanād
yat-prahvaṇād yat-smaraṇād api kvacit
śvādo 'pi sadyaḥ savanāya kalpate
kutaḥ punas te bhagavan nu darśanāt

"To say nothing of the spiritual advancement of persons who see the Supreme Person face to face, even a person born in a family of dog-eaters immediately becomes eligible to perform Vedic sacrifices if he once utters the holy name of the Supreme Personality of Godhead or chants about Him, hears about His pastimes, offers Him obeisances or even remembers Him."

Śrīmad-Bhāgavatam 3.33.6
[Devahuti to Lord Kapila]

---

aho bata śva-paco 'to garīyān
yaj-jihvāgre vartate nāma tubhyam
tepus tapas te juhuvuḥ sasnur āryā
brahmānūcur nāma gṛṇanti ye te

"Oh, how glorious are they whose tongues are chanting Your holy name! Even if bom in the families of dog-eaters, such persons are worshipable. Persons who chant the holy name of Your Lordship must have executed all kinds of austerities and fire sacrifices and achieved all the good manners of the Āryans. To be chanting the holy name of Your Lordship, they must have bathed at holy places of pilgrimage, studied the *Vedas* and fulfilled everything required."

Śrīmad-Bhāgavatam 3.33.7
[Devahūti to Lord Kapila]

---

rāma rāmeti rāmeti
rame rāme manorame
sahasra-nāmabhis tulyaṁ
rāma-nāma varānane

"I chant the holy name of Rāma, Rāma, Rāma and thus enjoy this beautiful sound. This holy name of Rāmacandra is equal to one thousand holy names of Lord Viṣṇu."

Bṛhad-Viṣṇu-sahasranāma-stotra, 72.335
(from *Padma Purāṇa, Uttara-khaṇḍa*)
[cited: *Śrī Caitanya-caritāmṛta Madhya-līlā* 9.32]
[Lord Śiva to his wife, Durgā]

---

sahasra-nāmnāṁ puṇyānāṁ
trir-āvṛttyā tu yat phalam
ekāvṛttyā tu kṛṣṇasya
nāmaikaṁ tat prayacchati

"The pious results derived from chanting the thousand holy names of Viṣṇu three times can be attained by only one repetition of the holy name of Kṛṣṇa."

Brahmāṇḍa Purāṇa
(quoted in *Laghu-bhāgavatāmṛta*, 1.354, by Rūpa Gosvāmī)
[cited: *Śrī Caitanya-caritāmṛta Madhya-līlā* 9.33]

---

tṛṇād api sunīcena
taror api sahiṣṇunā
amāninā mānadena
kīrtanīyaḥ sadā hariḥ

"One should chant the holy name of the Lord in a humble state of mind, thinking oneself lower than the straw in the street. One should be more tolerant than a tree, devoid of all sense of false prestige and ready to offer all respects to others. In such a state of mind one can chant the holy name of the Lord constantly."

Śrī Śrī Śikṣāṣṭaka (verse 3),
by Lord Caitanya, *Śrī Caitanya-caritāmṛta Antya-līlā* 20.21
[cited: *Śrī Caitanya-caritāmṛta Antya-līlā* 3.207]

---

bahu janma kare yadi śravaṇa, kīrtana
tabu ta' nā pāya kṛṣṇa-pade prema-dhana

"If one is infested with the ten offenses in the chanting of the Hare Kṛṣṇa *mahā-mantra*, despite his endeavor to chant the holy name for many births, he will not get the love of Godhead which is the ultimate goal of this chanting."

Śrī Caitanya-caritāmṛta Ādi-līlā 8.16

nāmāparādha-yuktānāṁ
nāmāny eva haranty agham
aviśrānti-prayuktāni
tāny evārtha-karāṇi ca

"Even if in the beginning one chants the Hare Kṛṣṇa *mantra* with offenses, one will become free from such offenses by chanting again and again."

Padma Purāṇa
[cited: *Śrīmad-Bhāgavatam* 6.3.24]

---

tad aśma-sāraṁ hṛdayaṁ batedaṁ
yad gṛhyamāṇair hari-nāma-dheyaiḥ
na vikriyetātha yadā vikāro
netre jalaṁ gātra-ruheṣu harṣaḥ

"If one's heart does not change, tears do not flow from his eyes, his body does not shiver, nor his hairs stand on end as he chants the Hare Kṛṣṇa *mahā-mantra*, it should be understood that his heart is as hard as iron. This is due to his offenses at the lotus feet of the Lord's holy name."

Śrīmad-Bhāgavatam 2.3.24
[cited: *Śrī Caitanya-caritāmṛta Ādi-līlā* 8.25]
[Śukadeva Gosvāmī to Mahārāja Parīkṣit]

---

duṣṭa mana! tumi kisera vaiṣṇava?
pratiṣṭhāra tare, nirjanera ghare,
tava hari-nāma kevala kaitava

"My dear mind, what kind of devotee are you? Simply for

cheap adoration you sit in a solitary place and pretend to chant the Hare Kṛṣṇa *mahā-mantra*, but this is all cheating."

Song by Śrīla Bhaktisiddhānta Sarasvatī Ṭhākura
[cited: *Śrīmad-Bhāgavatam* 4.28.33]

"The chanting of the Hare Kṛṣṇa *mantra* is present only on the lips of a person who has for many births worshiped Vāsudeva."

Padma Purāṇa [cited: *The Nectar of Devotion*]

---

pṛthivīte āche yata nagarādi grāma
sarvatra pracāra haibe mora nāma

"In every town and village, the chanting of My name will be heard."

Śrī Caitanya-bhāgavata, by Vṛndāvana dāsa Ṭhākura
[cited: *Śrī Caitanya-caritāmṛta Madhya-līlā* 25.264]
[Lord Caitanya]

---

kali-kālera dharma-kṛṣṇa-nāma-saṅkīrtana
kṛṣṇa-śakti vinā nāhe tāra pravartana

"The fundamental religious system in the age of Kali is the chanting of the holy name of Kṛṣṇa. Unless empowered by Kṛṣṇa, one cannot propagate the *saṅkīrtana* movement."

Śrī Caitanya-caritāmṛta Antya-līlā 7.11

nāca, gāo, bhakta-saṅge kara saṅkīrtana
kṛṣṇa-nāma upadeśi' tāra' sarva-jana

"My dear child, continue dancing, chanting and performing *saṅkīrtana* in association with devotees. Furthermore, go out and preach the value of chanting *kṛṣṇa-nāma*, for by this process You will be able to deliver all fallen souls."

Śrī Caitanya-caritāmṛta Ādi-līlā 7.92
[Īśvara Purī to Lord Caitanya]

āpane ācare keha, nā kare pracāra
pracāra karena keha, nā karena ācāra
'ācāra', 'pracāra',-nāmera karaha 'dui' kārya
tumi-sarva-guru, tumi jagatera ārya

"Some behave very well but do not preach the cult of Kṛṣṇa consciousness, whereas others preach but do not behave properly. You simultaneously perform both duties in relation to the holy name by your personal behavior and by your preaching. Therefore you are the spiritual master of the entire world, for you are the most advanced devotee in the world."

Śrī Caitanya-caritāmṛta Antya-līlā 4.102-3
[Sanātana Gosvāmī to Haridāsa Ṭhākura]

---

kali-yuge yuga-dharma-nāmera pracāra
tathi lāgi' pīta-varṇa caitanyāvatāra

"The religious practice for the age of Kali is to broadcast

the glories of the holy name. Only for this purpose has the Lord, in a yellow color, descended as Lord Caitanya."

Śrī Caitanya-caritāmṛta Ādi-līlā 3.40

---

nāhaṁ tiṣṭhāmi vaikuṇṭhe
yogināṁ hṛdayeṣu vā
tatra tiṣṭhāmi nārada
yatra gāyanti mad-bhaktāḥ

"My dear Nārada, actually I do not reside in My abode, Vaikuṇṭha, nor do I reside within the hearts of the *yogīs*, but I reside in that place where My pure devotees chant My holy name and discuss My form, pastimes and qualities."

[*Śrīmad-Bhāgavatam* 4.30.35]

"The chanting of the Hare Kṛṣṇa *mantra* is present only on the lips of a person who has for many births worshiped Vāsudeva."

Padma Purāṇa [cited: *The Nectar of Devotion*]

...yajñānāṁ japa-yajño 'smi...

"...Of sacrifices I am the chanting of the holy names [*japa*]..."

Bhagavad-gītā As It Is 10.25
[Kṛṣṇa to Arjuna]

avaiṣṇava-mukhodgīrṇaṁ
pūtaṁ hari-kathāmṛtam
śravaṇaṁ naiva kartavyaṁ
sarpocchiṣṭaṁ yathā payaḥ

The holy name chanted by non-Vaiṣṇavas is like milk touched by the lips of a serpent.

Padma Purāṇa
[cited: *Śrī Caitanya-caritāmṛta Antya-līlā* 1.101]

---

kṛṣṇa-nāma nirantara yāṅhāra vadane
sei vaiṣṇava-śreṣṭha, bhaja tāṅhāra caraṇe

"A person who is always chanting the holy name of the Lord is to be considered a first-class Vaiṣṇava, and your duty is to serve his lotus feet."

Śrī Caitanya-caritāmṛta Madhya-līlā 16.72
[Lord Caitanya to an inhabitant of Kulīna-grāma]

---

yāṅhāra darśane mukhe āise kṛṣṇa-nāma
tāṅhāre jāniha tumi 'vaiṣṇava-pradhāna'

Śrī Caitanya Mahāprabhu said, "A first-class Vaiṣṇava is he whose very presence makes others chant the holy name of Kṛṣṇa."

Śrī Caitanya-caritāmṛta Madhya-līlā 16.74

End of Appendix II

Appendix III
— Offenses To Be Avoided —
While Chanting The Holy Name

(*Padma Purāṇa Brahma Khaṇḍa* 25.15—18,
Ten Offenses to the Holy Name)

(1)

satāṁ nindā nāmnaḥ paramam aparādhaṁ vitanute
yataḥ khyātiṁ yātaṁ katham u sahate tad-vigarhām

To blaspheme devotees who have dedicated their lives to chanting the holy name of the Lord. The holy name, who is identical with Kṛṣṇa will never tolerate such blasphemous activities.

(2)

śivasya śrī-viṣṇor ya iha guṇa-nāmādi-sakalaṁ
dhiyā bhinnaṁ paśyet sa khalu hari-nāmāhita-karaḥ

To consider the names of Lord Śiva or Lord Brahmā to be on an equal level with the holy name of Lord Viṣṇu.

(3)

guror avajñā

To disobey the orders of the spiritual master or to consider him an ordinary person.

(4)

śruti-śāstra nindanam

To blaspheme the Vedic literatures or literatures in pursuance of the Vedic version.

(5)
artha-vādaḥ

To give some interpretation on the holy name of the Lord.

(6)
hari-nāmni kalpanam

To consider the glories of the holy name as imagination.

(7)
nāmno balād yasya hi pāpa-buddhir
na vidyate tasya yamair hi śuddhiḥ

To think that the Hare Kṛṣṇa *mantra* can counteract all sinful reactions and one may therefore go on with his sinful activities and at the same time chant the Hare Kṛṣṇa *mantra* to neutralize them is the greatest offense at the lotus feet of Hari-nāma.

(8)
dharma-vrata-tyāga-hutādi-sarva-
śubha-kriyā-sāmyam api pramādaḥ

To consider the chanting of the Hare Kṛṣṇa *maha-mantra* to be one of the auspicious ritualistic *mantras* mentioned in the *Vedas* as fruitive activity.

(9)

aśraddadhāne vimukhe 'py aśṛṇvati
yaś copadeśaḥ śiva-nāmāparādhaḥ

It is an offense to preach the glories of the holy name of the Lord to the faithless.

(10)

śrute 'pi nāma-māhātmye
yaḥ prīti-rahito naraḥ
ahaṁ mamādi-paramo
nāmni so 'py aparādha-kṛt

If one has heard the glories of the transcendental holy name of the Lord but nevertheless continues in a materialistic concept of life, thinking, "I am this body and everything belonging to this body is mine (*ahaṁ mameti*)," and does not show respect and love for the chanting of the Hare Kṛṣṇa *mahā-mantra*, that is an offense.

api pramādaḥ

It is also an offense to be inattentive while chanting.

END OF APPENDIX III

Appendix IV
— Captions to Photo Plates —

Plate I: 1 & 2. Lord Caitanya, the Golden Avatāra, the combined form of Rādhā and Kṛṣṇa, and Lord Nityānanda, Who is non-different than Lord Balarāma, descended to the earth in Navadvīpa-dhāma to introduce the *yuga-dharma*, the sublime method of self-realization for this age, the chanting of the *mahā-mantra*: Hare Kṛṣṇa Hare Kṛṣṇa Kṛṣṇa Kṛṣṇa Hare Hare Hare Rāma Hare Rāma Rāma Rāma Hare Hare. Their appearance was, in part, due to the sincere entreaties of Śrīla Haridāsa Ṭhākura.

Plate I: 2 & 3. Deities of Śrī Śrī Gaura-Nitai, pictured here at ISKCON's Rādhā Kṛṣṇa temple in the Westend of London, are now worshipped in temples and households throughout the world. Likewise, *harināma-saṅkīrtana*, the congregational chanting of the Holy Names of God, is a daily event in many cities around the globe. Pictured here in 1975, Srīla Prabhupāda leads the chanting of Hare Kṛṣṇa at the annual Jagannātha Rathayātrā festival in San Francisco, USA.

Plate II: 1 & 3. The divine personalities of the Pañca-tattva were the intimate associates of Śrīla Haridāsa Ṭhākura: Śrī Advaita Ācārya (the combined appearance of Mahā-Viṣṇu and Sadāśiva), Śrī Nityānanda Prabhu (the incarnation of Lord Balarāma), Śrī Caitanya Mahāprabhu (the Golden Avatāra, the combined form of Lord Kṛṣṇa and Śrīmatī Rādhārāṇī, the *yuga-avatāra*), Gadādhara Prabhu (Śrīmatī Rādhārāṇī Herself) and Śrīvāsa Ṭhākura (the eternal spaceman, the ever-traveling sage, Nārada Muni). Together, they established the Saṅkīrtana Movement.

PLATE II: 2. The deity of Haridāsa Ṭhākura at Siddha-bakula in Jagannath Puri. A picture of this deity features on the cover of this book.

PLATE II: 4. While Haridāsa Ṭhākura and Nityānanda Prabhu were delivering the residents of Navadvīpa by the chanting of the Holy Name, they encountered the brothers, Jāgai and Mādhāi, fallen members of *brāhmaṇa* families who had committed almost every conceivable sin. By the grace of Śrī Nityānanda Prabhu and Śrī Caitanya Mahāprabhu, the sinful brothers were delivered.

PLATE III: 1–3. Śāntipura, the ancestral home of Advaita Ācārya, was the home of Vaiṣṇava *dharma* prior to the descent of Śrī Caitanya Mahāprabhu. One of the *śālagrāma-śilās* in pictures 1 and 3 is reputed to be the *śilā* worshipped by Advaita Ācārya to cause the appearance of Lord Caitanya. The altar in Śāntipura is presided over by the golden form of Śrī Advaita Ācārya. Haridāsa Ṭhākura lived nearby in Phuliyā in a cave-like dwelling by the banks of the Ganges River. These two great personalities are credited with causing the descent of Lord Caitanya.

PLATE III: 4. When Haridāsa Ṭhākura moved to Navadvīpa from Phuliyā, he stayed near Śrīvāsāngam, the home of Śrīvāsa Ṭhākura (Nārada Muni), where the nocturnal *kīrtanas* of the Māyāpura Vaiṣṇavas (including Śrīla Haridāsa Ṭhākura) took place. Śrīvāsāngam is considered to be the birthplace of the Saṅkīrtana Movement.

PLATE III: 5–7. Śāntipura is now revered as a sacred place of pilgrimage where the Deity of Advaita Ācārya is worshipped, and where Śrīla Prabhupāda visited to pray for mercy before departing for America. Because it was in this place that the two stalwarts, Śrī Advaita Ācārya and Śrīla Haridāsa Ṭhākura successfully prayed for the appearance of the Lord, it is honored as a spiritually potent *dhāma* where prayers for the spread of the Saṅkīrtana Movement are answered.

PLATE IV: 1. Haridāsa Ṭhākura was born in the Jessore District and later moved to the forest of Benāpola. From there, he accepted the shelter of Śrī Advaita Ācārya in Śāntipura. The areas where his pastimes took place are indicated on the map which delineates the present boundary between West Bengal and Bangladesh.

PLATE IV: 2. Śrīla Haridāsa Ṭhākura chanted three *lakhs* (192 rounds) on his *japa* beads daily, without fail, until the end of his life.

PLATE IV: 3–4. Śrī Sanātana Gosvāmī, who initially stayed with Haridāsa Ṭhākura in Purī, later stayed in Vṛndāvana to fulfil the desire of Lord Caitanya Who ordered him to excavate the places of Kṛṣṇa's pastimes. There he established a wonderful temple to house the Deity of Śrī Madana-mohana, Whom we see him worshipping in this painting.

PLATE IV: 5. Śrī Kṛṣṇadāsa Kavirāja Gosvāmī, later wrote of Śrīla Haridāsa Ṭhākura's glorious activities in Śrī Caitanya-caritāmṛta.

PLATE V: 1. After leaving his home at a young age, Haridāsa Ṭhākura took up residence in the forest of Benāpola where he chanted continuously and worshipped Tulasī Devī. Rāmacandra Khān, an envious Vaiṣṇava hater, sent a beautiful young prostitute to lure Haridāsa Ṭhākura into worldly pleasures. However, she was converted into a spiritually advanced Vaiṣṇavī due to the extraordinary mercy of the Ṭhākura. She shaved her head and commenced chanting 300,000 names of Kṛṣṇa daily. Here she is seen surrendering all her worldly goods (which were distributed to saintly persons) and falling at the feet of the youthful Haridāsa.

PLATE V: 2. After leaving Benāpola, Haridāsa Ṭhākura came to live in Phuliyā, near Śāntipura. There, an officious Muslim cleric had the Nāmācārya arrested for the crime of conversion to Hinduism and brought before the Muslim king. In the Muslim lawbook, *Shariya*, composed some time after the *Koran*, this act of apostasy is punishable by death.

Haridāsa Ṭhākura was able to convince everyone in the king's council that his worship was of the same God that they all worshipped. However, the envious cleric who had caused his arrest and who had great influence with the king insisted that Haridāsa be beaten in 22 marketplaces. If he survived the beating, the kazi claimed that he would then accept Haridāsa as a *pīr*, a saint. Haridāsa survived and the kazi was doomed.

PLATE VI: Haridāsa Ṭhākura was severely beaten in 22 marketplaces by the king's guards, much to the consternation of the populace. Nevertheless, he never stopped chanting the Lord's Holy Name, and he not only survived the beating he received, but exhibiting the highest compassion, he prayed for the deliverance of his vicious oppressors.

PLATE VII: 1. During the time of the exhibition of the *mahā-prakāśa* in Mayapura, Śrī Caitanya Mahāprabhu revealed to Śrīla Haridāsa Ṭhākura that he had wanted to punish those who were beating Haridāsa, but because Haridāsa had prayed for the Lord to forgive them, He refrained from destroying the Ṭhākura's tormentors and accepted the beating on behalf of Haridāsa Ṭhākura. The Lord revealed the marks of the beating to Haridāsa on His own transcendental body.

PLATE VII: 2. While the *saṅkīrtana* partners, Haridāsa Ṭhākura and Nityānanda Prabhu, were attempting to deliver the demonic brothers, Jāgai and Mādhāi, Nityānanda Prabhu was struck with a clay pot, and the brothers Jāgai and Mādhāi, being threatened by the *cakra* of Lord Caitanya and realizing that they had made a grievous offense, surrendered at the feet of the two Lords.

PLATE VII: 3. The map depicts the transcendental *dhāmas* of Śāntipura, Phuliyā (just below Śāntipura) and Navadvīpa/ Māyāpura, where the transcendental pastimes of the Lord and His associates like Haridāsa Ṭhākura established the-Saṇkīrtana Movement.

PLATE VII: 4–6. Śrī Caitanya Mahāprabhu lead a successful

civil disobedience movement against the Chand Kazi with Haridāsa Ṭhākura at the head. Chand Kazi surrendered to the Lord and decreed that no one should henceforth interfere with the Saṅkīrtana Movement. Later, the Lord shaved his head and took *sannyāsa* from Keśava Bhāratī Mahārāja which created turmoil and grief for the residents of Māyāpura, especially the Lord's mother, Śacī.

PLATE VIII: After the Lord took *sannyāsa*, He established Himself in Purī, and Śrīla Haridāsa Ṭhākura followed Him, taking up residence there.

PLATE IX: 1–3. Considering himself unfit to enter the temple of Lord Jagannātha and following the order of Śrī Caitanya Mahāprabhu, Haridāsa Ṭhākura took up residence in Siddha-bakula, where he could gaze at the *cakra* of Lord Jagannātha's temple, and peacefully chant the Holy Name. It was there that Lord Caitanya visited him daily, delivering various forms of mercy.

PLATE X: 1–8. Siddha-bakula is now a transcendental place of pilgrimage where deities of Śrīla Haridāsa Ṭhākura and the Lord and His associates have been established. The serpentine and mystical *bakula* tree is reputed to have been planted by Lord Caitanya Himself to give shade to His beloved follower. A sign, for the benefit of English-speaking pilgrims, reputedly outlines a history of this famous tree as follows: "After taking *sannyāsa* at the age of 24 years, Lord Caitanya came to Nīlācala. After this period, the Lord's sincere devotee, Ṭhākura Śrī Haridāsa also came to Purī. Out of extreme humility, poor Haridāsa, in whom the *tṛṇād api sunīcena* verse was personified, never left his place of *bhajana*. Therefore, the most kind-hearted Lord Śrī Caitanya, the fulfiller of His devotees' desires, used to visit Ṭhākura Haridāsa, after seeing Lord Jagannātha daily. In order to provide shade to His dearest devotee, Nāmācārya Śrī Brahmā Haridāsa Ṭhākura, the most affectionate Lord Gaurāṅga, planted a used tooth stick of Śrī Jagannātha which suddenly grew up and appeared as a great shade-giving tree. Ṭhākura took 3 *lakhs* of Harināma under this divine tree daily. Under the shade of this sacred tree, Śrīpāda Rūpa Gosvāmī recited the *Lalita-mādhava* and *Vidagdha-mādhava* drama before Śrī Gaurāṅga and His followers. During his stay at Nīlācala, Śrīpāda Sanātana Gosvāmī were also staying with Śrī Haridāsa Ṭhākura. After the miraculous disappearance, *nirañjana*, of Śrī Haridāsa Ṭhākura, Śrī Caitanya carried his divine body on His lap and danced under this tree with *nāma-saṅkīrtana*. In the course of time, to construct the car of Lord Śrī Jagannātha, the ruler, Gajapati Mahārāja, ordered the tree to be cut. Siddha Jagannātha dāsa, the worshipper of this tree as well as a staunch follower of Śrī Haridāsa Ṭhākura, protested against it. But all of the protests of this *vairāgī* became fruitless against the royal might. Having been dumbfounded, the poor *vairāgī* fasted and lay flat under this divine tree. On the morning of the next day the royal officers found the tree hollow and returned without cutting it. From that day, ever awakening the sacred memories of the divine *līlā* of Lord Śrī Caitanya, as well as that of Śrī Haridāsa Ṭhākura, this holy tree is being worshipped as Śrī Śrī Siddha-bakula."

PLATE XI: 1 & 2. Śrī Caitanya Mahāprabhu and Śrī Nityānanda Prabhu in meditative states.

PLATE XI: 3. Lord Caitanya is seated in Purī with some of His intimate associates: Śrī Svarūpa Dāmodara Gosvāmī, Sārvabhauma Bhaṭṭācārya, and others. Śrīla Haridāsa Ṭhākura is not shown in this partial print; in the original, he is just to the right, gazing at the temple of Lord Jagannātha. King Pratāparudra is offering *daṇḍavats* to the Lord and His followers.

PLATE XI: 4. At the end of his life, Haridāsa Ṭhākura requested the Lord to allow him to pass away prior to the Lord's disappearance. The Lord fulfilled His desires, and Haridāsa Ṭhākura died in the sublime manner of the greatest *yogī* and devotee.

PLATE XII: After the disappearance of Haridāsa Ṭhākura, Lord Caitanya danced, holding the body of His beloved devotee in His arms.

PLATE XIII: 1–5. Śrī Caitanya Mahāprabhu personally bathed and prepared the Nāmācārya's body for being placed in *samādhi*. The *samādhi-mandira* of Haridāsa Ṭhākura is visited today by thousands and thousands of pilgrims. Śrīla Bhaktivinoda Ṭhākura composed wonderful prayers at this site glorifying Haridāsa Ṭhākura, while deeply meditating on the saint's life and pastimes.

PLATE XIV: 1 & 2. Prior to Lord Caitanya's appearance, Haridāsa Ṭhākura lived near Śāntipura in Phuliyā in a cave-like dwelling established for him by Śrī Advaita Ācārya. In this place he chanted over 300,000 names daily. Here, he was arrested by the kazi; here, he returned after being tortured; here, the bejeweled serpent gave way to the saint; and here, he chanted and prayed for the appearance of the Lord.

PLATE XV: 1–4. The site of Haridāsa Ṭhākura's *bhajana-kuṭira* in Phuliyā is visited by many pilgrims today, and a deity of the Nāmācārya has been established and the site has been renovated by the International Society for Kṛṣṇa Consciousness (ISKCON).

PLATE XVI: The deity of Haridāsa Ṭhākura at Siddha-bakula in Jagannath Puri.

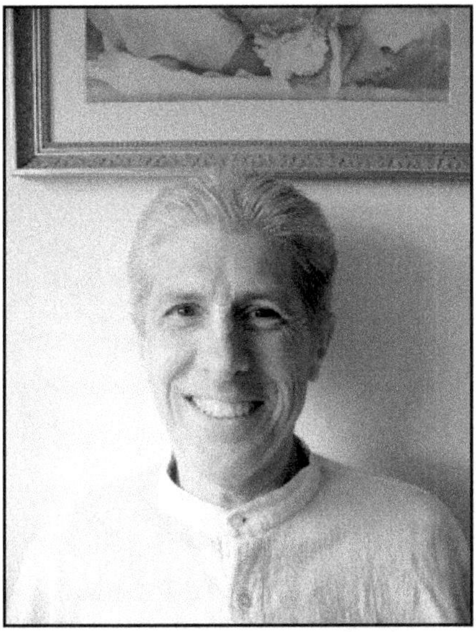

Rūpa-Vilāsa Dāsa (Robert MacNaughton) was born in Colorado, USA, in 1945. From an early age he was attracted to Eastern philosophy, which led him to receive initiation from His Divine Grace A.C. Bhaktivedanta Swami Prabhupāda in 1972. He is a well-known lecturer in ISKCON (The International Society of Krishna Consciousness) and has written a number of books on Gauḍīya Vaiṣṇava saints, including *A Ray Of Vishnu, The Seventh Goswami, Nāmācārya, Without Fear,* and *Bābājī Mahārāja.* He was a secondary school English teacher for many years and pioneered education in ISKCON. The author has five grown children and currently lives in the UK with his wife Śarad-bihārī (Sara MacNaughton). He continues to write books and his expanded and revised edition of *The Seventh Goswami* is soon to be published by the BBT (Bhaktivedanta Book Trust).

Hare Kṛṣṇa
Hare Kṛṣṇa
Kṛṣṇa Kṛṣṇa
Hare Hare
Hare Rāma
Hare Rāma
Rāma Rāma
Hare Hare

www.ingramcontent.com/pod-product-compliance
Lightning Source LLC
Chambersburg PA
CBHW060038100426
42742CB00014B/2633
* 9 7 8 1 8 8 0 4 0 4 5 1 5 *